SENIOR SECRETARIAL DUTIES
AND OFFICE ORGANISATION

TO MY MOTHER

SENIOR SECRETARIAL DUTIES AND OFFICE ORGANISATION

EVELYN AUSTIN, A.C.I.S., F.S.C.T.
*Senior Lecturer in commercial and professional subjects,
Harrow College of Technology and Art*

MACDONALD AND EVANS

MACDONALD & EVANS LTD.,
8 John Street, London WC1N 2HY

First published September 1974
Reprinted January 1976

©

MACDONALD AND EVANS LIMITED
1974

ISBN: 0 7121 1932 9

Filmset in Photon Times 11 on 12 pt. by
Richard Clay (The Chaucer Press), Ltd., Bungay, Suffolk
and printed in Great Britain by
Fletcher & Son, Ltd., Norwich

PREFACE

THIS book is designed specifically for candidates studying for a senior secretarial qualification. It is particularly suitable for those who hope to find and hold responsible positions in the office field, and will prove invaluable to anyone studying for the following examinations:

London Chamber of Commerce Private Secretary's Diploma.
London Chamber of Commerce Private Secretary's Certificate.
Royal Society of Arts Diploma for Personal Assistants.
Royal Society of Arts paper Personal Secretarial Practice III.
Royal Society of Arts paper Secretarial Duties II.

In addition, much of its content will be valuable to candidates sitting for:

London Chamber of Commerce Junior Secretary's Certificate.
Royal Society of Arts paper Office Supervision III.
Royal Society of Arts paper Office Practice I and II.

Students for professional examinations such as those mentioned below will find parts of this book directly related to sections of their syllabus in office management, office administration, office methods, clerical procedures and secretarial practice.

The Institute of Administrative Management Diploma in Administrative Management.
The Institute of Cost and Management Accountants paper Office Management.
The Institute of Chartered Secretaries and Administrators paper Secretarial Practice I (present scheme), and Office Administration (new scheme).

At the end of each chapter are two types of question: first, those requiring only brief answers—these are designed to test the student's understanding of the preceding chapter. Secondly, there are past examination questions requiring more detailed answers, designed to emphasise aspects of the syllabus often favoured by examiners and to give practice in answering questions under examination conditions. Approximately twenty minutes should be spent answering this type of question.

Aspiring secretaries will find much practical advice and information within these pages, regardless of whether or not they intend to take an examination in the subject, and it is hoped that experienced secretaries may also find material to interest them, to provoke and stimulate thought. If this book accompanies the secretary throughout her training, aids her in gaining the examination awards she requires, and finds a home in her desk drawer at the office from where she takes it out often to use as a reference book, then it will have attained every aim it set out to achieve.

In the firm belief that students of the calibre required to pass senior secretarial examinations have minds capable of a depth of understanding I have adopted a somewhat more sophisticated approach in some chapters than is usual in books on secretarial subjects. I feel no apology is necessary—let the reader be the judge.

April 1974

ACKNOWLEDGMENTS

MY grateful thanks are due to the London Chamber of Commerce (Commercial Education Scheme), and to the Royal Society of Arts, for their kind permission to reproduce questions from past examination papers and extracts from examination syllabuses; to Government Departments for the helpfulness of their officials and for making available to me current literature and notices; to the Post Office for the helpfulness of their officials and for their kind permission to reproduce illustrations and information contained in literature issued by them; to the Institute of Shorthand Writers for making available to me current literature; to Barclays Bank Ltd., and Lloyd's Bank Ltd., for permission to reproduce extracts from their literature; and to the manufacturers of office machinery and equipment who offered illustrations and literature and gave permission for these to be reproduced.

I should also like to record my gratitude to the undermentioned persons who contributed directly to the writing of this book:

My publishers for their helpfulness and guidance.

Past employers who made it possible for me to gain knowledge and experience which could be recorded for the benefit of students.

Students who made me aware of the real need for a book such as this.

My mother for her patience and forbearance during the period the manuscript was being written.

Other persons without whose encouragement and continued interest this book might never have been written.

CONTENTS

The Organisation; Departments in an Organisation; The
Merging of Functions; The Secretary's Duties; The Place
of Each Department Within the Company; Organisation
Charts: Types of Employers and Conditions of Work;
Loyalties; The Relationship Between the Office and the
Organisation

Background; The Place of the Junior, the Shorthand-
typist and the Secretary Within an Organisation and
Their Responsibilities to it

Relations With the Public; Relations With Superiors;
Relations With Fellow Employees; Job Satisfaction;
Conclusion

Correspondence; Abbreviations and Spelling

Direct Communication; Cultivating a Pleasant Voice
and Manner; Selecting the Means of Communication;
Transport

LIST OF ILLUSTRATIONS

CHAPTER 1

THE OFFICE

THE ORGANISATION

ORGANISATIONS are often described as "concerns," "businesses," "corporations" and by various other names. They are of course made up of a number of individual persons who have banded together with a common purpose, but as soon as this association of individuals has occurred a new body begins to take shape: the organisation. It takes on an identity entirely of its own and sometimes, as with registered companies, the law recognises this artificial being, which is in fact allowed to own property, to employ workers, to borrow money, to sue (or be sued) in legal proceedings, even to sign its name (by having its common seal applied to documents) and indeed to do most things which a real person may do. But even associations which are not legally recognised in their own right take on a separate identity from the people forming it. Thus a group of persons may form a club, say, for the purpose of meeting periodically and exchanging views on any subject of common interest. Very soon *the club* organises the meetings, the outings, the speakers and other activities. Millions of societies exist to serve those who are interested in the different aims of the society, but before very long, it is *the society's* aims, activities, headed notepaper which confirm its separate identity from those who attend its functions.

It is possible to divide all kinds of organisations broadly into two categories: (*a*) those which are formed for the purpose of making a profit which can (at least in part) find its way into the hands of those involved and (*b*) those which are formed to promote aims or activities or interests without making a profit. It will be seen that both categories *serve* those who are involved in them; in the one case by making money and in the other by pursuing a common interest or ideal. Into category (*a*) may be placed such concerns as large and small businesses and partnerships which are engaged in commerce and industry, producing goods, selling them or providing a service.

Into the second category go all the clubs, societies, companies and associations which pursue objects other than financial gain. Examples are The Institute of Qualified Secretaries Ltd., Leagues of Hospital Friends, Music Societies, Drama Societies, Tennis clubs, etc.

It is with the industrial and commercial organisations that this book is mainly concerned.

It is interesting to note that although the profit that such businesses earn finds its way into the hands of their shareholders by way of dividend, these shareholders are not necessarily the persons who originally formed the company, neither in many cases do they work for the company or show any interest in it other than cashing the dividend warrants! However, the organisation with its separate identity now assumes responsibilities of its own. We speak of "company image"—the picture it conjures up in people's minds of stability, prestige, glamour, and so on, or of unreliability and irresponsibility. (Note that it is not the shareholder who induces this impression.) The organisation (Fig. 1), especially if it is a large one, gives a livelihood to many workers: a host of factory workers who produce its goods; a large number of office workers who keep the records which are vital to the smooth running of the business; a directorate who manage the company and decide on its policy. (Note that it is not the shareholders who provide work for all these people.) In itself, this is a huge responsibility to the workers, but like a widening ripple this responsibility spreads to the satellite businesses which rely on the company for orders, to shopkeepers and small villages or even towns

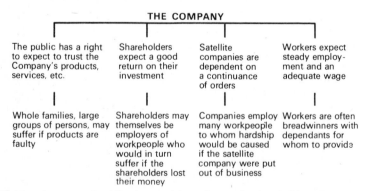

THE COMPANY

The public has a right to expect to trust the Company's products, services, etc.	Shareholders expect a good return on their investment	Satellite companies are dependent on a continuance of orders	Workers expect steady employment and an adequate wage
Whole families, large groups of persons, may suffer if products are faulty	Shareholders may themselves be employers of workpeople who would in turn suffer if the shareholders lost their money	Companies employ many workpeople to whom hardship would be caused if the satellite company were put out of business	Workers are often breadwinners with dependants for whom to provide

Fig. 1.—A company's obligations: to its employees, its shareholders, those who depend on it for their business and the public at large.

which may have sprung up to serve the company's employees. There is also an obligation to the company's shareholders who will be sorely disappointed if their dividend is less than the interest they might have received from elsewhere. The position would be even worse if business were so bad for the company that the value of the shares dropped so that shareholders could only sell their shares at a loss.

DEPARTMENTS IN AN ORGANISATION

In order to give effect to the teamwork and co-ordination which is essential to the achievement of any but the simplest objectives, the organisation usually divides its functions into a number of units. These may be known as groups, sections or—more commonly—departments; each department normally has a departmental head or manager who controls a number of subordinate staff. The departments are logically arranged according to the business of the organisation. The following are examples of some common classifications within a trading company.

1. SALES DEPARTMENT
According to the size of the organisation and the volume of work, this department may be sub-divided into, for example, Home Sales and Export Sales. There will probably be a Sales Manager in charge of all Sales, Area Sales Managers in charge of sales made in certain geographical areas of the country, and Sales Representatives in each of the areas. There usually are of course also a number of assistants at all levels, both technical and clerical. In such a department, the work consists mainly of bringing in orders, and a secretary employed here will probably be concerned with sending out quotations, giving delivery dates and following up to ensure that delivery promises will be met. Price lists will have to be compiled and kept up to date. Her chief will set sales targets, and will want to compare targets with actual achievements, which may involve figure work and display typing. The secretary may come into contact with sales representatives, agents or customers from foreign countries; she may have to arrange meetings, and make travel arrangements for her chief. If Sales Promotion is dealt with within the Sales Department, there may be sales promotion campaigns: there will be diaries or other gifts and gimmicks such as keyrings, ball point pens, pencils, etc. to order and

distribute by way of maintaining goodwill with old customers and to endeavour to establish new ones. Where the launching of a new product is undertaken, there may be press conferences to arrange.

2. PURCHASES DEPARTMENT

In this section is carried out work dealing with the organisation's purchases, e.g. raw materials for manufacture of goods or the purchase of stocks of goods for re-sale at a future date. The Chief Buyer will be concerned to keep in touch with old suppliers and to discover new ones; to ensure that a smooth flow of supplies is available and that alternative suppliers are at hand in the event of the failure of the regular ones to supply as contracted. The Chief Buyer will, of course, have subordinate assistant buyers to cope with the more routine buying and to train for eventual promotion to Chief Buyer.

A secretary working here may have to make arrangements for meetings between her chief and suppliers and between her chief and other executives within the company; she may have to see to her chief's travel arrangements (for not all suppliers will be close at hand). She may also be concerned with some figure work, e.g. comparison of prices, bulk buying discounts, etc.

3. ACCOUNTS DEPARTMENT

Apart from the annual accounts, periodical profit and loss accounts are usually prepared, thus enabling the management to keep a finger on the pulse of the firm's trading success. If the department is a large one, the various accounting functions will be sub-divided, e.g. into Sales Ledger, where the debtors' accounts are kept, Purchases Ledger, where the creditors' accounts are kept; Nominal Ledger, and so on. There is often a Costing Section, which sometimes merits a department of its own. The Chief Accountant may himself be quite remote from the various sub-divisions, but this is not necessarily so.

In whichever of the accounting divisions the secretary happens to work it is quite likely that some of her duties may consist of typing figures, receiving visitors and dealing with senior members of the organisation on behalf of her chief. She may have to attend committee meetings with her chief, and if there is need for him to travel, she will probably see to the travel arrangements for him. The external auditors in their periodical visits to the firm will be greatly concerned with her department and may indeed make their temporary home there. The secretary may therefore have to arrange additional accommodation for them and her knowledge of the firm and of her department will certainly be of value to them.

4. THE COMPANY SECRETARY'S DEPARTMENT

The Company Secretary must not be confused with a private secretary. The Company Secretary is a senior member of the organisation. Sometimes his function is fulfilled by the accountant; sometimes he has a seat on the Board of Directors. His knowledge of accounting and legal matters makes him a valued adviser to management. In his department much administrative work is carried out, e.g. insurance matters, negotiations for bank overdraft and loans, statutory returns to the Department of Trade and business with shareholders.

The private secretary who works here may be concerned with receiving such visitors as insurance agents, bank managers and senior company officials. She may have access to much confidential work such as minutes of Board Meetings, staff matters and company accounts. She may have to make arrangements for directors' meetings and for shareholders' meetings. Sometimes she accompanies her chief to these functions.

5. THE PERSONNEL DEPARTMENT

This is responsible for all matters concerning the recruitment, selection and (sometimes) the training of staff. Salary scales and matters of company policy affecting staff are dealt with in this department. For example, the company may have a policy of allowing advances on salary or loans to certain staff. Salary reviews and promotions either originate in the Personnel Department or, having originated in some other department, are implemented by the Personnel Department. The private secretary who works here will have access to staff files in which personal and confidential matters are found. She will have knowledge of salary scales and promotion prospects for staff. She may have to arrange appointments with applicants for posts and to help them with any pre-interview form-filling that might be required.

If there is no separate training department, her chief may be concerned with the induction and training of staff and the secretary may have to book a lecture hall, arrange a tour of the factory or offices, etc.

6. RESEARCH AND DEVELOPMENT DEPARTMENT

Companies must constantly try to improve their products, and this department is therefore vitally important if competition with rival companies is to be effective. If the company is a manufacturing concern, there will be experts in this department who are employed in improving the product. Better quality material might be used (at greater cost to the company) giving increased satisfaction to customers (and therefore greater sales); alternatively, cheaper but possibly more attractive material might be used, giving enhanced visual appeal to a prospective purchaser. Standardisation of parts used in different machines might give more economic opportunities for bulk buying. These are only a few examples of the work carried out by technical people in the Research and Development Department.

The secretary who works here will learn much about the technical side of her company's products. There may be committee meetings to arrange (and possibly to attend); visitors to receive; travel arrangements to make.

7. WORKS (OR PRODUCTION) DEPARTMENT

Here is carried out the actual business of producing the goods manufactured. The secretary's chief may be the Works Manager, in which case he will have direct responsibility for the factory work. Her work may be concerned with delivery schedules, production control, sales schedules and stocks of goods. She may have to arrange meetings for her chief with senior officials and with factory personnel. Her chief will necessarily work in close liaison with other departments such as the Sales Department and the Research and Development Department. The members of these other departments will hold conferences with her chief, and he may be requested to travel on behalf of the firm, in which the case the secretary may be concerned with his travelling arrangements.

8. DEPARTMENTS IN CONCERNS OTHER THAN MANUFACTURING ONES

The examples given above are not exhaustive, and it will be seen that they are drawn mostly from a manufacturing concern. However, much the same sort of divisions or departments exist in other types of organisations. For example, pharmaceutical concerns will be concerned with selling their goods—chemicals—(Sales Department), with buying raw materials—ingredients—(Purchases Department).

A record must likewise be kept of debtors, creditors and profits (Accounts Department) and new drugs will be brought out on to the market after development and testing (Research and Development Department). The same principles apply to any type of business organisation.

THE MERGING OF FUNCTIONS

According to the needs of the particular concern, a greater or smaller number of departments will exist. Some may have different names but they will essentially perform the same functions as the departments just described (Purchases Department is sometimes called Buying Department; Personnel Department is sometimes known as the Staff Department). When the secretary becomes familiar with her particular company there will be no difficulties, since she will soon learn the names of the various sections.

In the smaller organisations, it is not unusual for certain functions to be grouped together. Thus Home Sales Department and Export Sales Department might come under the one heading of Sales Department. Similarly the Accounts Department might house all the various sub-divisions of accounting, and so on. In a small concern, the volume of work would not warrant keeping a member of staff entirely employed on one aspect of work.

THE SECRETARY'S DUTIES

It will be noticed that while the functions of the various departments are totally different, some of the general duties of a secretary are identical, no matter in which department she finds herself. Whether her chief is the Accountant or the Sales Manager or even a more junior executive, she will have to arrange for any meetings he has to attend; to make reservations and other travel arrangements necessary; to deal with callers, both personal and telephone; to keep her chief's business diary, remind him of any appointments or other facts that might escape his memory and to type his letters and do his filing. Thus while her chief's function is individual, and different from that of any other executive in the company, her own stock-in-trade—her secretarial training and experience—will be useful to any executive in any department.

The immensely satisfying conclusion that emerges is that the private secretary can choose whatever line of business she finds most interesting, and indeed there is no reason why she should not eventually progress to executive secretary or personal assistant or even graduate to administrative work, leaving behind her the more mundane aspects of her secretarial work. That is the justification for the statement that a secretarial training opens the door to a vast number of commercial and government posts.

THE PLACE OF EACH DEPARTMENT WITHIN THE COMPANY

Each separate department is of vital importance to the firm as a whole, each contributing to the more efficient buying, selling or other purpose for which the firm exists and all merging together as a team to achieve the firm's objects. It is a curious fact, however, that each head of department and every loyal secretary attaches more importance to his/her own department than to any other! For example, the Accounts Department staff will claim that they keep a finger on the pulse of profit trends and that without periodical profit and loss statements, accurate costing and budgetary control, the firm would soon go downhill. There is certainly much truth in this statement. However, the Sales Office staff will claim that if their department did not find the customers to buy the firm's products the firm would soon be out of business, and certainly no one can dispute the validity of this statement. But the Production Department staff will almost certainly maintain that unless they ensured smooth production of the goods in the first place, there would be nothing to sell! There is more than a modicum of truth in that!

To continue round the circle, the Sales Office staff would reply that it would be useless for Production Department to ensure that the goods are produced if Sales Department were not there to provide the necessary outlets!

The truth of the matter is, of course, that each department is a part of the whole organisation and that they work together *as a team* for the benefit of the firm. However, intimate knowledge of a particular department makes it appear more important than any other in the eyes of its staff and while this is a good thing and fosters pride in one's work, it should be realised that each department is only a part—albeit a most important part—of the whole team.

ORGANISATION CHARTS

An organisation chart (Figs. 2 and 3) is a graphic representation of the "set-up." It will display the hierarchy, it will show who is responsible for a whole division, and will depict the sub-sections within it. Thus it becomes relatively easy to discover to whom one should report, who is one's immediate superior and who is the ultimate chief. A formal chart will merely show the designations of the individuals it portrays, thus no names appear, only functions, *e.g.*

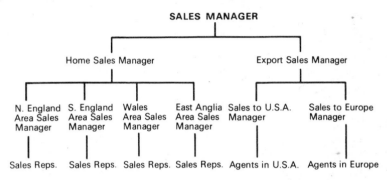

Fig. 2.—Organisation chart of a company's sales force.

Sales Manager, Sales Representatives, etc. In some businesses, however, a more intimate type of chart is used which gives the names of the persons who fulfil certain functions, *e.g.* John Brown, Sales Manager, or A. Bee and C. Dee, Sales Representatives. Occasionally, a small photograph of the individual accompanies his name and designation. It will be appreciated that the latter type of chart, although much less formal and much more informative, needs constant revision to keep it up to date. Indeed, any organisation chart needs periodical review since no business remains absolutely static for any length of time. The time and trouble involved in keeping an organisation chart up to date is the price which must be paid for the service it renders to those who need to refer to it.

TYPES OF EMPLOYERS AND CONDITIONS OF WORK

1. INDIVIDUAL EMPLOYERS

The secretary's chief or superior may or may not be her employer also (*i.e.*, the person who pays her). It may be that he employs her

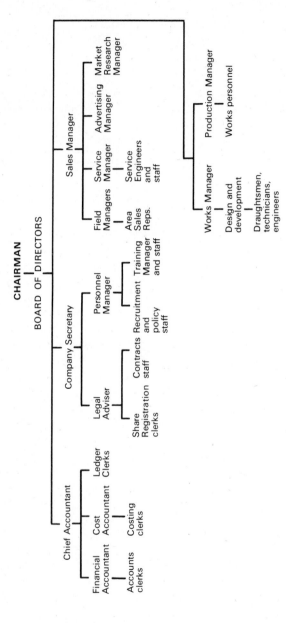

Fig. 3.—Organisation chart of a manufacturing company.

directly or that he is himself an employee within an organisation and holds a sufficiently senior position to warrant the assistance of a secretary. A writer who works in his study at home is an example of an individual employer. So is a sole trader, *i.e.* a man who works in business and is his own boss.

Sometimes an organisation is made up of a partnership of several individuals. As the term "partnership" implies, there are two or more persons associating together in business for a common commercial purpose. The actual number of partners for general commercial purposes (excluding solicitors, accountants, etc.) is limited by law to twenty persons (*Companies Act* 1967), but there is no limit to the size of the business itself and the number of persons employed by a partnership will naturally vary with the volume of work involved.

2. CORPORATIONS

(*a*) *Introduction.* This type of organisation is regarded at law as a legal entity, quite distinct from its members (*e.g.*, the shareholders who in effect, but not in law, own the business), from its directorate (*e.g.*, the people who manage the business) and from its employees.

The concept of corporate personality for an association of individuals evolved from the days when, because it was too costly for one person to finance an enterprise, the necessary finance for fitting out ships for trading purposes or for exploring distant lands was put up by several persons who pooled their resources and formed a company in which each had a stake. If the venture proved successful, profits were shared among those who had a stake in the venture, *i.e.* the shareholders. From these early beginnings grew the joint stock company (commonly known as the limited company) as we know it today.

Since corporations are regarded at law as legal entities they have legal rights and obligations. The assets which a corporation has, *e.g.* its plant and machinery, its fixtures and fittings and its bank balance all belong to the corporation and not to its shareholders. When it trades successfully and makes a profit that too belongs to the corporation (but in practice a proportion of the profits is usually distributed to the shareholders in the form of a dividend). If the corporation makes a loss, the burden normally lies on the corporation and not on the shareholders who have invested in it.

(*b*) *Addressing a corporation.* It now becomes easier to understand why such concerns are not normally addressed with the prefix Messrs., as a partnership always is.

Compare: J. Brown & Company Ltd. (a corporation)
  with   Messrs. Jones and Brown (a partnership of two persons)
  and   Messrs. Jones, Brown & Co. (a partnership of more than two persons).

Since Messrs. is an abbreviation of the French word "Messieurs," which means Gentlemen, it would not be strictly accurate to address a corporation—a single entity—by the prefix Messrs. which implies the plural. Custom has made it permissible, however (but it is not really accurate), to use the word Messrs. in addressing a corporation whose name includes proper names. Thus in practice it might be permissible to write Messrs. John Brown & Co. Ltd., but there is no excuse at all for using Messrs. to address companies with names like The Magic Typewriter Co. Ltd., The Blue & White Carbon Co. Ltd., Electrical Fittings Ltd.

3. THE SMALL EMPLOYER

Many corporations are so small as to be no different in their capacity as employers from an individual employer or a small partnership, and conditions of work, generally speaking, in any small office may be described as follows:

(*a*) *Advantages:*

(*i*) *Variety of work.* Because the volume of work is not so great as to keep the secretary occupied entirely on secretarial duties, she has the opportunity of learning a great deal about her employer's business. She learns the various aspects of work required to run the business; new fields are opened to her and she gains experience which will stand her in good stead for the rest of her working life.

(*ii*) *Security.* Her intimate knowledge of her boss's business renders her an invaluable member of his staff. She may become indispensable to him, and be secure in her post.

(*iii*) *Promotion.* Her salary will increase with the degree of importance of her duties. If she has learnt so much about the business that she can run it (or certain aspects of it) with a minimum of supervision she will be in a position to command a very high salary. Eventually, she may even discard her secretarial work to become an assistant or a partner.

(*iv*) *Rules.* Where there are relatively few employees there can be greater flexibility of rules—indeed formal regulations may be non-existent. In slack periods the chief may allow his secretary to go home early or he may give her time off for shopping, but he would expect her to work late or to take work home in peak periods.

(v) *Team spirit.* Where the working group is small each member becomes well known to the others; a team spirit may be fostered and a "family atmosphere" prevails.

(b) *Disadvantages:*

(i) *Additional duties.* The secretary may not like to take on duties other than those for which she has been trained: making the tea may be beneath her; doing the book-keeping may be beyond her.

(ii) *Coping with emergencies.* Because there are few other employees on whom to call, the secretary will have to cope with emergencies. If there is an influx of work, she will have to work late or come in to the office at weekends.

(iii) *Lack of welfare schemes.* A small employer cannot afford such benefits for his employees as a canteen on the premises, a sports and social club, loans or advances to employees and elaborate staff training schemes.

4. THE LARGE EMPLOYER

The criticism has often been levelled that in a large concern the employee is cloaked in anonymity, that he is merely a "number on the payroll," and that the atmosphere is impersonal. To a very limited extent this criticism may be valid, but all large groups are normally divided into smaller units—departments—and it is the department that becomes the secretary's own world within the universe which is the company. Certainly, she may be just a "number" to the Chairman or to other persons far removed from the department, but within the group which forms her department she is a very important member of the team.

(a) *Advantages:*

(i) *Definite rules.* Rules and regulations are laid down and usually strictly adhered to. This means that the employee knows exactly what is expected of her and what to expect of the employer.

(ii) *Specialisation.* Because the volume of each aspect of the work is greater, there is scope for an employee to specialise in that aspect which interests her most, *e.g.* a medical secretary may choose which branch of medical work to make her career in.

(iii) *Promotion.* An employee who becomes a specialist in his/her field becomes more valuable to the employer and is remunerated accordingly. Also, owing to the size of the large concern, there must obviously be more posts at all levels, including the higher échelons, to fill.

(*iv*) *Welfare*. Under this heading may be grouped all those fringe benefits which it is in the power of the large employer to offer: social club, canteen, medical facilities, staff training schemes.

(*b*) Disadvantages:

(*i*) *Limited scope*. If the secretary is kept within the limits of one department, she finds it harder to learn about the various other aspects of work involved elsewhere. Her knowledge of the company, although specialised, is limited.

(*ii*) *Routine*. Over-specialisation could lead to a dull routine, *e.g.* *typing pools*.

(*iii*) *Rules*. Rules and regulations must be strictly observed.

(*iv*) *Limits to salary*. There will probably be salary scales laid down, beyond which a secretary—however efficient—may not climb. (In fairness, it should be said that such salary scales would normally be very generous at the higher end of the scale.)

LOYALTIES

Where the secretary finds herself working for a company, she must remember that her chief is also employed by it and may have little or no control over certain regulations unless he is a very senior executive or a director. Within his own department he may be the head of the team, but when the whole organisation is viewed, the chief is still an employee. He may be a relatively senior or junior employee, but he is not a free agent and it would be unreasonable for the secretary to expect her chief to change rules or to award salary increases where such matters are outside his control. Beyond issuing a recommendation, there may be little he can do.

However, while he is technically not her employer, he does remain the secretary's immediate superior and so she has a dual loyalty: to her employer and to her chief. Normally, there is no conflict in these two loyalties. While the secretary is serving her chief she is serving the company and the two aspects are usually parallel. Exceptional circumstances may arise where the secretary is at variance with the company but not with her chief. Or conversely, she may object to her chief's activities but be quite happy with those of the company. Such examples are very rare indeed, but they are conceivable. It might be that the secretary disagrees with her firm's policies or objects, *e.g.* the export of arms and ammunition (if the secretary is a pacifist), or its employment policy, *e.g.* no women in high executive positions. Similarly, it is conceivable that her loyalty to her chief might be taxed if she discovered that he was stealing from the firm, or that he was spreading untrue and damaging rumours about the firm to outsiders.

If such a situation did occur, the secretary would have to use her good judgment, her practical common sense and her conscience to guide her in any action to be taken. Remedies might be to mention the matter to the chief, to ask for a transfer to another department or to leave the firm altogether, as dictated by the particular circumstances.

THE RELATIONSHIP BETWEEN THE OFFICE AND THE ORGANISATION

1. PURPOSE OF THE OFFICE

It is easy to appreciate that in a manufacturing company the factory workers who actually make the product are vital to the organisations; they are productive. If selling is the business of the company, the salesmen are the "productive" people; if the business be advertising, then the copywriters are those who produce the firm's "goods." What place, then, does the office have? Large and small "offices" accommodating hundreds of clerical staff engaged day in day out in taking dictation and transcribing on the typewriter, in filing and retrieving correspondence, in posting the accounting ledgers, in dispensing petty cash, in answering the telephone and manning the switchboard, in supervising staff and in being accountable to management—are they all useless, a burden, a parasite? Certainly, they are "non-productive" in the sense that they do not actually make anything, but without the office staff to sort, store and retrieve records, to provide effective communication between internal departments and between those departments and "outsiders," to produce work schedules, to progress orders, to keep accounts, to pay wages and salaries, the "productive" work of the business would be done under such chaotic conditions that it would grind to a standstill before very long.

If there were no wages clerk to calculate the wages, make out payslips, collect the cash and distribute the pay packets, would there be many workers left? If there were no clerks to open and sort out the mail promptly, to check delivery dates, to follow through orders to ensure prompt deliveries, would there be many customers left? If there were no typists to cope with correspondence, would many letters be sent off? The argument could go on and on. The office, then, does serve a useful purpose: IT PROVIDES A SERVICE.

2. CLERICAL FUNCTIONS

Without the services of the office staff to collect all the information as it comes in by telegram, telex, telephone, direct conversation and by letter; without the services of the office staff who have to sort this information, record it as necessary on charts, in ledgers and in books; without those people who interpret the information and make it more meaningful (figures turned into reports, figures transformed into charts, reports incorporated into statistics, questionnaires processed and turned into reports) it would be difficult for the *management of an organisation to have all the information necessary* to enable it to take the right decisions, form the policies and take the action required to make a success of the concern.

Providing the right information at the time it is required (and not a day later) means that someone in the office has to sort all the information, and classify it so that it may be retrieved without difficulty immediately it is wanted. The system is devised, the rules are made, the equipment is bought, the entries are made, and the *classifying and storing* is effected. All this is done by office personnel.

Business concerns are subject to legal requirements, the disregard of which could lead to heavy fines being imposed and even the possible winding up of the concern. For example, companies, especially those registered with limited liability, must by law send returns and copies of their accounts to the Department of Trade (*Companies Acts* 1948–1967); certain insurances are compulsory (*Employers' Liability (Compulsory Insurance) Act* 1969); employees must be given a written statement of their terms of employment (*Contracts of Employment Act* 1972). All this means that someone in the office must attend to these *legal requirements*.

Protecting the organisation does not end at looking after the legal side of the business. It is necessary to *protect its property* against loss, theft, damage, obsolescence, fire, and so on. Someone in the office must negotiate the necessary insurance, someone has to make and enforce the rules for the safekeeping of valuable property, someone has to decide what provisions to make in the accounts. Once again, that someone finds a place in the office.

It may therefore be said that the office service:

(*a*) *Collects information:* The office is a centre into which information pours from a variety of sources *via* a number of different means of communication.

(*b*) *Sorts and classifies information:* Unless this information is systematically sorted for further processing, it may be too plentiful, too disjointed and unrelated to be of any value.

(*c*) *Records information:* If records are not maintained properly, it may be impossible to refer to important documents, to check on vital information.

(*d*) *Processes and interprets information:* It is sometimes necessary to work on figures before they become really meaningful. Statistics must be interpreted; computer input must be processed; output must be interpreted. The information must be reduced to its most meaningful form if management is to be made aware of danger signals, of business trends, of a true and fair assessment of the state of the business.

(*e*) *Diffuses information:* It is the business of the office to see that those who might need it, get information. Not only members of internal staff will require information, but "outsiders" also. Thus customers will want to know prices and delivery dates; insurance companies must have accurate and complete information about the business's valuable assets, and so on. Only through effective communication can the information be properly diffused. It is for the office to select the means of communication (letter, telephone, telegram, telex) and to make these methods effective.

(*f*) *Protects the business and safeguards its assets:* The concern must be protected from defaulting (not complying with the law). This means that minute books must be kept up, licences taken out, returns must be registered, insurances must be effected. The property of the organisation must likewise be protected against fire (proper equipment), against loss and theft (proper precautions), against obsolescence (proper depreciation).

Short-answer Questions

1. Which is the more important department of a company: the Production Department or the Sales Department?

2. Name five departments (or functions) within a company.

3. What is the purpose of an organisation chart?

4. Why should you not use the abbreviation "Messrs." when addressing a registered company?

5. Give three advantages and three disadvantages of working for a small concern.

6. How does the office contribute to the achievement of the aims of an organisation?

7. Mention three functions of the office.

8. The office does not produce or make anything; what, then, does it do?

9. Give two examples of clerical work, other than shorthand and typing.

10. Would you prefer to work for an individual employer or a corporation? Give reasons for your answer.

Past Examination Questions

NOTE: Approximately twenty minutes should be spent on each question.
L.C.C. = London Chamber of Commerce; R.S.A. = Royal Society of Arts.

1. There are duties which are common to most secretarial posts. List some of these with comments on each.   (*L.C.C.*)

2. "The office performs a service of record and communication." Explain this statement by referring to the type of records maintained by the office and the necessity for adequate diffusion of information.   (*L.C.C.*)

3. You work for a large company.

    (*a*) Who would fix your wage scale?

    (*b*) If salaries had been paid monthly by cheque and are now to be paid by credit transfer, what department would be responsible for organising the detailed work to enable the change to be made?

    (*c*) If you were asked to verify the date of the next Board meeting, whom would you ask?   (*R.S.A.*)

4. How would you expect the nature of your work to differ if you were:

    (*a*) secretary to the owner of a retail business selling photographic equipment to the public;

    (*b*) secretary to the sales manager of a limited company manufacturing photographic equipment?   (*R.S.A.*)

5. "Two functions of an office are the receiving and issuing of information." By what means is information received and issued?
          (*R.S.A.*)

6. After five years' experience as a shorthand-typist you apply for and are offered two secretarial posts:

(*a*) secretary to the manager of a small manufacturing company on a local trading estate;

(*b*) secretary to the sales manager of a big manufacturing company at their head office in a large city.

State which you would choose; list the reasons for your choice; and mention any advantages which may be lost by refusing the alternative post. (*R.S.A.*)

7. Your brother has been working as a mechanic in a small, privately owned garage. He is now joining one of the large motor manufacturers which is a public limited company. He asks you what differences he will find. You point out that obviously, there will be a far greater number of employees. Give three other differences which will, in some way, affect your brother. (*R.S.A.*)

8. If you were offered the following jobs with similar salaries, which would you choose and why?

(*a*) An author of detective stories and other novels wants you to work for him at his home, going there each day. He tells you that in addition to dictating his books to you, he would dictate correspondence, expect you to do the filing, answer the telephone and make appointments for him.

(*b*) A large business organisation is prepared to employ you as a shorthand-typist in its central purchasing department. If you show any promise, they are prepared to train you in the work of the department so that you may become a junior buyer. (*R.S.A.*)

9. What would you consider to be the advantages and disadvantages of working as secretary to:

(*a*) an executive in a large business organisation;

(*b*) an individual who is not a member of a business organisation (*e.g.*, a Member of Parliament or a doctor)? (*R.S.A.*)

10. "A large organisation has a number of departmental heads, while the sole trader undertakes many of their functions himself." An antique dealer employs one office and three sales assistants. List (*a*) the executive functions the dealer is likely to undertake himself, and (*b*) those which he might hand over to an agency or professional specialist. (*R.S.A.*)

CHAPTER 2

THE OFFICE WORKER

BACKGROUND

ABOUT one hundred years ago women office workers were practically unheard of and all clerical work was done by male staff. Records were maintained by hand; mechanisation in the office, *e.g.* accounting machines, were unknown and copying was done in laborious handwriting (no typewriters) first with a quill pen, then with a metal-nibbed pen (fountain pens and ball point pens are comparatively recent developments). Working conditions were drab (Fig. 4) and an abundance of labour (there was no compulsory school leaving age) did nothing to induce employers to improve the lot of the worker.

It was not until the First World War that women workers began to appear in clerical positions. Until that time, women who remained unmarried and had no private income normally found work as domestic servants or as shop assistants or governesses and teachers. Little else was available to them except perhaps laundry and dressmaking work. During the Second World War the shortage of men and an increase in work—both administrative and industrial—gave women a chance to really come into their own and they have never looked back since!

A growing awareness of the dignity of the worker, coupled with some decades of full employment and a shortage of manpower, have contributed towards the drastically changed working conditions which prevail today. From a situation where the employer was able (although he did not always do it) to extract as much work as possible from his workers, we have progressed through a period of paternal concessions granted by the benevolent employer, to the present day where the worker is protected by such legislation as the *Offices, Shops & Railway Premises Act* 1963, the *Contracts of Employment Act* 1972, the *Redundancy Payments Acts* 1965 and 1969 and the *Equal Pay Act* 1970. A prolonged shortage of certain

OFFICE STAFF PRACTICES

1. Godliness, cleanliness and punctuality are the necessities of a good business.

2. This firm has reduced the hours of work, and the clerical staff will now only have to be present between the hours of 7 a.m. and 6 p.m. on weekdays.

3. Daily prayers will be held each morning in the Main Office. The clerical staff will be present.

4. Clothing must be of a sober nature. The clerical staff will not disport themselves in raiment of bright colours, nor will they wear hose, unless in good repair.

5. Overshoes and top-coats may not be worn in the office, but neck scarves and headwear may be worn in inclement weather.

6. A stove is provided for the benefit of the clerical staff. Coal and wood must be kept in the locker. It is recommended that each member of the clerical staff bring 4 pounds of coal, each day, during cold weather.

7. No member of the clerical staff may leave the room without permission from Mr. Rogers. The calls of nature are permitted and clerical staff may use the garden below the second gate. This area must be kept in good order.

8. No talking is allowed during business hours.

9. The craving of tobacco, wines or spirits is a human weakness, and as such, is forbidden to all members of the clerical staff.

10. Now that the hours of business have been drastically reduced the partaking of food is allowed between 11.30 a.m. and noon, but work will not, on any account, cease.

11. Members of the clerical staff will provide their own pens. A new sharpener is available on application to Mr. Rogers.

12. Mr. Rogers will nominate a senior clerk to be responsible for the cleaning of the main office and the private office, and all boys and juniors will report to him 40 minutes before Prayers, and will remain after closing hours for similar work. Brushes, brooms, scrubbers and soap are provided by the owners.

13. The new increased weekly wages are as hereunder detailed:-

Junior boys (to 11 years)	1/4d.
Boys (to 14 years)	2/1d.
Juniors	4/8d.
Junior Clerks	8/7d.
Clerks	10/9d.
Senior Clerks (after 15 years with the owners)	21/-d.

The owners recognise the generosity of the new Labour Laws, but will expect a great rise in output of work to compensate for these near Utopian conditions.

As issued in an office in Lichfield in 1852, name of firm not known.

Fig. 4.—Office staff practices.

types of clerical labour, notably secretarial labour, has induced employers to compete with one another in offering attractive conditions of work and increasingly higher salaries.

Office workers may be broadly classified into three categories: managerial staff; administrative staff; clerical staff.

1. MANAGERIAL STAFF

Into this category fall the directors, Chief Accountants, Company Secretaries, departmental managers and other executives and junior managers. These are the people who are sometimes known as "top management," "middle management" and "junior management." They make the company's policies; they take important decisions; they give the orders; they also accept the responsibilities.

2. ADMINISTRATIVE STAFF

These are the supervisors; the people who see to it that policies coming from top management are implemented. They sift through any problems before allowing them to go to higher management. The administrative staff are concerned with greater detail of work than higher management who generally deal in broad outlines. They are the supervisors of the lower ranks and the personal assistants to the higher ranks.

3. CLERICAL STAFF

The clerical staff are the people who deal intimately with the detail of the day-to-day work. Into this category fall the vast armies of typists and book-keepers, of secretaries and filing clerks, of audio-typists and telephone order clerks, of shorthand-typists and accounts clerks. It is interesting to note that the Institute of Administrative Management have published a booklet on Clerical Job Grading, in which all classes of office workers are arranged in six grades, ranging from the junior messenger to the senior person with a professional qualification.

THE PLACE OF THE JUNIOR, THE SHORTHAND-TYPIST AND THE SECRETARY WITHIN AN ORGANISATION, AND THEIR RESPONSIBILITIES TO IT

Just as each department of a firm is a part of the whole company, so every member of staff within a department is a part of the departmental team.

1. THE OFFICE JUNIOR

She may only be employed on such mundane tasks as messenger work (distributing and collecting mail), making the tea, typing envelopes and filing under supervision, but without her services some other employee—perhaps the secretary—would have to attend to this work. Although without doubt the secretary could do such simple tasks efficiently, her own more sophisticated work would of necessity have to be delayed if the junior were not there to play her part. No one should look down on the office junior: her tasks may be simple ones but they are essential to the smooth running of the department. It is not always the case that the junior's tasks are very simple ones, and they invariably require the application of intelligence, a sense of responsibility and often the use of initiative. Sometimes it falls to the junior to operate simple office machinery such as a photocopier, a duplicator or a franking machine. Sometimes it is she who maintains the postage book, entering particulars of mail received and/or despatched. She soon learns how each member of the department prefers his tea: strong, weak, with or without sugar or milk; that Mr. X takes pure milk (perhaps for stomach ulcers); that Mr. Y likes a biscuit with his tea; that the private secretary will go without her tea altogether if she is not handed it with a kind "now do give yourself a breathing space Miss Smith." It is the junior who knows that the postman usually calls a few minutes late for the mail, therefore: "you might just get this letter in if it is really urgent." It is the junior who is sent to buy stamps, envelopes, etc. and so "Why, yes of course Mr. A., I'll buy a birthday card for your daughter while I'm out." These matters may seem trivial when viewed individually but they all go towards the making of a contented and efficient team within a department.

2. THE SHORTHAND-TYPIST

Sometimes the junior is promoted to shorthand-typist. Often, however, the post is offered to an outside applicant who possesses the necessary skills. The shorthand-typist's work is of a somewhat more complicated nature than that of the junior. For example, instead of filing under supervision it is likely that once she has learnt how the system operates, she will be left to do her own filing. She may supervise some of the junior girls' work, *e.g.* show how to establish a routine for the collection and delivery of mail, explain the filing system, and so on. She takes dictation from her chief, leaving the straightforward copy-typing to be done by the junior. The shorthand-typist can be of great assistance to her chief. There is hardly an employer in existence who will not appreciate a helpful comment from an intelligent stenographer when he hesitates in his dictation, searching for the appropriate word. The shorthand-typist soon learns his style, is able to supply the word or phrase that is so tantalisingly on the tip of his tongue. She can take some routine work off her boss's shoulders. Such instructions as "write to Mr. Brown—the one who came to see us yesterday—not the other Mr. Brown . . . you can find his address when you get back to your office," or "find out from previous correspondence on file why we refused to buy our stationery from XYZ Co., and then let me know so that I can write a further letter," or "with reference to your quotation for (you can look this up later) . . ." allow a competent shorthand-typist to help a busy executive to get through a day's work with maximum speed and efficiency.

3. THE SECRETARY

With the junior clerks and shorthand-typists taking most of the routine work from the secretary, her working day can be spent doing those tasks which only she can perform with efficiency. Her more intimate knowledge of her chief's work enables her to anticipate his requirements, to supervise the work of her juniors (but not do it herself) and indeed to take on as much of her employer's own work as he is willing to delegate to her and she is able to cope with. She will arrange his appointments, make his travel arrangements, book hotel reservations, remind him of important matters, arrange his meetings, shield him from unwanted visitors and generally deal with the hundred and one items which are necessary to make her chief's working day as trouble-free as possible.

It must be emphasised here that a secretary cannot hope to be of maximum service to her employer in the first few weeks of working for him. It takes an accumulation of knowledge and experience gathered over months, even years, and stored meticulously in the secretary's brain before she can be at her peak of efficiency. Mere high speeds in shorthand and typing indicate worthwhile manual dexterity and brain co-ordination but these skills alone do not make an efficient secretary.

4. CONCLUSION

It will be appreciated that the tasks of the junior, the shorthand-typist and the secretary as described above are examples only. In practice, they will vary with the type of business and department in which the employee finds herself and also with the degree of intelligence and ambition which she possesses, as well as with the amount of trust and confidence which her superior is willing to place in her. However, whatever their respective duties, each grade of employee has her place in the team which makes up the department. All should work in close liaison and co-ordination towards the achievement of the common objective: the smooth running of the department; for to work as individuals in a vacuum without regard to the manner in which their own particular work fits into the whole must necessarily cause delays and inefficiencies in the office.

Short-answer Questions

1. In what ways are office workers protected from an unscrupulous employer?

2. List five tasks which an office junior might be asked to perform.

3. How can a secretary help her chief (other than by typing his letters)?

4. Why are conditions in the office so different nowadays from the situation 100 years ago?

5. What do you understand by "clerical work"?

6. How does a shorthand-typist contribute towards the smooth running of her department?

7. Give three examples of designations applicable to the "top management" category of office worker.

8. What part does the administrative staff play in the office?

9. Give three examples of designations which might apply to "administrative staff."

10. List five classes of specialist clerks.

Past Examination Questions

1. At a conference the speaker, who had been talking about the promotion of staff in his business, was asked why women were given

so few opportunities for promotion. He replied that this was largely the fault of the women themselves. He stated that most girls took office jobs to earn some money and fill up the time between school and marriage, and that they were not prepared to undergo further training or to accept responsibility.

(a) *For both men and women candidates:* Do you think this is a fair description of most of the girls you know?

(b) *For women candidates only:* How do you feel about it in relation to yourself?

(c) *For men candidates only:* Describe how you hope to use your training in secretarial duties in the development of your career.   (*R.S.A.*)

2. You have been asked to look after a school-leaver who has been attached to your department. She has speeds of 80 w.p.m. in shorthand and 35 w.p.m. in typewriting. List the points you would make in advising her how to improve her skills and how to become a useful member of the department.   (*R.S.A.*)

3. It has been suggested that a junior should be engaged to assist you in the everyday routine matters and some correspondence. The post has been advertised and you are asked to interview applicants. What qualities will you look for and what questions will you ask?   (*L.C.C.*)

4. The term "Secretary" is nowadays used very loosely and wrongly and is often applied to shorthand-typists and even to office juniors. What, in your view, does this term mean and what do you consider to be six of the main requisites of a secretary?   (*L.C.C.*)

5. The private secretary's work is mainly concerned with assisting her immediate employer. Describe some aspects of her job which demonstrate how this aim can be achieved.   (*L.C.C.*)

6. "A secretarial post calls for much initiative because it is possible for a good private secretary to save her employer a great deal of time by the quick anticipation of his requirements and possible future action." Justify this statement.   (*L.C.C.*)

7. What do you understand by Secretarial Duties, and what training do you consider you need in order to undertake these duties?   (*R.S.A.*)

8. Some employers complain that every young shorthand-typist who works for one man calls herself a private secretary. What

training, experience and knowledge do you consider a private secretary should possess? (*R.S.A.*)

9. Describe the working function of (*a*) a personal assistant to the managing director of a company, (*b*) a shorthand-typist working for several junior executives. (*R.S.A.*)

CHAPTER 3

HUMAN RELATIONS IN THE OFFICE

No one works in an office in complete isolation, and even where there are few employees and where the secretary occupies a room all to herself, she still frequently comes into contact with other persons, *e.g.* members of the public who have business dealings with her chief; her own immediate chief and his superiors and/or subordinates; her colleagues—other secretaries or clerical workers and junior employees. All these people come into personal contact with the secretary but there is a greater number still whom she may never meet and yet with whom she may enter into written or spoken communication. The relationship she establishes (Fig. 5) with every one of these individuals produces a subsequent effect. This effect may be quite remote from the secretary and her work situation—indeed

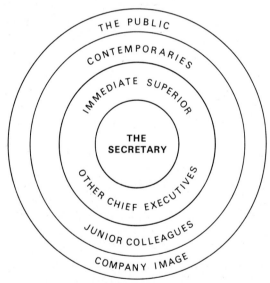

Fig. 5.—The secretary is concerned with developing and maintaining good relations with the public, with superiors and with fellow employees.

she will probably not be aware either of the implications of her actions or of their subsequent effect, but this does not make them any less real, or any less important.

RELATIONS WITH THE PUBLIC

Not all visitors who find their way to the secretary's office will necessarily be in a sunny frame of mind. They may have had difficulty in finding the premises; they may have been wrongly routed from the reception desk in the hall; they may reflect a nervous or belligerent attitude towards the impending interview—or they may be suffering from acute toothache! The secretary must be able to "handle" visitors: she may have to placate the angry man; to indulge the difficult customer; to put the nervous interviewee at his ease. Her duty is threefold: to the individual callers—she must treat them in the manner they have a right to expect; to her chief—her handling of the situation, the impression she presents of poise, efficiency and a pleasant disposition can set the mood for the interview with her boss; to her company—in a broad sense she has a duty to enhance her company's image, to increase its esteem in the eyes of the public.

Like an ever-widening ripple, the secretary's attitude towards members of the public who have dealings with the company will have repercussions far afield.

RELATIONS WITH SUPERIORS

Situations will occur daily in the secretary's dealings with her employer which call for tact, discretion and finesse. She should try to remember that her chief is an individual person as well as her boss. He is motivated by much the same human "wants" as other employees; he is subject to much the same stresses and strains as other individuals. An appreciation of this fact will lead to a deeper understanding of human behaviour. However, while the secretary must realise that her chief comes to the office from a background which is entirely personal—*e.g.* he has a married life which is entirely separate from the office; he is pleased (or disappointed) at the results of the local by-election; his child has caught measles or has failed in the G.C.E. exams; he is worried about his old and ailing mother; he has just had his dog put to sleep; his dentist has told him all his teeth must come out—she will, if she aspires to perfection, take care to show that as far as she is concerned his personal life is absolutely private. If he wants to talk about it, by all means lend a sympathetic ear. If he complains that his wife doesn't understand him, you may make soothing noises—BUT DON'T GO BEYOND THIS. To allow relationships to become personal must detract from the business relationship in the end.

Christian names may sound friendly and cheerful, but it is suggested that, with the chief at any rate, the secretary should not allow the relationship to become so personal. If he wishes to call his secretary by her christian name, certainly he is entitled to do so, but unless he specifically asks her to call him by his first name, she should not become so "pally." Even a young boss will gain dignity from being addressed as "Mr." and it is just not done for his superior to hear him being called "John" by his secretary. By preserving an atmosphere of dignity the secretary will be promoting efficiency: if a junior (who usually models herself on the senior secretary's behaviour) hears the boss being called "John" she may follow this example herself.

The question of going out with office colleagues or with the boss may pose some dilemma. There is no law against making personal friendships in the office, neither is there one against meeting a colleague outside the office on a social basis: indeed, a very large proportion of friendships begin in this way (and many men use the office as a hunting ground). However, the social aspect should be kept quite separate from the business side and talking "shop" is to be avoided if efficiency and respect are to be maintained in the office. And there is always the danger of being suspected of talking shop or giving away confidential information if it becomes known that the secretary is meeting a colleague outside the office. (A "don't care what they think" attitude is not the answer: the perfect secretary *does* care.)

There can be no harm in accepting an invitation from the chief if it comes as a reward, or as a means of thanking a secretary who has performed some extra service for her chief, over and above "the line of duty"; but to become too friendly outside the office may prove embarrassing in the long run and impair the efficiency of the chief/ secretary team.

The ideal relationship is one which has developed after months (not to say years) of working together *as a team*. The secretary should feel able to speak frankly to her boss; to "sense" his moods— even to anticipate them. She should have learnt whether a little "mothering" annoys him or not. If not, by all means she may buy him sandwiches if he has no time to go out to lunch, or she could sew on a button for him, or she could brush his coat before he goes to an important meeting, but this "mothering" must not be carried too far. To be for ever "clucking" after him like a worried hen is the surest way of irritating all but the most spoiled of employers.

If her opinion is asked, then the secretary should give it unreservedly, even if it differs from the chief's own, but she should not sulk if it is not acted upon. Even if her opinion is not asked for, a senior secretary might venture to give it if the issue is important enough; if she is rebuffed she should not sulk. The ideal secretary never sulks. Her chief may give her cause, but she should not show anger, irritation or impatience. It simply doesn't help. Either he won't notice, or he will pretend not to notice (which has the same effect) or he too will sulk, making the atmosphere impossible to work in! Try to cultivate a cheerful disposition (even if you don't feel cheerful, you can pretend). But a hint, or a straightforward remark is permissible to clear the air or to avoid perpetuating an unacceptable state of affairs.

RELATIONS WITH FELLOW EMPLOYEES

In her relations with her contemporaries, *i.e.* colleagues in similar positions to her own, the secretary will find that a sound, friendly relationship will help the smooth running of her work. Often, she may have to telephone her opposite number in another firm or another department of the same firm, to make or cancel an appointment or to ask for information, and a pleasant, helpful manner will invite reciprocal action.

Every employee in the organisation is an individual in his/her own right, leads a private life outside the office and is subject to the stresses and strains that life creates, both in the office and at home. An appreciation of this fact will lead to the realisation that each employee (even those the secretary doesn't like) is earning his living in the best way he knows. Petty jealousies should not be allowed to take root (and it is amazing how easily they can grow and multiply in an office). One girl notices that another appears to enjoy privileges exclusively; she wonders why, becomes jealous, behaves unreasonably. In fact, there may be very valid reasons for the apparent privileges: indeed, there usually are. Look at the following examples.

(*a*) One secretary is allowed more flexibility in timekeeping (she comes in later and often leaves earlier) than the other girls. So much is obvious. What is less apparent is that she may have explained her private reasons for requiring the extra time to her chief; if it is only for a short period, he may permit this temporary adjustment of working hours. Alternatively, the girl might have agreed to a reduction in salary or to forego her annual holiday.

(*b*) An employee discovers that her contemporary in another department is earning more than she is. There is not necessarily injustice in the administration of salary scales. Could it be that the "other girl" is better qualified, has had longer service with the firm, is more capable?

A secretary should never try to gain favour at someone else's expense—a reputation for that sort of thing is just about the worst possible thing that could happen to a girl in the office. Not only will she be disliked and mistrusted by her colleagues, but her chief will not like to have a secretary with this nasty trait. It is not suggested that every individual in the office must be liked and respected, but if the secretary cannot like them all, she can at least hide her dislike for them. Here lies the perfect practice ground for cultivating tact and diplomacy.

Relations with juniors merit special notice, too. Juniors come with dispositions that are sunny, brash, timid, reserved . . . the adjectives could go on and on. But the same thing applies to the lowliest junior as to the chief executive. There is a home life quite separate from the office life. There are brothers and sisters, parents and boyfriends all of whom are unknown to office personnel but who nevertheless exert their influence over the junior's behaviour in the office.

For example, a disinclination to work late to finish a "rush" job could indicate a "couldn't care less" attitude, but on the other hand there might be any one of a number of reasons why the junior hesitates when asked to stay late: she might have aged parents who rely on her help when she comes home from work; she might have to fetch a younger brother or sister from school; she might have a mother who worries herself sick if her daughter is even a few minutes late; she might have to attend evening classes; she might have an exciting "date." And so on. An appreciation of the "human element" will cause a senior secretary to give plenty of notice before requiring overtime; to allow the junior to telephone her home from the office to say she will be late—indeed she should suggest it—and to let her go at the earliest opportunity.

Quite apart from the respect which the junior has a right to expect, it will be in the secretary's own selfish interests to cultivate good relations with her because of the interdependence of individuals within an organisation. For example, if the office junior is late in arriving with the morning's mail, or has made a mistake in its distribution, it is largely in the senior secretary's own hands as to how this error is pointed out to the junior. An impatient frown, and a harsh word could freeze the timid junior, produce tears and make for confusion when dealing with the next day's mail; or it could infuriate the spiteful junior who might deliberately sabotage the secretary's routine just to "get even," *e.g.* by inserting the wrong letters in the In Tray, by "losing" an important file or by delaying the commencement of work by making the secretary's office the last in the delivery rounds; or it could induce the junior to hand in her notice, with the consequent trouble of finding a replacement and training the new girl all over again.

There are, of course, ways of dealing with each of the possible developments outlined above, but none will be resolved without frustration or at the very least waste of time on the secretary's part. How much simpler to point out kindly and clearly the junior's mistake in the first place, thus earning that girl's co-operation, loyalty and respect.

The best way to deal with any awkward situation is for the secretary to try to put herself in the other person's place and to ask herself how she would have liked the matter dealt with. Juniors and superiors alike are individual persons, quite distinct from the role they play in the office. After office hours, they do not curl up in a filing cabinet for the night, but go home to their wives and families or to their parents.

JOB SATISFACTION

Individuals seek from the work situation satisfactions which are common to the majority of workers (Fig. 6). They want pleasant superiors and colleagues, responsible and interesting work, security and an adequate wage packet, adequate status with prospects for promotion, tasks which are commensurate with their ability and pleasant surroundings and working conditions.

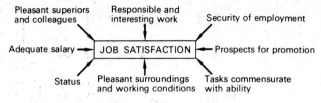

Fig. 6.—Job satisfaction.

Workers want an understanding boss, one who is approachable. Do you know this type—he consents to see you, asks you to sit down and the minute you start to talk he glances at the clock, fidgets with papers on his desk, gives you the impression he isn't really listening? An employee wants a boss who does *not* do these things. Workers also require pleasant companions from their work situation. It's not against the rules to exchange views with a colleague, to chat for a few minutes. (But it *is* wrong to spend ages chatting in the cloakroom or applying make-up.) Just as the secretary will want her chief to be pleasant, understanding, appreciative, so will her own juniors hope to find these qualities in her. She should try to avoid appearing impatient, cross or "flustered," even if—as will surely happen—she sometimes feels it.

A little bit of good acting can be of tremendous help. Credit should be given if credit is due. Appreciation for a job well done *must* be shown. Above all, be approachable. This is in your own interest, for if a junior is too frightened to ask questions her work may be done badly, resulting in wasted time.

1. RESPONSIBLE AND INTERESTING WORK

In an ideal world, there should be no need for anyone to work at uncongenial tasks or at low levels of pay, but even in our imperfect situation when one takes into account that about half our waking life is spent at work it is surely foolish to accept dull and tedious work for the sake of slightly higher rates and many workers do in fact accept employment offering somewhat lower rates of pay because the job content is interesting. This is not to say that all tasks which go to make up a complete job have to be challenging and interesting, but the job *as a whole* must be, otherwise the worker becomes frustrated, bored and unresponsive. The work must also be responsible: there is an element of satisfaction in knowing that one is capable of handling responsible work. Responsibility savours of integrity, maturity, capability. For example, tedious work could be responsible work if accuracy is an essential part of it *and* the worker realises this. Secret work might not necessarily be interesting work (*e.g.*, it might be too technical for the secretary to understand, or it might be coded) but it is responsible work. There is a satisfaction in the knowledge that one is thought responsible and dependable.

A happy employee must exercise her capabilities. Do you know this type of boss: he gives you a job to do and then promptly checks on your progress, your accuracy, your understanding of the task so minutely that he might just as well have done it himself? What is the use of all the training a secretary has undergone if she is not allowed to use it, if her initiative is stunted before she has a chance to apply it? The intelligent superior will delegate a task and allow the subordinate as much freedom to complete the job as is consistent with preventing mistakes which might cause harm either to the firm or to the subordinate.

The same reasoning applies, of course, to the secretary's juniors: having shown them how to do a task and having ensured that they are capable of doing it, she should then allow the young people to get on with the job and give them a chance to prove themselves. (This, incidentally, has a dual benefit: it gives satisfaction to the junior and will prove useful to the secretary who is thereby training them to become more useful to her.) If the job is eventually well done it does no harm to show appreciation—everyone responds to encouragement (the secretary herself will have realised this when she feels "on top of the world" at a good word from her own boss).

2. SECURITY OF EMPLOYMENT

Even in times of full employment, the worker wants to feel secure in his job. Even if he knows that he can find another job without any trouble, the worker still wants to feel that it is for *him* to decide when to make a change: that he can "hand in his notice" at the time when it suits him to do so. It is extremely disconcerting to any but the most thick-skinned individual to be told that he is no longer needed in his job; it is a matter of dignity and of self-respect which has no relation to the availability or otherwise of other jobs.

For this reason the secretary should never threaten a junior with the possibility of losing her job. Even if this is known to be true it should not be revealed without the superior's permission; and to even allude to such a serious step when there is no real justification is downright unkind. The secretary can do no better than ask herself how she would react to such treatment.

3. AN ADEQUATE SALARY

Man (the worker) must satisfy certain basic needs. He must satisfy his hunger and thirst; he must have warmth and shelter from the elements. When these basic needs are satisfied, he can turn to other "wants." He can seek pleasure in the way he satisfies his hunger; he can choose how he will keep warm; he can decide to decorate the walls of his cave. In a sophisticated society, it can be assumed that the basic wants are no longer the same as those of primitive man. (They are really, but the assumption is that the "wants" have been satisfied over several stages.) Take the example of hunger: the basic need would be to stop the pangs; the second stage might be with which food to stop the pangs (*e.g.*, which food gives most pleasure); after that might come a decision as to what surroundings to eat the meal in (*e.g.*, home, restaurant, country picnic), and so on.

The worker's salary is a means of satisfying his needs. He needs an adequate salary in order to maintain the standard of living to which he is accustomed. But given enough money to maintain such a standard of living, he does not necessarily want more than that. He must now choose whether to accept an "adequate" salary and gain other benefits (*e.g.*, pleasant surroundings) or whether to take a higher salary (more than enough) and, perhaps, perform dangerous work.

If "adequate" is taken to mean that it satisfies the worker's accustomed standard of living, then most people give very serious considerations to other factors.

4. ADEQUATE STATUS

What's in a name? Apparently, quite a lot. Advertisements in the daily papers usually try to make the job sound attractive by giving it a higher status than it merits. How many people call themselves secretaries when in fact they are really performing clerical duties such as shorthand and typing, possibly keeping the petty cash and answering the telephone? Nevertheless, human nature being what it is, we like to think well of ourselves and we like others to think highly of us, too. Therefore a little bit of psychology can go a long way towards making employees contented. If there are no immediate prospects for promotion, there might be time to reward a deserving employee, expressing appreciation of her good work, suggesting a slight change in the job content and upgrading her status. Thus a junior messenger could graduate to clerk/typist. A clerk/typist could become a specialist clerk, *e.g.* costing clerk, wages clerk, etc. Finally a shorthand-typist could be promoted to junior secretary. It is the senior secretary who might suggest such action to the chief, and it is certainly her job to keep the wheels of her section well oiled. By sensing the morale of the employees, by keeping aware of their progress, she can contribute enormously to the smooth running of her office.

5. PROSPECTS FOR PROMOTION

There comes a time in the office life of any employee when he asks himself: where do I go from here? If the employee does not see promotion with reasonable certainty in the not too distant future you can be sure that he *will* go from here; and you will have to train his replacement all over again. (The surest way to get rid of any but the dullest employee is to make it obvious that there is no prospect for promotion.) Even if promotion cannot be imminent, it is usually worthwhile to show an able employee how this can be achieved, *e.g.* by gaining an additional qualification (a shorthand-typist could attain higher speeds, an accounts clerk could work towards a professional qualification). This acts as a spur to the worker; he starts to work towards a goal, learns more, becomes a more useful employee and eventually gets the promised promotion (which is by now very well deserved). However, a word of caution is necessary: do not set impossible goals. The "carrot" is well worth attaining, but if it is too hard or impossible to reach, then the result will be a defeated, deflated and bewildered employee. It is advisable and always possible to get experienced help in guiding employees.

6. TASKS COMMENSURATE WITH ABILITY

Although many employees do not realise this, the worker is happiest at his work when he feels confident that he can cope with it. Efficient secretaries develop a certain poise and a capable appearance when they have been at their job long enough to know that they will be able to cope with whatever emergencies or crises the day will bring, when they have confidence in their own ability to deal with the day's pressures. The same applies at any level. The secretary's chief and her juniors are subject to the same emotions and stimuli, to the same responses. To give a junior clerk work that is too difficult for her will make her bewildered, unhappy and discontented. This is not to say that all tasks must be easy ones, but the secretary should try to introduce harder or more complicated work gradually, taking time and trouble to explain clearly not only how the task should be done, but giving extra information, *e.g.* why it is important that it should be done in a certain way; what would be the consequences if it were not done so; what will happen to the work when it leaves the junior. A fuller understanding of the job will ensure that fewer mistakes are made.

Similarly, the secretary herself should try to find out the place of her work within the framework of the organisation as a whole. This will enable her to perform her own duties far more satisfactorily than if she merely views each task as an entity in its own right. As ability to perform the job grows, so the intelligent employee will require to be fed with more important or more complicated work. To be important, work does not have to be complicated: thus it is not complicated to make a decision, but it is important that the decision should be the right one. Executive or "top" secretaries often have to make decisions on behalf of the chief. A copy typist, on the other hand, could eventually graduate to the more complicated display required in tabular statements, balance sheets, and so on.

The important point to remember is that an employee must know that he can (or will soon be able to) cope with the work which he is set.

7. PLEASANT SURROUNDINGS AND WORKING CONDITIONS

No one likes to work in poky little offices, badly lit, damp, etc. To a large extent, recent legislation has improved working conditions in offices (the *Offices, Shops and Railway Premises Act* 1963) but it must be remembered that the Act lays down *minimum* standards. The secretary may not be able to change the actual location of the premises, but she can do a lot towards making the office a pleasanter place. Keeping the office tidy is an obvious example; bringing in a pot plant or flowers is another. But she might be able to do more: she could persuade her chief that it is time to redecorate; she could bear in mind the design and appearance of any furniture (*e.g.*, desks, cabinets) that she orders, and the layout of office furniture. She can see to it that junior clerks are trained to keep the office tidy and clean; that they have a place to keep biscuits or sandwiches they may bring to the office. Otherwise, she is liable, on going to a filing cabinet for a file, to find her fingers closing round a half finished packet of crisps!

Many offices now offer amenities and services to the employee such as the running of a sports and social club; medical advice; schemes for loans or advances on salary; training facilities, and so on. It is important that employees should be aware of the benefits in which they might be entitled to participate. The secretary should try to become familiar with them and ensure that any newcomers to her department are made aware of their existence.

It is impossible to gauge the degree of importance attached to any of these "needs" by a worker. Indeed, in some instances, the worker may not be aware that he seeks these satisfactions from his work. In any case he will be influenced by personal background, past experience and individual traits. Thus one worker may place "prospects for promotion" higher on his list of priorities than "pleasant surroundings." Another may place "pleasant superior and colleagues" before "status." However, if a generalisation may be attempted, it might be illustrated as in Fig. 7.

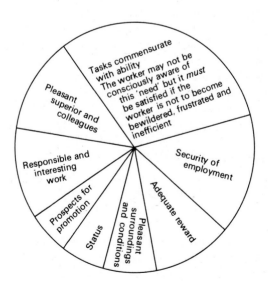

Fig. 7.—What goes into job satisfaction.

CONCLUSION

The important facts that emerge from this chapter are the importance of maintaining good relations both with "outsiders" and with "colleagues"; the satisfactions which individuals seek from their work situation; and how the leaders or supervisors have a duty to help to achieve desirable objectives.

Short-answer Questions

1. What qualities are needed on the part of a secretary to ensure that she does not "snap" at a junior?

2. With whom is it important that the secretary should maintain good relations in the office?

3. List six personal attributes desirable in a secretary.

4. Why might the chief appear to be bad tempered for no obvious reason?

5. In what ways is a secretary dependent (*a*) on her juniors and (*b*) on her "opposite number" in another department?

6. What should you do if the boss asks you to go out to dinner with him?

7. It is necessary to ask your junior assistant to work late one evening; how would you tackle the matter?

8. What would most employees require of their work situation?

9. If you discover that your married boss has a girlfriend, what, if anything, should you do?

10. Suggest ways in which your attitude could influence employees to remain long-term with your firm, and not look for a better job.

Past Examination Questions

1. What qualities are needed on the part of both employer and secretary to make an ideal working relationship?   (*L.C.C.*)

2. Your firm has been taken over and the person for whom you work is to be promoted to a position where the secretarial work has been done by the same person for many years. She is to retire in eighteen months' time and it has been suggested that you should join the typing pool for this period in the hope that eventually you will join your employer. What will you do and why?   (*L.C.C.*)

3. A junior typist is frequently late. She offers different excuses, some of which sound genuine, but more often than not prove to be untrue. Despite this failing, she is a good, industrious worker with a higher than average standard of efficiency. As secretary to the departmental manager, how would you deal with this situation?

(R.S.A.)

4. Owing to the rebuilding of part of the premises, typists have been given desks in a room next to yours and you have been asked to keep an eye on them. The typists complain that the room is badly lit and inadequately heated. As they will be there for some months, you feel something should be done about it. Write a report to the Office Manager. (R.S.A.)

5. You work for a secretarial agency. An important client, who is a friend of the owners, telephones to say he is going abroad the next day for a few days, and that he would like to come to the Agency to dictate a few letters before he goes.

He does not arrive until 5 p.m. You take him into the room where clients dictate their work. He does not begin dictating at once, but talks to you about his trip. When he does begin, it turns out that he wants not only to dictate, but also to have a number of forms filled in and documents photocopied. All this takes time to explain.

It is a rule of the Agency that staff may not work after 6 p.m. unless another member of the staff is on the premises.

At 6 p.m., Jane, one of the junior typists, asks to speak to you, and when you are outside the office, she tells you that she has offered to stay until you have finished and that she will be working in the typists' room.

At 7 p.m., you ask the client if there is much more to do, and he asks you to stay on for a little while in order to finish.

At 7.30 p.m., he is still dictating and shows no signs of nearing the end. You have not had a meal since 12 noon, and you know that Jane has a long journey home. You do not want to offend the client. What would you do? (R.S.A.)

6. What would your reactions be if you went for an interview for a new job and learned that you would work for a middle-aged woman, and also that you would be in charge of two boys, one a messenger and the other a photo-copying machine operator? (R.S.A.)

7. Mary, your young duplicating operator, has been on a week's course to learn to use an offset duplicating machine. She has come top of the class and your employer, who is away ill, wishes to write

and congratulate her. He asks you, by telephone, to prepare a letter for his signature, congratulating Mary. Write the letter.   (*R.S.A.*)

8. You are in charge of a number of junior staff. Your immediate superior criticises individual juniors in full hearing of other employees. How would you try to overcome such unpleasant episodes?

(*R.S.A.*)

9. You work for a Personnel Officer. While she is on holiday you are left to deal with emergencies, although you are, of course, able to ask the advice of executive members of staff. A telephone operator does not turn up for work for two days and neither telephones nor writes. Decide what you would do in these circumstances and write a memorandum describing your actions so that the Personnel Officer will be fully informed on her return.   (*R.S.A.*)

10. A junior from another department comes to you in an unhappy frame of mind. She says she "can do nothing right" in the eyes of the head of her department. The head of that department is a woman senior to you. What could you do?   (*R.S.A.*)

CHAPTER 4

COMMUNICATION: I

CORRESPONDENCE

It is probably true to say that dealing with correspondence forms the bulk of a private secretary's work. Just as the sound of her voice over the telephone creates an impression—pleasant or otherwise—on her listener, so the wording, format and neatness of the letters she sends out on behalf of her employer create an impression on the recipient. It is very tempting to adopt the attitude that "nothing but the best" must be allowed to leave the office; that letters containing errors must be retyped and that if the boss changes his mind after the letter has been typed, he must not be allowed to make the alteration with pen and ink. However, to be a perfectionist, although laudable in theory, is just not feasible in practice. The intelligent secretary must establish a high standard for her work and must then maintain that standard, but she will realise that to achieve 100 per cent accuracy at all times is unrealistic in terms of economy and—for that reason— inefficient in the real sense of the word. This may sound like heresy to the typist who takes pride in her work, but a moment's thought and an intelligent interpretation of the foregoing advice will show it to be sound. Is it really worth falling behind with the rest of the work in order to retype a letter which contained an error that could have been erased? If the boss decides to make a small alteration by hand, will you risk incurring his annoyance as well as delay in posting by suggesting that you retype the letter? The answer is of course "no." But this advice must be applied intelligently, and the secretary must decide what is "mailable" work. Experience here, as in every other area of the secretary's job, is a great teacher; the chief's advice is invaluable; a colleague's opinion is helpful; and the secretary's own good judgment must be trusted.

43

1. WRITING LETTERS

There will be occasions when the secretary must write letters for her chief. Correspondence which she is able to deal with might be delegated to her: in these cases, she would compose the letters and present them typed and ready for signature to her chief. The secretary would be well advised to study and cultivate her boss's own style of writing so that the recipient of the letter is not aware that the chief has not given his full attention to it. With daily doses of dictation from her chief, it will not be difficult for a secretary to acquire his style of writing.

In other instances, the secretary may have to write letters in her own name but on behalf of her chief. Here she will of course allow free rein to her own style of expression, and will merely indicate at the foot of her letter that it has been written by someone else on behalf of the chief. The following phrases are commonly used.

EXAMPLE 1

> Yours faithfully,
>
> *Mary Smith (Miss)*
>
> Secretary to John Brown, Sales Manager.

EXAMPLE 2

> Yours faithfully,
>
> *Mary Smith (Mrs.)*
>
> *for* John Brown,
>   Director.

EXAMPLE 3

> Yours faithfully,
> X.Y.Z. COMPANY LTD.
>
> *Mary Smith (Miss)*
>
> Signed by Mr. Brown's Secretary
> in his absence.

NOTE:

If you do not indicate "Miss" or "Mrs." you will be causing some perplexity to anyone who wishes to reply to you personally, and you deserve to be addressed as M. Smith, Esq.!

If a letter is dictated by the chief but he is not able to sign it personally, this can be indicated (if desired) in the following manner.

.EXAMPLE 4

```
            Yours faithfully,
            X.Y.Z. COMPANY LTD.

            Mary Smith (Miss)
  for  J. Brown, Director.
            Dictated by Mr. Brown and signed
            in his absence.
```

It will be noted that the word "for" is used rather than the abbreviation "p.p." or "per pro." Per pro, the abbreviation for *per procurationem*, means not merely "by permission" but "with the express legal authority," and few secretaries will have such authority, *e.g.* where a power of attorney has been given. It is therefore more correct to sign letters merely "for" the chief, *i.e.* on his behalf.

To give a more personal touch to letters, the salutation

```
"Dear ..."
```

is used, a blank space being left after the word "dear" for the writer to insert by hand his correspondent's name. This style is adopted where the addressee is known personally to the writer and it is desired to give the letter a personal touch, even though it has been typewritten. In this case, the correct complimentary close would be

```
"Yours ...."
```

The word "sincerely" would be written by hand, and no designation usually follows the signature, as the writer is sufficiently well known to the addressee.

The next step towards the formal business letter is the letter which starts

```
"Dear Mr. Jones"
```

or

```
"Dear John"
```

the complete salutation being typed, *i.e.* the name is not inserted by hand. The corresponding ending here would naturally be

```
"Yours sincerely"
```

(again in typescript). After that, of course, comes the familiar

```
"Dear Sir/Yours faithfully"
```

which requires no comment, but what of the ending

```
"Yours truly"?
```

Does it have a place in the business letter, and if so with which salutation should it be coupled? Opinions vary, but I feel that it belongs with the opening of "Dear Sir" or even possibly "Dear Mr. Jones," if the tone of the letter is not sufficiently formal to merit a close of "Yours faithfully," nor yet sufficiently familiar to warrant "Yours sincerely." Where it is desired to convey a tone somewhere between these two endings, "Yours truly" may be used. It will be appreciated that the dividing line is very thin, and personal preference is usually the guiding factor.

To reflect fully the typist's competence, the outgoing letter must be displayed to the best advantage. Neat, accurate typescript is not in itself sufficient to create the best impression on the recipient of a letter; it is necessary to adopt a layout which shows an awareness both of the latest "fashion" and of what is pleasing to the eye.

Thus the size of paper selected should be appropriate to the length of the letter. The text should be attractively displayed, with insets being symmetrically indented, double line spacing used if it is necessary to spread a very short text over the page, and headings or sub-headings underlined for emphasis.

There are several methods of displaying written material and any method which serves the purpose of making the communication clear and attractive is acceptable, but the typist should be consistent throughout the letter. Thus, if a subject heading is used for each new matter dealt with in the letter, and the first heading is underlined, so should they all be underlined. Similarly, if the block method is used on the first page, then this method should be adopted throughout.

Compare the following styles.

```
Ref:  AB/CD/123                                    1st January, 1974


Dear Sir,

        This letter is an example of the indented style of display.

        Note that each new paragraph is indented by six character spaces,
i.e. half an inch of elite type.  If the type were pica, it would be
correct to indent the paragraphs by five character spaces.

        The complimentary close is indented to approximately half way
across the page and the designation is meticulously centred over the
writer's name and the complimentary close.

        The name and address of the recipient are typed at the foot of the
letter, a practice more commonly used in official (government) corres-
pondence than in commerce.  Note the indentation which, although con-
sistent with the style of indented paragraphs, is unnecessarily elaborate
and time-consuming.  This was once the rule for official letters but is
now giving way to a more modern style.

                                   Yours faithfully,
                                   X.Y.Z. COMPANY LTD.

                                        (J. Brown),
                                        Director.

A. Bee, Esq.,
   1 Blank Street,
      London, EC2 6NY
```

```
Ref:  AB/CD/123                                    1st January, 1974


A. Bee, Esq.,
1 Blank Street,
London, EC2 6NY.


Dear Sir,

        This letter is typed in a mixture of the block and the indented
styles of display.

        The paragraphs are still indented by half an inch; the compli-
mentary close and designation are still centred, but the name and
address of the recipient of the letter appear at the top of the letter
(much more sensible since there is always the danger that the typist
may omit this at the end of the letter) and there is no indentation
(neater and quicker to type).

        Note the omission of the full stop at the end of the date.

                                   Yours faithfully,
                                   X.Y.Z. COMPANY LTD.


                                        (J. Brown),
                                        Director.
```

```
1 January 1974

Ref:  AB/CD/123


Mr. A. Bee
1 Blank Street
London  EC2 6NY


Dear Sir

This letter is an example of the fully blocked style.

The great advantage is the saving of time and effort since the typist
does not have to indent the date, the paragraphs or the complimentary
close.  Note the brevity of the date and the lack of punctuation through-
out especially in the date (the beginnings of this will have been noted
in the preceding example where the final full stop in the date was
abolished) and in the address.

How many key depressions has the typist saved when this letter is
compared with the first example?


Yours faithfully
X Y Z COMPANY LTD


J Brown
Director
```

2. THE INTERNAL MEMO

This is used in inter-office or inter-branch communications. The object is to convey written information and/or instructions in the most economical manner, saving both time and money.

To save money, the quality of paper used for memos may be inferior to that used for outgoing letters. Sometimes it may be possible to obtain large quantities of paper of an unusual colour at a substantial discount, and provided this colour is not likely to cause eyestrain, there is no objection. In many companies the printing of memos is undertaken internally, using the offset lithographic process, the stencil method or some other available means. Even though the result might not be entirely professional (much depends on the process used and the skill of the operator) the saving is certainly worthwhile for internal correspondence.

To save time, the memo form is pre-printed with the words

```
MEMORANDUM, To, From, Date, Ref, Subject.
```

and all variable information is written concisely, using a brief style. It is quite permissible to render the date 1.1.74 (Consider the number of typing strokes saved compared with 1st January, 1974.) Some organisations allow "Mr." to be omitted from the addressee's name; there is no salutation or complimentary close and it is not essential for the writer's full signature to appear at the end of the memo. However, it is usual (and this practice is recommended) to identify and give authority to the memo by initialling it at the end, usually over a row of dots.

3. REPORTS

These differ vastly in style and presentation from letters. The generally accepted rule is for the report to show at a glance (*i.e.*, at the beginning) the writer, the addressee, the date and the subject. Below this information, the text itself follows a generally accepted pattern:

(*a*) Terms of reference (the scope of the report).
(*b*) Research (what has been done).
(*c*) Findings (this is the result of (*b*) above).
(*d*) Action or recommendation (as appropriate).

The following example incorporates the above rules.

To: Secretarial students   From: Miss E. Austin
    1 January 1974

                            SPECIMEN REPORT

(Terms of Reference)   In accordance with your request I have made
                        an investigation into report writing in this country.

(Research)   Copies of reports made by office personnel to
                        their superiors have been obtained and a study of
                        the more commonly adopted styles has been made.

                        It appears that:

(Findings)   1. The subject heading is a great time-saver since
                        it enables the superior to determine at a glance
                        whether this particular piece of documentation
                        needs to be dealt with immediately or whether it
                        could safely be shelved for a short period.

                    2. It is only sensible to insert the addressee's
                        name in a prominent position since this enables
                        a person to see at once whether the report is
                        indeed in the right hands.

(Recommendation)   I recommend therefore that the format represen-
                        ted in this report be adopted throughout the company
                        and that instructions to this effect be issued to
                        our Typing Pool Supervisor forthwith.

                                                . . . .

The above report closely resembles the format of a memo, as indeed it should since it is intended to be an internal report. It sometimes happens that a report is submitted with a covering letter, or that it is not addressed to an individual but to several persons, or to a section of the public. In such cases, the recipient's name will not necessarily appear on the report itself; it is also permissible for the writer's name to appear at the end of the report. It will be seen that there are no hard and fast rules. The overriding consideration should be: "How can I best display my report so that the recipient will be able to identify it in the shortest time possible?"

4. SUMMARIES

It may happen that the secretary is asked to summarise lengthy reports or newspaper articles and the following few pointers should prove helpful.

(*a*) If you don't understand what the article is about, don't attempt a summary! Far better to admit frankly to your boss that it is just too difficult for you.

(*b*) If you have read through the report or article, and you do understand it, ask yourself: "What is it all about?" The answer should give you a title for it. Try to keep the title brief.

(*c*) Read through the article again and underline those parts of it which you think are important enough to be included in your summary.

(*d*) Read it through again and satisfy yourself that you have done (*c*) above correctly.

(*e*) Now compose your summary from the underlined sentences. Read over your work to ensure that it does not sound stilted; it is not enough to just copy out each sentence you have underlined; you must not make it sound disjointed.

(*f*) Unless you are answering an examination question which particularly requires a certain number of words in your summary, or particularly requires you to use your own words, use the amount of words and the phrasing which in your opinion makes the best summary. If, however, you are answering an examination question which requires the summary to be "in your own words," you may find it helpful to ask yourself "what does this paragraph mean?" By answering that question, you will have the meaning in your own words.

5. STYLES OF ADDRESS

Not many examiners now require candidates to answer formally how they would address individuals ranging from the Queen to the nobility and members of the clergy; nor is it considered essential for a good secretary to have this knowledge at her fingertips. But she should know where to find this information if required. Modes of address will be found in typists' desk books, some typing textbooks and such reference books as Pears Cyclopaedia and Black's *Titles and Forms of Address*.

The following information would, however, be useful to the secretary in her everyday work:

(*a*) Husband and wife are jointly addressed by the husband's Christian name and surname, *e.g.* Mr. and Mrs. Albert Brown.

(*b*) A married woman is generally addressed by her husband's Christian name and surname, *e.g.* Mrs. Albert Brown.

(*c*) A widow may be addressed by her own Christian name and her late husband's surname, *e.g.* Mrs. Mary Brown. This is necessary to avoid possible confusion with her son's wife.

(*d*) A divorced woman may take her ex-husband's surname. (If it is known that she prefers to resume her maiden name, her wishes should of course be respected.)

(*e*) Limited liability companies should be addressed by the name of the company, *e.g.* the Magic Typewriter Company Ltd.

(*f*) Partnerships take the preface Messrs., *e.g.* Messrs. John Brown & Co.

(*g*) The prefix Mr. is now generally accepted as synonymous with Esq., and either may be used.

So far as business letters are concerned, as mentioned earlier in this chapter, if the writer wishes to give his letter a semi-personal tone he may begin it with

```
Dear ...
```

in typescript, and insert the name.

6. DRAFTING ADVERTISEMENTS

To produce results, an advertisement must be arresting, explicit and brief. Let us take as an example an advertisement to fill a vacancy for a shorthand-typist. If it is not eye-catching, it may be missed by a number of suitable applicants; if it is not sufficiently informative, many would-be applicants may misunderstand or decide not to apply; and if it is not fairly brief a number of possible applicants may not bother to read the whole of it. Although it is wise to keep the advertisement short, this must not be at the cost of withholding interesting information. For example, would-be applicants are usually highly interested in the salary offered, and to state "good salary offered" is not as informative as "salary range £1,000–£1,500." Similarly, if it is possible to include some information about the duties, more applicants might be attracted. Compare

```
"Secretary required.   Interesting work."
```

with

```
"Secretary required.   Duties include meeting overseas visitors
 at airport."
```

7. LETTERS OF APPLICATION

So far as the secretary is concerned, an application for a post may well be one of the most important letters she has to write in her career, and it is well worth spending some time over the draft. The following hints should prove helpful.

(*a*) Should such a letter be typed or handwritten? There are two schools of thought: those who feel it should be handwritten say that an employer may be looking for neat handwriting, that he may find therein a clue to the personality of the applicant, that handwriting lends just the right "personal" touch to a formal business letter. Those who advocate a typed application maintain that the employer sees a "sample" of what he is buying when he receives a neat, well displayed, typed letter, that the employer is not a graphologist, and that a letter of application is a business letter, not a personal one. I must confess that my own views are in sympathy with this.

(*b*) An increasingly popular method is to write a brief covering letter and attach to it a separate form showing the "curriculum vitae." When drafting the covering letter, try to visualise the employer's needs, rather than your wants. Your letter should convey the impression that the applicant will just fit his requirements. If you can show that his requirements happen to suit you too, then you are in a strong position. For example:

"The location of your offices is particularly convenient as my home is within very short walking distance."

"I am pleased to note from your advertisement that day-release is offered as I would very much like to continue my studies."

"I have always been interested in legal work - at college I gained distinction in the examination in General Principles of Law - and feel that the post of legal secretary would exactly match my interests."

But beware of making your letter too long: a businessman is a busy man.

On a separate sheet of paper, fill in neatly all the information that you think your employer will want to know about you. The following is a suggested format:

(*i*) *Name.* (Do not forget to insert here as in your covering letter whether you are "Miss" or "Mrs.").

(*ii*) *Address.*

(*iii*) *Age.*

(*iv*) *Education.* (It is not necessary to go into detail on primary education; secondary and/or further education is sufficient.)

(*v*) *Academic and vocational attainment.* A list of certificates and other qualifications gained should be given. Do not forget any special awards, *e.g.* medal, distinctions, etc.

(*vi*) *Past experience.* Experience in irrelevant occupations should be played down, but full details of knowledge and experience relevant to the employment being sought should be stated. mention also any special aptitudes (if relevant), which your past employers were able to exploit, *e.g.* figure work, languages.

(*vii*) *Present employers.* (It is not essential to divulge this information at the application stage, but you will probably be asked for their name if you are called for interview.) You may insert a special request that your employers are not to be contacted for a reference without your prior permission, which will certainly be given if you are actually offered the job.

(*viii*) *Other relevant information.* This is reserved for any special points you want to emphasise, *e.g.* if a car driver is preferred, you may like to state that you have a "clean" driving licence; if the job involves travelling, you may like to say that you have no home ties and are completely mobile; and so on.

ABBREVIATIONS AND SPELLING

1. COMMON ABBREVIATIONS

When typing abbreviated words, it is usual to insert a full stop after the abbreviation, thus: div. (dividend), l.c. (lower case). Certain abbreviations such as degrees or other qualifications are written with a full stop between the letters, thus: B.A. (Bachelor of Arts), and it is important to insert the full stop in the correct position. Abbreviations such as LL.B. (Bachelor of Laws) should be noted carefully. In some instances, the letters used in two abbreviations can be the same, but have different meanings according to whether they are in upper or lower case. Sometimes the use of a solidus or a full stop will indicate the distinction. Examples are given below, followed by a list of the more common abbreviations and their meanings.

```
a/c   =  account
A/C   =  account current

pp    =  pages
pp.   =  per procurationem

P.P. =  parcel post
```

```
a.m.       =  Ante meridiem (before noon)

a/v        =  Ad valorem (according to the value)

c.i.f.     =  cost, insurance and freight

c/o        =  care of

E. & O. E. =  errors and omissions excepted

e.g.       =  exampli gratia (for example)

et seq.    =  et sequentia (and the following)

f.o.b.     =  free on board

i.e.       =  id est (that is)

l.c.       =  lower case
```

n.b.	=	nota bene (take good note)
nem. con.	=	nemine contradicente (no one contradicting)
per pro.	=	per procurationem (with the authority of)
pro tem.	=	pro tempore (for the time being)
q.v.	=	quod vide (which see)
R.S.V.P.	=	Répondez s'il vous plait (reply if you please)
u.c.	=	upper case
viz.	=	videlicet (namely)

In some cases, it is necessary to take great care in distinguishing abbreviations. Compare

B. of E.	(Bank of England)	B/E	(Bill of Exchange)
l. c.	(lower case)	L/C	(Letter of Credit)

However, most offices have their own phraseology and there is rarely any danger of confusion after the secretary has gained some experience.

Many employers who draft their letters by hand employ an abbreviated system of writing which only they (and an intelligent secretary) can transcribe! Can you decipher the following?

2. SPELLING

There is only limited benefit in telling a girl to look up a word in the dictionary. If she is in doubt as to the correct spelling, then the dictionary must certainly be consulted, but in many cases a weak speller simply does not know that she is spelling inaccurately and does not therefore look up words in the dictionary. This is a difficult problem, but it is not insurmountable; the best solution is of course to improve your spelling. This can be done in several ways:

(*a*) *By reading:* If you see a word written accurately often enough, you will—with no conscious effort—learn to write it accurately yourself. Have you noticed how some people who are not sure how to spell a word write it down both ways and then decide which *looks* correct?

(*b*) *By learning from your mistakes:* Keep a list of words which you have misspelt at some time or other and look over it frequently.

(*c*) *By reading through the following list and trying to memorise the important points made:*

accommodate	two "m"s.
acknowledg(e)ment	acceptable with or without an "e."
judg(e)ment	acceptable with or without an "e."
all right	there is no such word as alright!
grammar	never grammer!
separate	never seperate!
apologise organise mechanise emphasise	"z" or "s" is acceptable.
supervise	always "s."
supervisor	always "-or."
adviser	always "-er."

the effect of reading is to affect her eyes.

effect	noun verb
affect	"effect" can also be used as a verb: to effect a change.
precede	to go before—and "e" comes before "o" in the alphabet!
proceed	to go along.
stationary	to remain still: a car is stationary—note the "a" in both car and stationary!
stationery	what letters are typed on—note the "e" in letters and stationery!
practise	the verb.
practice	the noun.
license	the verb.
licence	the noun.
advise	the verb.
advice	the noun—there is rarely any difficulty here, so why should there be with the others?
principal	head, main, capital—all with an "a" in them.
principle	theory—with an "e."

3. BUSINESS JARGON

It is now considered unnecessary, indeed out of date, to employ clichés and such jargon as

```
"your esteemed order," "your letter of the 10th ultimo," "assuring
you of our best attention at all times."
```

and others. The modern idea is to write *briefly* (businessmen do not want to waste their time ploughing through hundreds of words), and in *plain* English (the business letter is not the place to show off one's knowledge of uncommon words).

The skill in letter-writing lies in marshalling ideas and paragraphs into such an order and under such headings that the information is conveyed in the clearest possible way, and in achieving exactly the "tone" of letter desired. The latter skill is not easy to acquire, since it will be readily appreciated that a string of words may have more than one *shade* of meaning and only when read in context can the tone be discerned. As in many other things, however, practice makes perfect.

Short-answer Questions

1. What is the difference between a memo and a report?
2. Why is the indented method of letter display less popular today?
3. What does "per pro." stand for?
4. When should it be used?
5. What is the first thing you should do when attempting to write a summary?
6. Give three rules to remember when drafting an advertisement.
7. What do the following abbreviations stand for.

R.S.V.P.

viz.

i.e.

8. Make up a sentence to show you understand the use of the word "practise."
9. What is meant by "official" correspondence?
10. How may a secretary indicate a letter has been composed and signed by her while her chief was away?

Past Examination Questions

1. The copying work in your office has increased materially and your employer is considering the purchase of a photocopying machine. He knows very little about photocopiers and has asked you to advise him on a suitable model. Write a memorandum to him setting out your recommendations and how you have obtained the information. (*L.C.C.*)

2. Reply to the following advertisement:

"Jill of all Trades." Are you seeking a job with a difference? A busy, young and charming Managing Director is looking for someone to soothe his troubled brow; personality and enthusiasm as much as competence in secretarial duties are prerequisites. Long, erratic hours rewarded by good salary. Full details please to Box. 2345 . . . (*L.C.C.*)

3. The Managing Director of your Company has asked you to visit the Business Efficiency Exhibition to report on any one piece of equipment which you feel is long overdue in your office. Prepare the necessary report.   (*L.C.C.*)

4. Your employer has drafted the following notes to show possible ways of reducing the cost of stationery as this has been rather high in your office recently. Amplify these notes by replying in memo form:

(*i*) Printing costs might be reduced if we did our letterheads, memos, etc. Do we need to buy any new equipment or can we manage with our existing machines?

(*ii*) I am sure there is much wastage in the internal issue of such items as shorthand notebooks, ball point pens, etc. Can we tighten up here?

(*iii*) It might be possible to obtain better rates from our suppliers. Please see what you can find out about bulk buying and cash discounts.   (*L.C.C.*)

5. Give the correct spelling of any of the following words which you think to be misspelled: definately, predictible, discription, pronunciation, incidently, occurrence, privilege, acknowledgable, noticeable, interminible, invisible, adviser, advisory, promotor, prevalent.   (*R.S.A.*)

6. Rewrite this letter in better style:

Dear Sir, Thank you for your communication of 10th inst., which came to hand today. The aforesaid letter is receiving our prompt attention, but we respectfully beg to point out that owing to a recent strike we are unable to deal with the same within this week. Assuring you of our best attention at all times and trusting that you will continue to favour us with your esteemed orders, Yours faithfully,"   (*R.S.A.*)

7. Your employer has arranged for someone to come to measure several rooms which are to be carpeted, but, in spite of several telephone calls, no one has appeared. Write an appropriate letter, which you will sign yourself, to the firm concerned.   (*R.S.A.*)

8. Your employer has a party of foreign visitors whom he must entertain. He proposes to take them to the Science Museum. The following is an extract from an official guide book. From it, prepare a

paragraph of not more than 100 words which will indicate to the visitors what they will see.

"The Science Museum is the the national museum of science and industry. It is historical in method and illustrates by its collections the development of physical sciences and their applications in industry. The collections are rich in original pieces of scientific apparatus and of transport and industrial machinery, and these are supplemented where necessary by facsimile copies, scale models, demonstration exhibits, transparencies and diagrams.

Many of the exhibits can be operated by visitors or demonstrated in action to them. Others have been sectioned so that their internal structure can be clearly seen.

HOW TO REACH THE BUILDINGS

The main entrance to the museum is in Exhibition Road. There is a second entrance to the principal building at the eastern end of Imperial Institute Road, and at the western end of Imperial Institute Road will be found the entrance to the separate Western Galleries, in which the Aeronautics collection is temporarily exhibited. Access to the Library is through the Imperial College building in Imperial Institute Road.

The Museum is within a few minutes' walk of South Kensington Station on the District and Piccadilly railways, and a similar distance from bus routes, numbers 9, 46, 52 and 73.

LECTURES

Free public lectures are given daily (except Sundays) at 11.15 a.m. and 3.15 p.m. The morning lectures normally consist of conducted tours of particular galleries; the afternoon lectures are given in the Theatre. Many of the lectures in the Theatre are augmented by short sound films. The subjects of the day's lectures are indicated on the notice board in the Entrance Hall, and monthly programmes may be obtained at the Catalogue Stall.

Special lectures or lecture-tours can be arranged for

schools or other organised parties on weekdays between 10 a.m. and 5 p.m. without charge. Applications should reach the museum at least a week before the proposed visit.

HISTORY

The formation of a museum of science was first proposed by the Prince Consort after the Great Exhibition of 1851, and in 1857 collections illustrating foods, animal products, examples of structures and building materials and educational apparatus were placed on exhibition in a large corrugated iron building which had been built by the Royal Commissioners of the Exhibition of 1851 on the site of what is now the Victoria and Albert Museum.

In 1864, a collection of naval models and marine engines was lent by the Admiralty, and by 1873, when the exhibits belonging to the Admiralty were transferred to Greenwich, there remained a large number of important objects which formed an interesting collection illustrating ship and boat construction and marine engineering. This has been continually extended, until today it is one of the most important collections of its kind in existence.

The collections of scientific instruments and apparatus were first formed in 1874, but it was only after 1876 that they became important. The Special Loan Collection of Scientific Apparatus which was exhibited in the Museum during that year brought together examples of apparatus from various countries, and a large number of these were acquired for the museum.

Subsequently many additions were made, including, in 1900, the Maudslay Collection of machine tools and marine engine models, and, in 1903, the Bennett Woodcroft Collection of engine models and portraits.

In 1912, it was decided to rebuild the Science Museum in three blocks. Progress was delayed by the 1914–18 war, and it was not until 1928 that the first of the new blocks was formally opened by His Majesty King George V."   (*R.S.A.*)

9. Rewrite this letter in good style:

Dear Sir, Thank you for your letter of 30th ult, which came to hand to-day. Your esteemed order for which we thank you, is receiving our prompt attention. The goods you require, which you desire to receive so urgently, were not all available at the time of the receipt of the order, and we have had to send away for same which we hope will soon be here and which we will send on to you as soon as received. Again thanking you for your esteemed order and hoping to be of service to you at all times. Yours faithfully.   (*R.S.A.*)

10. Because of the increased volume of work in your office, it is proposed to appoint a junior shorthand-typist to work under you. Draft the advertisement to appear in the press, and give your employer a short note on what you consider to be the necessary qualifications and personal attributes of the person to be appointed, together with some questions which he can put to candidates at an interview.   (*R.S.A.*)

CHAPTER 5

COMMUNICATION: II

DIRECT COMMUNICATION

THE conveying of thoughts, ideas, information and instructions may be effected in several ways. Direct face-to-face verbal communication is usually the easiest way of conveying exactly the right information, since one has at one's disposal a *choice of words*, which is supported by a *tone of voice*, and when these are used simultaneously with *facial expression* and *gesticulation*, we have the quickest, easiest and most accurate method of communication (Fig. 8). However, this is not

WHEN GOOD IS BAD

	Medium	Meaning
This is a good piece of work	Words	It's good
This is a good piece of work (sounding pleased)	Words + inflexion of voice	It's really good
This is a good piece of work (sounding sarcastic, frowning and tearing up the work)	Words + inflexion of voice + facial expression + gesticulation	It's bad

Fig. 8.—Direct verbal face-to-face communication makes use of four media.

always the most practical method. For example, it creates no permanent record (as is well recognised in law, where libel (written defamation) is clearly differentiated from slander (oral defamation)). There may therefore be difficulty in referring to a verbal communication at some future date. Direct face-to-face communication may also be so slow as to be impractical. If A wants to communicate with B using this method and B is located at the North Pole, A will have to delay his communication until he has travelled to B's location!

There are of course many ways in which these drawbacks may be overcome. If you want verbal communication over some distance,

63

you may use the telephone. Here you have at your disposal *choice of words* and *tone of voice*, but you cannot convey the visual impression of a frown, and if you use your hands when talking (gesticulation) the effect is wasted on the other party. It will be seen in this situation how much more important the available media of words and voice have become.

It is not of course always necessary to communicate verbally. Indeed it may be essential to have a written record. Now you have only *choice of words* at your disposal, and it is solely through the choice of words that you can convey the desired "tone." The recipient of your letter will have no means of discovering what you want to tell him other than the words you have used, so in letter-writing the use of words is all-important. It is of course easy to combine written communication with speed, and Mr. A will not have to be sent to the North Pole to hand Mr. B a written communication!

1. TELEGRAMS

These may be sent inland or overseas. As the charge is calculated on the number of words used, it will be seen that the essential work involved in composing a telegram lies in making it as brief as possible without sacrificing clarity. A *telegraphic address* is a great word-saver, since it usually consists of only two words. The Magic Typewriter Company, Limited, 1 Blank Street, London W1N 1AB might be condensed into MAGITYPE LONDONW1 (note that the first word denotes the name of the company, the second the town). The finer points of punctuation may be safely omitted, and normally only full stops indicated (by the word STOP). Finally, and this is the greatest test of your skill, use a single word instead of a phrase wherever possible.

I would like you to do this:	PLEASE DO THIS
This must be done without any delay at all:	THIS MUST BE DONE IMMEDIATELY
I shall arrive on Monday next, 25th September, Brown	ARRIVING 25 SEPTEMBER STOP BROWN

Telegrams may also be dictated to the operator over the telephone, but in this case great care must be taken to see that no word has been misunderstood. Whether the telegram is dictated verbally over the telephone or the written form handed in over the Post Office counter, a written copy should always be taken for the file, otherwise there will be no written record of the communication.

2. THE TELEPRINTER AND TELEX

There is now a sophisticated telex system operated by the Post Office. This combines speed with written communication. If you can imagine a *written telephone conversation*, then you have telex! Firms subscribe to telex as they do to telephones; there is a telex directory where "Answer Back" codes or numbers may be looked up, and subscribers may communicate with one another simply by dialling the appropriate code, where necessary, and the subscriber's number, in much the same way as they would dial a telephone number.

Try to imagine a *typewriter* and *telephone* combined, and you have a teleprinter. A teleprinter (even the name implies a telephone which prints!) looks somewhat like a large typewriter with a telephone dial. The idea is to dial the number of the subscriber you want to call and when you receive his "answer back" code you type the message, which is received and printed "over the line" at his end almost instantaneously. If necessary, a reply may be sent immediately. Teleprinters may be rented from the Post Office. There is a rental charge, and an additional charge is made for calls on a time and distance basis. The teleprinter is capable of typing at high speeds, and where complicated or difficult messages are to be sent long distances it is worth investing in a teleprinter with automatic facilities whereby the message is typed once slowly with the teleprinter in "local", and corrected if necessary by the operator, and then sent automatically at the high speed. This is possible because a punched paper tape is prepared simultaneously with the first (slow, careful) typing, and it is this tape which is then put through the machine for transmission at the high speed.

Firms which do not wish to subscribe to the telex system may wish to hire, say, two teleprinters (one for Head Office and one for a branch office). They may then communicate freely with one another over a private circuit, but not with other telex subscribers. Telex operates inland and in most overseas countries.

The advantages of the telex system are many:

(*a*) *Speed*. The message is transmitted instantaneously.

(*b*) *Permanency*. A permanent written record is obtained—indeed if required several copies may be taken, as with an ordinary typewriter.

(*c*) *Availability*. Like the telephone, telex may be used at any time of the day or night, provided of course that the recipient has left his machine switched on ready to receive messages.

(*d*) *Little training is required.* A good typist can easily be "converted."

(*e*) *Accuracy.* Since the message is in written form, it may be checked and errors rectified.

3. THE TELEPHONE AND THE SWITCHBOARD

There are not many fully-fledged secretaries who have not had to use a switchboard at some time in their career. Those who have already become friends with this intricate-looking piece of equipment agree that it is not difficult to learn to operate and that once the technique has been mastered it can be quite good fun. The great secret is not to get flustered if the switchboard becomes busy. If the lights flash or the buzzers buzz—let them—until you have dealt with the call in hand. But this does not mean letting them wait a long time. If you can't put a call through immediately you can usually "hold" it and answer the next one, asking the first caller to "wait one moment, please." *Always* have a pad and pencil available and *never* keep requests for numbers in your head; put them down on the pad and cross them off methodically after dealing with each one.

Apart from the efficiency of this approach you should remember that S.T.D. (Subscriber Trunk Dialling) can become expensive if calls are unduly prolonged. The charge is calculated on a time basis, and any time that a caller is kept waiting is wasted money. This may be a drawback of S.T.D., but on the credit side:

(*a*) it encourages speedy handling of calls, which makes for efficiency; and

(*b*) it enables a subscriber to dial his own trunk calls without resorting to the operator—again a saving of time.

In some systems, the switchboard operator is used mainly for taking incoming calls and putting them through to the appropriate extensions. She can be by-passed, however, for outgoing calls, since these may be dialled direct from the internal extension. Similarly, one extension may communicate with another by direct dialling. This does not mean that no telephone contact with the operator may be had by the user of an extension: he merely has to dial the operator's extension number. It will be appreciated that this system releases the operator from dealing with all internal calls and the majority of outgoing calls. This system is known as P.A.B.X. (Private Automatic Branch Exchange), and there are a number of P.A.B.X. systems designed to meet the needs of a variety of business firms.

P.M.B.X. (Private Manual Branch Exchange) makes use of the operator for all calls: extension-to-extension, extension-to-outgoing call, incoming call-to-extension. Here there is no automatic connection to an exchange without going through the operator, and consequently there may be a greater delay.

Some organisations find it useful to install a telephone system which does not provide connection to external lines. In this system internal extensions may be connected only to one another and to the operator. This is known as an internal telephone system.

(*a*) *Switchboard rules.* There are a few rules which any person operating a switchboard *must* observe:

(*i*) If you ask a caller to wait because the extension he wants is engaged, reassure him from time to time with such phrases as "I am sorry to keep you waiting, extension 39 is still engaged," or "the line is still engaged, would you prefer to call back?"

(*ii*) Always have a pad and pencil and do not fail to write down requests for calls. It is only too easy to forget if the switchboard suddenly becomes busy.

(*iii*) Keep another pad for incoming messages and *do not fail* to pass them on. A suitable message form is shown in Fig. 9.

(*iv*) *Never* listen in on a conversation. It is just as bad as

```
┌─────────────────────────────────────────────────────────┐
│                   TELEPHONE MESSAGE                       │
│                                                           │
│  To:                      From:                           │
│                           Date:         Time:             │
│  Message:                                                 │
│                                                           │
│                                                           │
│                                                           │
│                           Call taken by ............      │
└─────────────────────────────────────────────────────────┘
```

Fig. 9.—Telephone message form.

opening someone's private letters and is unpardonable. If you happen accidentally to overhear part of a conversation, try to forget it. In any case, the person at the other end can usually tell if someone is listening in!

(*v*) Do not make or accept any private calls of your own (genuine urgent calls are of course excepted). If you are caught it creates a terrible impression.

(*b*) *Telephone services.* The following are some of the services available:

(*i*) *Motoring.* A report on road conditions.

(*ii*) *Music.* A different record each weekday evening and two on Sundays.

(*iii*) *Food.* A different recipe each day.

(*iv*) *Business news.* A Financial Times Index and business news summary updated seven times daily during weekdays.

(*v*) *Time.* A speaking clock gives the correct time of day or night.

(*vi*) *Cricket.* The prospects of play and score are given during Test and other important matches played in the U.K.

(*vii*) *Events.* "What's on in town and around" gives a selection of the main events of the day in and around London.

(*viii*) *Weather.* Up-to-date forecasts are available.

NOTE: The Speaking Clock, Weather, Recipe, Motoring, Test Match and Dial-a-Disc Services are available at many centres in the provinces; the Teletourist Service is available in Edinburgh. Full details of the Services and the numbers to call are given in local directories.

(*ix*) *Advice of duration and charge (A.D.C.).* The cost of a call made *via* the operator and its duration will be notified on request for a small fee.

(*x*) *Telephone credit cards.* For a small fee per quarter a subscriber can be supplied with a card which enables him to make calls and send telegrams from any telephone without payment at the time.

(*xi*) *Morning alarm calls.* The operator will call you in the morning, or at any other time. A small charge is made.

(*xii*) *Personal calls.* These may be booked *via* the operator for a small charge. This may work out cheaper than S.T.D.

since only one personal fee is payable however many attempts are made to connect the call during a period of 24 hours. Time begins to run when the callers are brought into communication.

(*xiii*) *Freefone.* This makes it possible for incoming calls to be accepted on a transferred-charge basis. This could be useful, *e.g.* where customers have to call the office but it is desired that the office and not the customer should pay for the call. A quarterly charge is made in addition to the charge for the call. Transferred-charge calls are in any case available for a small additional charge per call. This means that the subscriber called (not the caller) pays for the call, but the subscriber's agreement must be obtained each time.

(*xiv*) *Fixed-time calls.* A call may be booked in advance for connection at a specified time (traffic conditions permitting). A small charge is made.

(*xv*) *Transference of calls.* This is obtained by giving advance notice of requirements. Callers dialling the subscriber's number are then transferred by the operator to another number as requested by the subscriber.

(*xvi*) *Telegrams.* Both inland and international telegrams may be telephoned, and a request made for delivery by telephone. Overnight telegrams may be dictated from 8.00 a.m. to 10.30 p.m. for delivery by post the next day. De luxe greetings telegrams may be delivered by hand on attractive cards. These may be dictated in advance for delivery on a specified date. International telegrams may also be dictated to Post Office Overseas Telegraphs.

(*xvii*) *London Radiophone service.* This is a service whereby equipment located in a car (*e.g.*, on the dashboard or in the upholstery) allows a connection to be made with an external telephone. The equipment is privately manufactured and rented (*i.e.*, not rented from the Post Office) but the Post Office requires a licence to be taken out (payable quarterly); other expenses are of course the cost of each call, which is somewhat higher than normal telephone call charges. The system operates through the Post Office operator. Thus if the person in the car wants to call an outside number, he must first get through to the operator who will connect the call. Similarly, an outside caller must first go through the operator before contacting the person in the car. Conversation is one-way only, by means of push-buttons on the apparatus. This service is not to be confused with the system widely used by taxi drivers. It will be appreciated that London Radiophone should only be used by someone in a chauffeur-driven car or if the car is stationary—otherwise it would be impossible to keep both hands on the wheel.

(*xviii*) *On board ship services.* There is a "ship-to-shore" and "shore-to-ship" service, which enables communication to be made between ships at sea and persons on land. This communication may be either by radiotelegraphy or radiotelephony. A businessman on a sea voyage could thus maintain contact with his office staff, but it will be appreciated that the ship must be fitted with the appropriate equipment.

(*xix*) *Express messenger.* This is a service operated by most principal Post Offices. Items are collected and delivered during normal business hours, at customers' request.

(*xx*) *Telephone calls to countries overseas.* Where the subscriber has I.S.D. (International Subscriber Dialling) facilities, a call may be made by dialling direct to telephone numbers on most exchanges in Europe, Canada and the U.S.A. If the calls have to be booked *via* the operator, the caller must know how to get through to the International Exchange Operator. (This information can be easily ascertained from the telephone directory, *e.g.* from London the caller dials 104 or 105 for European countries and 108 for such countries outside Europe as the West Indies or Brazil.) If the call is booked *via* the operator, the caller may specify details as to the time he would like it to be put through, *e.g.* as soon as possible, at a given time, (but no guarantee can be given that this latter request will be met precisely) not before a given time, and so on.

(*xxi*) *Station call.* A station call means that the exchange operator puts through the call from the home telephone to the distant telephone and lets the number ring. Time begins to run when the distant telephone receiver is lifted and the connection is made. This service is cheaper than the personal call.

(*xxii*) *Personal call.* Here, the caller is connected by the operator to the individual he wants to speak to at the distant telephone number, but it is not necessary for the caller's own name to be specified.

(*xxiii*) *Person-to-person call.* In this case, the caller's name must be given in addition to the name and telephone number of the person called. Thus the person called is asked by the operator if he wants to receive a call from a named individual.

It should be noted that both with the personal and person-to-person calls the caller may, if he wishes, specify a substitute if the first-named person called is not available and it is not essential actually to name an individual; thus an office department, an extension number or a person speaking a certain foreign language may be specified.

(*xxiv*) *Credit card calls.* This service is similar to the one offered on inland calls: calls may be made from any telephone in the U.K. and debited to the subscriber's own telephone account.

(*xxv*) *Collect (transferred charge) calls.* This service is also similar to the one offered on inland calls: the charge for the call, if accepted, is transferred to the account of the person called.

(*xxvi*) *Conference call.* These facilities are available with many countries: up to five parties in this country can be connected simultaneously on an international call, and in certain circumstances more than one party abroad can be connected.

4. THE INTERCOM

As its name implies, this is an instrument which facilitates communication, *e.g.* between an employer and his secretary when they are in separate offices. By means of push-button controls an employer is able to communicate with one or more of his employees. This is a kind of loudspeaker system, but there are variations, *e.g.* a central instrument where several persons in different locations may carry on a conversation. It will be appreciated that such equipment can be of great use in a business office, but the drawback is that the method is not a good one to use for confidential conversations. However, there are variations available to suit most requirements and the majority of offices find it necessary to install intercom equipment.

5. PAGING SYSTEMS

These are often referred to as "Tannoy" systems, after the well known loudspeaker system of that name. The main use of a paging system is to locate persons who are often away from their desks. Thus a factory with adjacent offices might often require personal visits by office staff, and with suitable equipment installed in the factory and office rooms, location of such staff becomes easy. The drawback here is that it is not practicable to give long messages over the loudspeaker and of course nothing confidential should be broadcast. The use is often restricted to "Mr. X is wanted on Extension 1" or "Will Mr. X please ring Extension 1." Loop paging is the term used to describe the "bleep" system widely used by hospitals and other organisations.

CULTIVATING A PLEASANT VOICE AND MANNER

There is already the beginnings of a feeling of insecurity when one picks up the telephone since one is so dependent upon the receiver of the call. Have you ever put through a telephone call to be told "One moment please" and then you wait ... and wait ... and wait ...? There are many variations of this game, for example the person intent on exasperating you may say "the line is engaged, will you hold?" and when you eagerly say you will, you hear nothing but a series of ominous clicks and then ... silence! You put a call through and hear the ringing tone; this is intercepted (indicating that your call has been received and time on S.T.D. begins to run) but you hear no more until in desperation you try again, but like a recurring nightmare your call is intercepted (indicating that your call has been received and time on S.T.D. begins to run) but you hear no more until in desperation. . . .

There was once a boss who took great pride in the way his telephonists answered incoming calls. Sometimes he would go out of the office and telephone his own number just to make sure. He was not a very popular boss and did not keep his telephonists very long. Never give your employer cause to resort to such tactics!

It is not difficult to cultivate a pleasant manner. Just put yourself in the shoes of your caller and you will soon know how best to tackle his particular problem. If the person he wants to speak to is not available ask him whether he would rather wait or try again later. Better still, ask if you may ring him back. Never keep a person "hanging on" without informing him periodically that you have not forgotten his existence. This may be done by "I'm trying to connect you" or "I'm sorry the line is still engaged" or some such soothing phrase. The words you choose will also affect the impression you make. Compare "XYZ Co., Good morning" with "Hello?" This emphasises the first rule: identify yourself. Rule 2 is also not difficult: be courteous. It doesn't hurt nor does it cost anything to say "please," "thank you" or "I'm sorry." The third rule is to be helpful. Remember that you represent your employer and the way you handle his calls may have a strong bearing on his recognition of your efficiency. A pleasing voice is one which is not high-pitched, nor rasping. You may be excused if you genuinely have a sore throat (though you shouldn't be using the telephone if you had) but otherwise try to pitch your voice low. Smile when you speak—although your caller can't see you, it is surprising how effective a "smiling voice" can be.

Finally if you have to take a message never, but *never*, forget to pass it on. This is the unforgivable sin. Use specially printed Telephone Message forms and write the message clearly. Better still, type it. Do not forget to show for whom the message is intended nor should you forget to sign it. And a message reading something like "will you please ring Mr. X when you return from lunch" without showing Mr. X's telephone number is sheer inefficiency.

There is a list of hints earlier in this chapter—refer to it—often.

Whether you are at the switchboard or in your private office, the rules are the same:

    (*a*) *Identify yourself.* "Mr. Brown's secretary speaking."
                                "Mr. Brown's office—may I help you?"
                                "Miss Smith speaking."
any of the above or variations thereof are acceptable.

    (*b*) *Be courteous.* "I'm afraid Mr. Brown is the only person who can help you and he won't be back before lunch. May I get him to ring you back?"

"I'm so sorry the information isn't available immediately but I can get it in time for tonight's post if that's any help."

"I'm so sorry Mr. Brown has to cancel his appointment with you but he isn't very well today and been advised to stay at home. When is it convenient to make another appointment?"

(Notice how a problem or difficulty is never presented without an attempt at a solution.)

    (*c*) *Never forget to pass on messages.*

SELECTING THE MEANS OF COMMUNICATION

When selecting a mode of communication, overall efficiency should be the guiding principle. Thus, if speed is essential a telegram should be sent even though the cost would obviously be higher. If it is not essential that there should be a written record then possibly a telephone call would serve the purpose better. If the company is a subscriber to telex, speedy and written communication is easily effected (provided the other party is also a subscriber).

With regard to paging or loudspeaker systems, thought must be given to the degree of urgency, the amount of noise which will be tolerated and the loss of confidentiality. Thus, some form of paging system is obviously essential in hospitals but unnecessary in a small office. On the other hand, if the offices are rambling and key personnel have to be contacted urgently it will be worth tolerating a certain amount of noise which inevitably disturbs employees who are not being called.

There is an infinite variety of machinery and equipment to suit almost every conceivable purpose. Thus if it is decided that a paging system would ideally suit the purpose except for the noise, battery-charged portable "bleepers" could be used; alternatively buzzers or flashing lights located at strategic points in the offices could be substituted for a loudspeaker.

Manufacturers are only too pleased to supply literature and to demonstrate their equipment and investigation into the cost and variety offered by different manufacturers would amply repay the initial trouble.

TRANSPORT

Apart from information and instructions which are communicated from one person to another, articles also need to be conveyed from one place to another, and the best means of conveyance must be selected. Sometimes the choice will be determined by the object which is to be sent; thus if it is a person who must be conveyed from one place to another, then letter post and even post office messenger are obviously eliminated! But if it is something like a precious stone, then these and other means (*e.g.*, private messenger) are available. If the article is large, a road haulage company or British Road Services or British Rail may be selected and a further determining factor might be the fragility of the article. It will be seen that, in effect, it is the *needs* which determine the means. If answers are found to the following questions, the choice becomes quite simple:

> How large is the article?
> Would it infringe postal regulations if it were posted?
> Is it fragile?
> Does it need any special care (*e.g.*, is it alive—a dog)?
> Does it contain secret information?
> How far is it going?
> How quickly must it arrive at destination?
> How much will it matter if it gets lost or damaged?

It will be noted that the all-important *cost* has been omitted from the questions which will determine the means of transport. This has been purposely left out because if it were essential for the article to arrive at a destination with the utmost speed, air transport would be chosen, regardless of the cost; similarly, if special care were necessary, messenger service would be the answer, even though it might be more costly than letter post. The only justification for inserting cost in the above list might be in answer to the question: how much money can we spare? And even then, the answer would have to be weighed against the risk involved in using the wrong means of conveyance.

Short-answer Questions

1. Why is it necessary to be more careful in the choice of words during a telephone conversation than during a face-to-face talk?

2. Why do most firms adopt a telegraphic address?

3. Name three advantages available to a subscriber to telex.

4. What do the initials S.T.D. stand for?

5. What information should appear on a telephone message form?

6. What skill is involved in composing a telegram?

7. How can a secretary discover the telex code of a firm her employers wants to contact?

8. What should be the first words you say when you answer the telephone in the office?

9. What is P.M.B.X.?

10. The telephone service offers "personal call" facilities. What is a personal call?

Past Examination Questions

1. What is meant by:

(*a*) S.T.D.; (*b*) inter-com; (*c*) a personal call when using the telephone; (*d*) an overnight telegram; (*e*) a reply paid telegram; (*f*) a transfer charge telephone call?   (*R.S.A.*)

2. In connection with the telephone, what do you understand by:

(*a*) a cheap rate period; (*b*) a transferred charge call?

(*R.S.A.*)

3. What would you say, when lifting the receiver, to an incoming telephone call? If the caller wished to leave a message for someone who was out, what would you do? What is a personal call, and how do you find the time of day by telephone?   (*R.S.A.*)

4. What is:

(*a*) a radio telegram; (*b*) an "intercom"; (*c*) a transferred call charge?   (*R.S.A.*)

5. Assuming your company has up-to-date equipment, suggest ways in which the Managing Director might communicate with:

(*a*) other managers in the building; (*b*) someone whose work takes him to all parts of the factory; (*c*) someone in a provincial branch office.   (*R.S.A.*)

6. Discuss and compare some modern methods of external communication employed in offices today.   (*L.C.C.*)

7. The system in an organisation is to allocate a secretary to each executive. The secretaries are accommodated in one large office while each executive has his individual office. Give examples to show how each secretary can conveniently be contacted by her chief.   (*L.C.C.*)

8. Your employer is away from the office and expects to return in two weeks' time. You receive a letter from a client, Messrs. Jones and Company to the effect that unless the Tender (on which your employer was working before going away on business) is submitted within one week, the opportunity of obtaining the order will be lost. The Tender was for the supply of five swivel chairs and five desk lamps; two dozen typists' chairs and two dozen typists' desks. The deadline for submitting the Tender is 3rd July, 1968. Draft a telegram informing your chief of the situation.   (*L.C.C.*)

9. While on holiday abroad you are involved in a serious car accident a few days before you are due to return. The driver of the car in which you were travelling is seriously injured and your injuries will keep you in hospital for a week. Send an overseas cable to your employer and follow this up with a letter. The overseas cable is to be set out in correct form. (*L.C.C.*)

10. Discuss the economic benefits and commercial advantages and disadvantages arising from the advent of S.T.D. (*L.C.C.*)

CHAPTER 6

DOCUMENTATION

PURPOSE OF DOCUMENTATION

THE documentation of a business is recorded in letters, books of record and special forms. Letters have been dealt with fully elsewhere in this book, but in a chapter dealing with forms it is worth noting that even outgoing letters are displayed in a certain format; they could in fact be categorised in the term "form": margins must be of a certain width; some of the information (date, reference, address) is always to be found in the same position, and they serve a purpose (presumably) of communicating or placing on record certain information.

Books of record are the bookkeeping records, the accounting ledgers (Accounts Department), the minute books and the registers of members (Company Secretarial Department), and a variety of other books maintained according to the needs of the particular firm.

The special forms are those necessitated by legal requirements (tax returns, company returns, applications for licences, etc.) and those used for the convenience of the firm and of persons dealing with the firm.

The purpose of a pre-printed form is to ensure that information which is required is actually entered (if the questions were not pre-printed, the information might be omitted); to eliminate the wastage of time in trying to remember what information to incorporate into the form (if it is pre-printed, you don't have to think afresh each time you complete the form); and mainly of course to *provide information.*

COMMON BUSINESS DOCUMENTS

In every office there are large numbers of forms in use, each designed to meet a particular need of the business concerned, and just as the business, and therefore the requirements, vary from firm to firm, so the forms used by each business will be different also. However, there are some documents which are commonly used in the majority of firms throughout commerce and industry. It is with these in particular that this chapter is concerned.

1. QUOTATION

This is usually sent to an intending customer in reply to an enquiry about goods. If, for example, a person has studied the catalogue and brochures of a certain manufacturer, and decides he would like to know more about those products he intends to buy, he then writes to the firm, asking for a quotation. This enquiry puts no obligation on the customer to buy, but as there is every indication that he may buy, the firm should deal very promptly with his enquiry. If at all possible, a quotation should be sent to the customer on the same day his enquiry is received, otherwise there is the danger that he may decide to buy from another firm which has dealt more promptly with his enquiry. The quotation should not only be sent out without delay, but should be neatly and clearly typed, and should contain enough information to enable the customer to decide whether to place his order or not. The following information is usually shown on a quotation, which may take the form of a letter or a pre-printed form:

Name and address of manufacturer, including telephone and telex numbers, telegraphic address and reference number (much the same information in fact as would appear on the firm's headed notepaper).

Name and address of the customer to whom the order is addressed.

Date.

Description of the goods which are the subject of the quotation.

Price of the goods *per unit.*

Price of the goods *in quantity, e.g.* per dozen.

Delivery dates, e.g. whether from stock or within so many weeks from receipt of the order.

Terms and conditions of payment, e.g. $2\frac{1}{2}$ per cent reduction may be offered to a customer who pays within one month from receipt of the invoice.

Carriage charges, e.g. postage and packing may be free on orders over a certain amount.

It is most important that all quotations should be followed up if, after a short period, no firm order has been placed by the customer, and for this reason a carbon copy should be retained by the firm.

2. ORDER

If the customer decides to place his order with the firm on the strength of the quotation received by him, he will send in to the firm a formal order setting out clearly what he wants to buy. If any special arrangements have been agreed subsequent to the issue of the quotation, he should refer on his order form both to the quotation and to the special arrangements. The order form usually contains the following information:

Name and address of customer, including such other information as would normally be shown on his headed notepaper.

Name and address of the manufacturer to whom the order is sent.

Date.

Description of the goods ordered (a full description may be given, but a reference to the listed catalogue number is adequate).

Quantity required.

Price.

Order Number (it is important that a reference number should be allocated to each order as this will be quoted on subsequent correspondence, invoice, etc.).

At least one copy of the order should be retained by the customer for filing and future reference, but in practice several copies are made (one copy would be passed to the Order Department for filing, another copy would be sent to the Accounts Department and a third copy would go to the Goods Inwards Department).

3. ADVICE NOTE

When the goods are ready to be despatched, it is usual to advise the customer by letter post that he may expect receipt of the goods. This is done by filling up an advice note which will show:

Name, etc. of the firm sending out the goods.

Name, etc. of the customer who is to receive the goods.

Date.

Reference number of the *advice note*.

Reference number of the *order*.

Description of the goods despatched.

Method of despatch.

At least one copy of the advice note should be retained for filing, but in practice again several copies are usually made (one copy (known as a delivery note) would accompany the goods, and another would be retained in the Goods Outwards Department).

4. DELIVERY NOTE (also known as a DESPATCH NOTE)

This contains substantially the same information as the advice note (often it is a carbon copy of the advice note on a form which is headed Delivery Note instead of Advice Note) and usually travels with the goods themselves. It is in fact packed with the goods in the same parcel. The purpose of this form is to enable the customer to check that the parcel does in fact contain the goods as stated in the delivery note.

5. CONSIGNMENT NOTE

This form also travels with the goods. It shows:

> *Consignor* (sender).
> *Consignee* (addressee).
> *Carrier's name and address* (*e.g.*, a road haulage firm, British Road Services, etc.).
> *Date*, and *reference number*.
> *Description* of the consignment, (*e.g.*, ten cases).
> Whether *carriage* is to be paid by the sender or the addressee.

Thus the carrier knows who is to pay his charges and he is also able to obtain a signature of receipt on the consigment note itself when he delivers the goods.

6. INVOICE

This is obviously an important document. It should be sent out promptly after the goods have been despatched (sometimes it is sent out at the same time as the goods). The selling firm makes out this document and sends it to the buyer. Its main purpose is to indicate to the buyer the amount he owes the firm for the goods received, so that in theory it might be sufficient to make out only two copies (one original for the customer and one copy for the seller's files), but in practice this form is used for other purposes and as will be seen it is useful to make several copies. The invoice must show the following information:

> *Name, address, etc.* of the seller.
> *Name, address, etc.* of the buyer.

Reference number of the invoice.
Date of the invoice.
Details of the goods purchased, *e.g.* quantity, description, catalogue list number.
Price per unit.
Total price.
Customer's order number.
Transport or other carriage charges, if applicable.
Discounts, or other special terms.

The original invoice will be sent to the customer, one copy will be retained in the sender's file and another copy will be passed to the Accounts Department. It is from this copy that the accounting entries will be made in the sales day book.

7. STATEMENT

A statement of account is usually sent out to debtors (customers) once a month. The statement shows the total amount owing by the customer. For example, he may have a small balance outstanding on his account; when he orders further goods, the invoice will show only the amount due for those goods, but the statement will indicate the total amount due, *i.e.* the balance outstanding plus the amount due for the recent order. Many firms pay when they receive the statement, and not the invoice.

The statement shows:

Name, address, etc. of the seller.
Name, address, etc. of the buyer.
Date of the statement.
Brief details of *transactions* and the *amount due on each.*
Total amount due.
Special terms, *e.g.* discount for payment within seven days.

8. CREDIT NOTE

If the goods are defective, or if for any other reason it is agreed between the buyer and the seller that he has been overcharged on the invoice, the seller will issue a credit note to the buyer. It is by this means that he reduces the balance due to him—he cannot alter the original invoice which has already been sent out.

The credit note shows:

> *Name, address, etc.* of the seller.
> *Name, address, etc.* of the buyer.
> *Date* of the credit note.
> *Brief details* of the reason for the credit (*e.g.*, empties returned, allowance for defective goods, etc.).
> Amount credited.

The original copy is sent to the customer and a copy will be sent to the Accounts Department for entry in the appropriate account.

9. DEBIT NOTE

As the name implies, this is the reverse of the credit note. If the seller has undercharged the buyer on his invoice, or if he has sent better quality goods which the buyer agrees to retain, or if for any other reason the amount shown on the invoice is less than that which should be due, the seller will make out a debit note and send the original to the buyer. The debit note shows:

> *Name and address, etc.* of the seller.
> *Name and address, etc.* of the buyer.
> *Date.*
> *Brief reason for the debit* (*e.g.*, goods undercharged on invoice No. . . .).
> *Amount debited.*

It is from a copy of the debit note that the appropriate accounting entries are made.

10. RECEIPT

Since the *Cheques Act* 1957, receipts are usually issued only if the customer specifically requests a receipt, or if he pays by cash (processing of cheques through the bank is now accepted as evidence of payment and receipt). When issued, the receipt should show:

> *Name, address, etc.* of the firm issuing the receipt.
> *Name, address, etc.* of the payer.
> *Number of the receipt.*
> *Amount received.*
> *Method of payment, e.g.* cash, cheque.
> *Signature* of the cashier.

11. PRO FORMA INVOICE

Although this contains substantially the same information as the invoice proper, a pro forma invoice serves a different purpose. It is not invariably used, but when it is used, it would probably be because there is some doubt as to the creditworthiness of the customer, thus the pro forma invoice is a polite way of requesting payment *before* the goods are actually despatched; alternatively it would be used if the goods are sent on "appro." (*i.e.*, approval, or "sale or return"). If the goods are returned, no invoice need of course be raised, but if the goods are retained, then the pro forma invoice is considered as a real invoice. Finally, the pro forma invoice is perhaps most often used in the export trade; it would show an indication of the price which the seller hopes his agent will realise for the goods, but as the amount actually remitted by the representative may in fact be larger or smaller it would obviously be wrong to raise a proper invoice in the first place.

12. REMINDER LETTERS

Unfortunately, not all customers (debtors) pay promptly, and it is usual for *reminder letters* to be sent out when payment becomes overdue. The procedure varies slightly from firm to firm, but briefly consists of a first letter, which politely assumes that the neglect to pay is merely due to an oversight and reminds the customer of his debt. If this letter meets with no response, a second letter, somewhat more strongly worded, may be sent. Finally, a third letter might be sent to the defaulting customer, threatening to place the matter in the hands of solicitors if payment is not received within a certain time. A demand for payment is often referred to as a "dun" in debt-collecting jargon, and the term "dunning" is applied to this work.

13. REQUISITION

As the name implies, this is a request for the issue of goods from the stores or the warehouse. A copy is of course retained in the issuing department, and the original is retained by the stores or the warehouse to account for the stock which has gone. Physical stocktaking is periodically (sometimes annually, sometimes more often) undertaken, and the requisition forms will be evidence that there has been no pilfering.

14. MULTI-SET FORMS

Since much of the information contained on some of the documents mentioned above is the same, it will be appreciated that time and energy is saved if only one entry is made on a three- or four-fold set of forms. Each copy is printed with the name of the form, *e.g.* Invoice, Advice Note, Consignment Note, and all but the last are carbon backed (or N.C.R.—*see* p. 152). Thus one typed entry will be sufficient to reproduce the information on all three or four carbon copies. However, it is usual for the invoice to show rather more information than some of the other forms, *e.g.* it is unnecessary for the advice note to show the price of the goods. This requirement is simply met: the forms are not completely carbon-backed, but merely coated with carbon strips over those areas which it is desired to reproduce on all forms. Below is set out in full the steps in a financial transaction from the raising of an invoice to the receipt of payment, and the route a transaction takes from receipt of customer's order to despatch of goods.

Financial transaction from the raising of an
invoice to the receipt of payment

1. On advice being received by the accounts department that goods have been despatched, an invoice is made out. The original is sent to the customer, to advise him of the amount due.

2. A copy is retained and filed in numerical order.

3. From a second copy an entry is made in the sales day book. At the end of the period the total amount shown in the sales day book (which includes of course the amount of this particular invoice) is "posted" (i.e., entered) to the credit of the Sales Account. The corresponding debit entry is made in the customer's personal account in the Sales Ledger.

4. A statement is prepared showing the total amount outstanding on the customer's personal account. This statement is sent to the customer.

5(a) If the customer does not pay promptly, he is sent a reminder.

5(b) If the customer sends a cheque in settlement, details of the payment are recorded (1) to the credit of the customer's personal account in the sales ledger, (2) to the debit of the cash book.

6. The cheque is banked.

7. A receipt is sent to the customer if he has specifically requested one.

The routing of a transaction from receipt of customer's order to its despatch

The sequence of a transaction may be shown as follows:

1. Customer's enquiry   The original is received by Sales Department, who take the next step.

2. Quotation   This is sent by the Sales Department to the potential customer. The quotation is kept active, or filed and marked "to be brought forward" so that it may be followed up if the customer does not place an order within a reasonable period.

3. Customer's order   The original is received by the Sales Department who will probably copy out the relevant details on a number of internal copies:

    copy 1 to Order Progress Department who will follow through the order;

    copy 2 to Works or Warehouse who will prepare the goods;

    copy 3 retained on file.

4. Customer's order copy 1   This is "chased" by the Progress Department whose job it is to ensure that delivery to the customer is not unduly delayed.

5. Customer's order copy 2   The warehouse gets the order ready and passes the goods to the Despatch Department. At this stage the warehouse may make out a new form which will show either the complete order, or as much of the order as is ready for despatch (e.g., some items might be out of stock). Copies of this new form are made out as under:

    copy 1 advice note sent to customer in advance of the goods;

    copy 2 despatch note sent in the case with the goods to enable the customer to check the contents;

    copy 3 consignment note (if applicable). This would be given to the carrier and would accompany the goods en route, but would be retained by the carrier who might ask the customer to sign it as evidence of receipt of the goods;

    copy 4 this is an advice to the warehouse that their request for despatch has been dealt with;

    copy 5 this is an advice to the Progress Department that the order or part order has been despatched;

    copy 6 this is an advice to the Sales Department to indicate despatch;

    copy 7 this is sent to the Accounts Department who will raise an invoice.

Short-answer Questions

1. What is the purpose of any form?

2. Name three forms commonly used in business.

3. Give an example of a reason why it might be necessary to raise a Credit Note.

4. Give an example of a reason why it might be necessary to raise a Debit Note.

5. What is the difference between an invoice and a pro forma invoice?

6. Why should the Stores Department keep a record of all requisitions received?

7. What information should be shown on a quotation to a customer?

8. At what stage is a statement sent to a customer?

9. Why are receipts for cheque payments not now sent out by most firms unless the payer specifically requests a receipt?

10. What does "dunning" mean?

Past Examination Questions

1. For what purposes are the following documents used:

(*i*) a pro forma invoice; (*ii*) a despatch note; (*iii*) an order form? (*L.C.C.*)

2. A London Retail Store writes to a wholesaler in Birmingham for the details and prices of certain goods, which are eventually bought, delivered and paid for. Enumerate the various commercial documents which are likely to be used in this transaction, giving a brief description of each. (*L.C.C.*)

3. What is an invoice and what uses are made of it by (*a*) the purchaser, (*b*) the seller of goods? (*R.S.A.*)*

4. A merchant receives an order for goods from a customer in London. What documents are likely to be employed in connection with this order, from the date the order is received to the time of receiving payment for the goods? (*L.C.C.*)

5. What is a credit note, and for what purposes is it used?
(*R.S.A.*)

6. What is the difference between a statement and an invoice? (*R.S.A.*)*

* Only part of a longer question included.

7. If a company sent short weight through error of its own employees, explain how the mistake might be rectified if it were not discovered until after despatch and receipt of the invoice.

(R.S.A.)

8. What is a credit note? Specify two possible cases for its use arising out of the purchase of nylon stockings, invoiced at £100 by Smith & Co., from the Universal Textile Warehouse Ltd.

(R.S.A.)

CHAPTER 7

READING AND CORRECTION OF PROOFS

IT may happen that the secretary is employed by an author, in which case she will probably have to read the printers' proofs and make herself familiar with the signs commonly used in the correction of proofs. But it is not only authors' secretaries who need to learn these signs—any line of business where work has to be printed will give the secretary an opportunity to use her knowledge: a commercial firm will have to prepare printed publicity material; a trading company will have to prepare printed copies of the Directors' Report for the shareholders; an educational concern will have to get the examination question papers printed—examples may be taken from advertising, publishing, and so on.

Proofs must be read over very carefully indeed as it is surprisingly easy to overlook a small error, and subsequent corrections may prove very costly.

The following abbreviations and signs are commonly used in the correction of proofs:

Abbreviation or sign used in margin	Corresponding sign shown in the printed text where a correction is necessary	Meaning of the abbreviation or sign
Caps.	three lines are placed under the word(s) to be corrected	Capital letters required
Rom.	A circle is placed around the word(s) to be corrected	Roman type to be used
Ital.	one line is placed under the word(s) to be corrected	Italics to be used
trs.	This sign is placed between the words or letters to be transposed	Transpose
run on	This sign links one paragraph to the next	No new paragraph required

Abbreviation or sign used in margin	*Corresponding sign shown in the printed text where a correction is necessary*	*Meaning of the abbreviation or sign*
spell out	A circle is placed around the abbreviated word	Spell out in full
centre	⌐ ⌐ This sign is placed to indicate position-ing	Centre
take over	[This sign is placed at the end of the line	Take word (or letter) from the end of one line to the beginning of the next
take back	⌐ This sign is placed at the beginning of the line	Take word (or letter) from the beginning of one line to the end of the preceding one
X	A circle is placed around the damaged character	Replace damaged character
9	A circle is placed around the word or letter to be corrected	Invert type
⌐	⌐ This sign is shown where required in the text	Move to the left
⌐	⌐ This sign is shown where required in the text	Move to the right
=	═══ This sign is placed through the lines to be straightened	Straighten lines
⌣	⌣ This sign is shown where the existing space is to be closed up	Close up
#	⋀ This sign (caret) is shown where the space is to be inserted	Insert space
E.&⋀ E.	⋀ (this sign (caret) is placed where the words are to be inserted)	Insert
/-/	⋀ (this sign is placed where the hyphen is to be inserted)	Insert hyphen

Abbreviation or sign used in margin	Corresponding sign shown in the printed text where a correction is necessary	Meaning of the abbreviation or sign
/–/	⋏ (this sign is placed where the dash is to be inserted	Insert dash
⊙	⋏ (this sign is placed where the full stop is to be inserted)	Insert full stop
,⁄	⋏ (this sign is placed where the comma is to be inserted)	Insert comma
(other punctuation signs may be similarly indicated)		
9/	/ (a line is placed through the word or letter to be deleted)	Delete
stet.	········ (a row of dots is placed under the words not to be altered)	Leave as printed (do not alter)
l.c.	A circle is placed around the letter or word to be corrected	Lower case
s.c.	═══ (two lines are placed around the word(s) to be corrected)	Small capitals required
w.f.	A circle is placed around the word or letter to be corrected	Wrong fount
N.P.	⌐ (this sign is placed in front of the first letter of the word commencing the new paragraph	New paragraph required

The following are some commonly used printers' terms and their meanings:

Author's proof	A proof which has been corrected by the author.
Copy	The author's typewritten text which is passed on for printing.
Fount	A set of type.
Galley proof	Impression taken before the pages have been made up.

Italics	Type resembling handwriting more than print.
Page proof	Impression taken after the pages have been made up.
Roman type	Plain type (not italics).

Short-answer Questions

1. Suggest two pieces of work which a secretary might have to proof read.

2. What does the caret sign mean?

3. How would you indicate that the wrong fount had been used?

4. What is the sign showing that the type has been printed upside down?

5. How would you indicate that a space was to be closed up?

6. How would you indicate that you wanted a space inserted?

7. What does trs. stand for?

8. What do you understand by three lines under a word?

9. What does "stet" mean?

10. How would you indicate that no new paragraph was required?

Past Examination Questions

1. What is meant by:

(*i*) a galley proof; (*ii*) a page proof; (*iii*) l.c.; (*iv*) ital.; (*v*) run on?

(*R.S.A.*)

2. In the correction of printers' proofs, give the recognised signs for the following instructions:

(*a*) change to small capitals;
(*b*) transpose two words;
(*c*) insert comma;
(*d*) insert full stop;
(*e*) insert space;
(*f*) invert type;
(*g*) move to the left;
(*h*) straighten lines;
(*i*) delete;
(*j*) take letter or word from end of one line to beginning of next line.

(*R.S.A.*)

3. You are required to correct the following proof, as for a printer.

He must b e experienced In retail selling? preferably at
Mana ĝer level, and in the tᵉlevision and domesticm-

appliance field. High basic salary plus commission and
   bonos, enables earnings in excess of £1,4o0 per annum
from commencement. There are excellent prospets for
promotion. (*R.S.A.*)

4. Give the following marginal proof signs:

   (*a*) delete; (*b*) leave as it is; (*c*) capital letter not required.
   (*R.S.A.*)

5. Explain

   (*a*) What is meant by a printer's proof and why proofs are
necessary;
   (*b*) Show how you would correct (in the text and in the margins)
six different mistakes in a proof. (*R.S.A.*)

6. Give four marginal proof correcting signs and their meanings. (*R.S.A.*)
   7. (*a*) What signs are used, in margin and in text, to indicate the
corrections needed in a printer's proof for: (*i*) insert full stop;
(*ii*) transpose; (*iii*) make spacing equal; (*iv*) close up; (*v*) change to
small capitals?
   (*b*) Why are standard proof correction signs essential?
   (*R.S.A.*)

8. What is meant by the following printing terms:

   (*a*) copy; (*b*) italics; (*c*) author's proof; (*d*) Roman type?
   (*R.S.A.*)

9. Correct, by means of marginal signs, etc. the printer's proof
shown below.

   In this course, we train yuo on the varous types of
machiness now in use in industry, So that you will be
familiar with the principles of any any make you are likely
to meet. We мill pro vide you with duplicated notes about
the machines, and you may retain thexe notes for your
future use. our training aims at improving your accoracy
and building up your operative speed. (*R.S.A.*)

CHAPTER 8

MEETINGS

PREPARATION FOR, AND PROCEDURE AT, MEETINGS

THE secretary's work in preparing for a meeting will vary with the type of meeting, the size of her company and the role of her chief at the meeting (he may be the convenor or merely attend as a member).

The type of meeting may range from a formal Annual General Meeting held once every calendar year in the life of a registered company to an informal committee meeting of a group within a department. The Annual General Meeting is a shareholders' meeting called yearly to transact such business as the election of the Directors, the appointment of the company's auditors, the consideration of the Directors' Report and Accounts and the declaration of a dividend. If the company has a large membership a suitable hall will have to be booked so that the estimated number of persons expected to attend may be accommodated. Notices of the meeting will have to be sent out to all those entitled to receive them, an agenda must be prepared and sent to those expected to attend, and on the day of the meeting the room itself will have to be prepared, *e.g.* additional copies of the agenda (for persons who arrive without their own), should be provided, all the necessary books and papers should be available for reference if required, including the Minute Book and the company's Memorandum and Articles of Association, and a sufficient number of ashtrays placed within easy reach of members' seats. If the membership is not too large, it might be helpful to provide pencils and writing paper as well.

The meeting may be a domestic affair (*i.e.*, internal) and yet formal. Directors' Board Meetings would come into this category. As these meetings are usually held several times in the year, *e.g.* at fortnightly or monthly intervals, and attendance is restricted to the Directors and Company Secretary, they are often held on the office premises, a special Board Room being reserved. Here the secretary's role in preparing for the meeting would be to see that the room was

94

suitably prepared, chairs arranged along the table, writing materials and ashtrays suitably to hand, with probably a copy of the agenda for those Directors who arrive without their copy. Any books or papers which might be required at the meeting should be available (including the Minute Book and the company's Memorandum and Articles of Association) and arrangements should be made to ensure that the Directors are not disturbed for the duration of the meeting.

Many meetings are of a more informal nature and occur with greater frequency. Thus weekly meetings of departmental heads might be held to co-ordinate the work of a large Branch Office; or a Sales Manager might hold monthly meetings with his Area Representatives to discuss sales programmes and targets; or a small sub-committee of the office social club might hold meetings to make arrangements for the annual outing.

IMPORTANT DUTIES

Even though a meeting may be somewhat informal, the business will proceed more satisfactorily if the proper procedure is observed. Before the meeting may commence, it must be ensured that a quorum is present and that a chairman is properly elected. An attendance book or sheet is passed around so that those present may sign their names; a record of those present is thus preserved. The Secretary, at the request of the Chairman, reads the Minutes of the previous meeting and if the members agree that it is a correct record, the Chairman signs these Minutes. They may then be used as evidence of the proceedings.

Motions, questions, etc. should always be put to the meeting through the Chairman and not direct to individual members. A motion is put to a meeting by a *proposer* and it is usual for another person, called a *seconder*, to endorse the motion. This procedure proves that there is at least one other supporter of the motion. Motions (sometimes called Resolutions in company meetings) may be discussed, amended and voted upon and it is the Chairman's duty to see that motions are in order (within the scope of the meeting), that amendments are properly made (*e.g.*, they must not be a mere negation of the original motion) and that the sense (the wishes) of the meeting (as ascertained by the votes) is properly determined.

Sometimes the feeling of the assembly is made known by cries of "Aye" and "No," and the Chairman will declare that "the Ayes have it" or "the Noes have it" according to the shouts heard. In company meetings, however, the Chairman will usually take a vote "on a show of hands," the members raising one hand to indicate their vote clearly. It will be appreciated that voting on a show of hands is not necessarily the fairest way of taking the sense of the meeting, since such a vote takes no account of the weight of a member's interest. Thus, a shareholder who has a single share has the same (one) vote on a show of hands as another shareholder who has one thousand shares. For this reason, provision is usually made in the regulations of organisations (and in the *Companies Acts*) for a poll to be demanded. Where the requisite number of persons are not satisfied with the way a voting has gone, they may demand a poll and the Chairman is obliged to grant it. A poll takes account of the members' interests according to their rights; thus if each share is accorded one vote, then the holder of a single share will only have one-thousandth part of the voting power of the shareholder who owns one thousand shares. Members who wish to vote but are unable to be present at the meeting may appoint another person, known as a *proxy*, to vote on their behalf, provided due notice is given to the company. If the proxy is instructed how to vote, he must follow the instruction. It is permissible, however, for him to be given a free hand, in which case he will vote as he thinks fit. The attendance of the donee (the real member) at the meeting revokes the power of his proxy.

Most regulations give the Chairman a casting (an additional) vote, so that if the votes cast for and against a motion are equal, he can resolve the deadlock by using his casting vote.

1. PRINCIPLES OF MINUTE-TAKING

Unless you are specifically asked to take down "verbatim" minutes, it will be a waste of energy to attempt to do so as well as a waste of transcription time. Verbatim minutes are word-for-word notes of the proceedings and are not normally required. They would cloud the real business which was transacted by their sheer profusion, making the work of extracting only the relevant information much more difficult.

When taking minutes of a meeting, it is necessary for the secretary to be alert to the real business transacted. Notes should not take detailed account of the actual discussions, but only of the decisions reached. This does not mean that at this stage the rough notes should not contain any detail—this will help when writing up the minutes— but only just enough detail should be included of the events leading up to the decisions to enable the secretary to write up an accurate record. This is more easily said than done, since in practice much discussion goes on, some members voicing first one opinion then being persuaded to reverse it, and sometimes even digressing from the subject under debate, until the secretary (no one could blame her!) loses track of the discussion. If this happens, it is important not to lose heart as well! A brief check with the Chairman before the meeting proceeds to the next business should settle the matter. The secretary might look enquiringly at the Chairman, and ask "how have we left it then?" with her pencil poised to take the Chairman's dictated note which is to go on record. Since accuracy is one of the first essentials of minute-taking, it is important that you should not feel too timid to ask if you are not sure that you have followed the discussion to its conclusion.

It is generally recommended that the actual minutes should be written up as soon as possible after the meeting, while the secretary still has the proceedings fresh in her mind. This will help enormously when drafting the minutes. The draft is then agreed with the Chairman and finally circulated to members before being finally written up in the Minute Book. Sometimes, of course, the minutes are not circulated but read out at the next meeting when, if the members agree that the minutes are an accurate record, the Chairman will sign them. If the minutes have been circulated to the members before the next meeting, they may, in order to save time, agree that the minutes "be taken as read," whereupon the Chairman will append his signature. Many authorities feel that once the minutes are agreed and signed, all other copies and drafts should be destroyed, so that there can be no question of conflicting evidence at a later date.

The main points to remember when taking down minutes of a meeting are then:

(*a*) *Accuracy is essential.* If you are not absolutely sure that you have understood the discussions or that you have taken down an accurate record, check with the Chairman there and then. Do not leave it until later.

(*b*) Exercise your skill in sorting out the opinions, discussions and occasional red herrings from the *real decision reached.* This is a real test of the secretary's skill which, as with many other spheres of her work, improves with practice.

(*c*) The names of the *proposer and seconder* of a motion should usually but not invariably be included, but it is not necessary to show the names of those who voted for or against the motion. Occasionally there may be a special request from an individual *e.g.* to place on record the fact that he voted against the motion, and this may be allowed.

(*d*) Where the number of *votes are counted*, these should be shown.

(*e*) It is permissible, and sometimes desirable, to show *how a motion has been carried, e.g.* unanimously, or *nem. con.*

(*f*) When the minutes from the original rough notes are being written up it should be shown very clearly what the motion was (it is usual to insert the actual wording of the motion).

EXAMPLE 5

The directors considered the short list of applications for the post of Company Secretary and it was

> RESOLVED that Mr. A. Bee be asked to attend for a final interview on IOth December next.

EXAMPLE 6

After some discussion on the relative merits of Brighton, Eastbourne and Hastings for the annual outing, it was

> RESOLVED that Brighton be selected and the secretary was instructed to inform the staff accordingly.

EXAMPLE 7

Mr. Cee proposed and Mr. Dee seconded

> THAT the date for the annual social club outing to Brighton should be fixed at 15th June 19.. The resolution was carried by fourteen votes to two.

(*g*) The draft minutes should be *finally agreed* with the Chairman before being circulated and entered in the Minute Book.

(*h*) Minutes should be *headed, consecutively numbered and indexed* for easy reference. Alterations should be avoided, since these would have to be initialled by the Chairman.

(*i*) When the minutes are finally written up in the Minute Book, all previous drafts, copies, etc. should be destroyed.

2. STANDARD TERMS

adjournment

the continuation of a meeting at a subsequent date. Not to be confused with a postponement, which means putting back the original meeting to a later date. Strictly speaking, once a meeting has been properly convened, it may not be postponed; but it may be held briefly and then adjourned.

Ad hoc

special purpose (an *ad hoc* committee is formed for one special purpose, and when this has been accomplished, it is dissolved).

agenda

an itemised list of the business to be transacted at a meeting. The order of the business should normally be as shown in the agenda, as some members might be inconvenienced if they had made arrangements to attend for only that part of a meeting where the business concerning them was due to be transacted.

alternates

the Articles of Association of some companies may make provision for the appointment of "alternate" Directors (a person to take the place of an absent Director).

By order of the Board

a phrase commonly used in notices of meetings to indicate the authority for convening the meeting.

casting vote   a second vote which the regulations of an organisation may give to the Chairman of a meeting. This vote may be used in the event of a tie in the voting. Some authorities believe that if the feeling against a motion is so strong that half the votes are against it, the Chairman should use his casting vote against it and thus not disturb the *status quo* (the existing position).

Convenor   the person properly authorised to call a meeting.

Co-opted member   a person who has been brought into membership through the votes of the existing members (*e.g.*, where it is desirable to co-opt a person because of his specialised knowledge in a certain field).

ex officio   by virtue of the office held.

in attendance   persons who are at a meeting other than by right are said to be in attendance. The term is usually applied to the secretary.

Madam Chairman   the accepted manner of addressing a woman who chairs a meeting.

nem. con.   the abbreviation for *nemine contradicente*, which means "no one contradicting." Thus a motion is said to be carried nem. con. if no votes are cast against it. Some members may have abstained from voting either for or against the motion, but so long as no votes were cast against it, the motion may be said to be carried nem. con.

poll

a means of voting which takes account of the voter's interest, *e.g.* one vote *per* share held (not *per* person).

proxy

a person appointed to attend at a meeting and vote on behalf of a member who is unable to be present.

quorum

the number of persons required to hold a valid meeting. Generally, the minimum number of persons required to form a quorum is two, but the rules of each organisation invariably make their own special provisions.

reference back

where information submitted to the main body by a committee is considered to be inadequate or to require further research, it is said to be "referred back" (to that committee for further work).

resolution

when a motion has been carried, it becomes a resolution. However, the *Companies Act* 1948 refers to resolutions instead of motions,

<table>
<tr><td></td><td>and the words are now sometimes used synonymously.</td></tr>
<tr><td>show of hands</td><td>a means of indicating a vote: holding up one hand.</td></tr>
<tr><td>unanimous</td><td>where all the members present vote for a motion, it is said to be carried unanimously. (In this case, there must be no abstentions.)</td></tr>
</table>

3. STYLES OF MINUTING

When the minutes are being written up from the first rough notes, they follow a generally accepted style. The first sheet would be headed with the date, time and place of the meeting and would of course indicate the name of the organisation.

EXAMPLE 8

MINUTES OF THE TWENTYFIFTH ANNUAL GENERAL MEETING OF XYZ COMPANY LIMITED, HELD AT 1 BLANK STREET, LONDON, EC2 4BY, ON 10th JANUARY, 197.. AT 12 O'CLOCK NOON.

EXAMPLE 9

XYZ COMPANY LIMITED
SOCIAL CLUB COMMITTEE
MINUTES OF THE MEETING HELD AT THE COMPANY'S REGISTERED OFFICE, 1 BLANK STREET, LONDON, EC2 4BY, ON 10TH JANUARY 197.. AT 12 O'CLOCK NOON.

After the heading, those present at the meeting must be shown. This usually takes the following form:

EXAMPLE 10

Present: Mr. A. Bee, Chairman
                Mr. C. Dee
                Mr. E. Eff
                Mr. G. Aitch

In attendance: Mr. I. Jay, Secretary

It will be noted that the Chairman always heads the list, the other members' names often being shown in strict alphabetical order. Persons who have been invited to attend for a specific purpose usually have the words "by invitation" written after their names. The secretary (of the meeting, not necessarily the private secretary) is shown last.

Minutes should be numbered consecutively, and each minute should be given an appropriate heading. The usual order is:

1. *Apologies for absence.* Apologies received from those unable to be present are tabled.
2. *Minutes of the meeting dated. . . .* These are the minutes of the previous meeting and are either read out, approved and signed by the Chairman as correct, or "taken as read," agreed and signed by the Chairman as correct.
3. *Matters arising from the previous minutes.* Any business arising from the previous minutes is dealt with at this stage.
4. The business of the meeting is now dealt with in the order in which it appears on the agenda. Each minute is given a separate number and heading, *e.g.* 4. Correspondence, 5. Consideration of Financial Statement.
5. *Any other business.* Under this heading comes business discussed or validly transacted which has not figured in the agenda. It will be appreciated that matters of importance may not be validly transacted unless due notice was given in the agenda. "Any other business" is therefore restricted to minor matters or to the agreement that certain important matters be put on the agenda for the next meeting.
6. *Next Meeting.* The date, time and venue for the next meeting are recorded.

Sufficient room should be left at the end of the minutes for the Chairman's signature. The date on which he signed the minutes should appear beside his signature.

There are three main styles of minuting:

(*a*) *Minutes of Resolution.* This is a somewhat cryptic style which merely shows what resolutions were taken. After all, that is really the only object of the minutes.

EXAMPLE 11

```
4.  Appointment of Assistant Secretary.  Mr. A. proposed, Mr. B.
    seconded and it was RESOLVED that Mr. C. Dee be offered the
    post of Assistant Secretary with effect from 1 January 197...
```

(*b*) *Minutes of Narration.* These minutes literally "tell the story."

EXAMPLE 12

4. <u>Appointment of Assistant Secretary</u>. The Secretary tabled a
   short list of candidates for the post of Assistant Secretary.
   It was agreed that an accounting qualification was essential
   and after some discussion Mr. A proposed and Mr. B seconded
   THAT Mr. C. Dee be offered the post of Assistant Secretary
   with effect from 1 January 197... The secretary was instructed
   to write to Mr. Dee accordingly.

(*c*) *Verbatim Minutes.* This is an actual record of all that was said at a meeting.

EXAMPLE 13

4. <u>Appointment of Assistant Secretary</u>.

   Mr. Brown (Secretary): "I have here the short-list of five
   candidates who were interviewed for
   this post." (Copies are circulated.)

   Mr. A : "It is my opinion that a man who has not
   got an accounting qualification will
   not meet our needs."

   Mr. E (Chairman) : "Yes, but surely you would accept a
   similar qualification - the second man
   on the list seems to have made a very
   favourable impression."

   Mr. B : "The last one on the list seems to have
   everything we want. His age is just
   right too."

   Mr. E : "You will be the one who has to work with
   him, Brown, what do you think?"

   Mr. Brown : "I was most impressed with Mr. C. Dee,
   the last candidate on the list."

   Mr. C : "I agree - we couldn't do better than
   engage him."
   (Murmurs of assent)

   Mr. E : "Well, gentlemen, shall we take a vote?"
   (Pause)

Mr. A	:	"I propose that Mr. C. Dee be offered the post of Assistant Secretary with effect from 1 January 197..."
Mr. B	:	"Seconded."
Mr. E	:	"How many for? Three, and my vote makes it unanimous then. Carried unanimously."

4. THE MINUTE BOOK

It used to be the practice to write up the minutes by hand in a bound book and indeed many officers still feel that there is less opportunity for tampering with the minutes if a bound book is used. However, if a loose-leaf form is adopted, this allows the minutes to be typed instead of written by hand and the advantages of speed, neatness and legibility are gained. Providing adequate precautions are taken to safeguard the minutes, a loose-leaf book is perfectly acceptable. (The *Companies Act* 1948 recognises this for minutes of company meetings.) The usual practice is for the sheets to be numbered consecutively, and accounted for by the Company Secretary. The book itself is generally fitted with a lock (the Company Secretary and a Director having custody of the keys), and is kept in the office safe.

The Company Secretary must not be confused with the private secretary. The former is an important executive of the company. He often acts as adviser to the Board of Directors, especially on matters relating to company law, and is sometimes the Chief Accountant of the Company. It is he who attends Board Meetings and General Meetings of the company.

Short-answer Questions

1. What is the difference between a Board Meeting and an Annual General Meeting?

2. Name two methods of taking a vote on a motion.

3. What is a casting vote?

4. What is a quorum?

5. Why is a proxy sometimes appointed to attend a meeting?

6. What remedy is available to a person who is dissatisfied with the result of a vote on a show of hands?

7. Explain: *nem. con.*; unanimous; proxy; poll.

8. What are "verbatim minutes?"

9. What is the difference between a Company Secretary and a private secretary?

10. Make up a sentence to show you understand the meaning of "*ex officio.*"

Past Examination Questions

1. The minutes of meetings of a Social Club have hitherto been written up by hand in a bound book. It has now been decided that the minutes in future are to be typed. What advantages does this present and how is the new minute book to be kept?   (*L.C.C.*)

2. At a meeting shortly to be held by your company many visitors who are not entitled to vote have been invited. Suggest a procedure to be followed on the day of the meeting to ensure that a separate record is obtained of members and visitors present and that those voting on a show of hands are in fact members entitled to vote and not visitors.   (*L.C.C.*)

3. The following items appear on the agenda of a meeting to be attended by your chief: (*i*) Absences; (*ii*) Minutes of previous meeting; (*iii*) Finance; (*iv*) Contract with Jones & Co.

Expand each item to show how it might appear in the Minute Book, inventing any detail you think necessary.   (*L.C.C.*)

4. (*a*) As secretary to your firm's Sports and Social Club, prepare the notice and agenda for their Annual General Meeting on 29th September.

(*b*) To whom will you send copies and when?   (*L.C.C.*)

5. The following is an extract from a report of a meeting. Explain the meaning of the words in italics.

The *ad hoc* committee reconvened on 16th June after its *adjournment* on 9th June.

The meeting continued with a discussion of the *amendment* to the *motion* for revision of the *quorum*. This alteration to the *Standing Orders* was passed *nem. con.*

(*R.S.A.*)

6. You are secretary to the committee of a local music and drama club. Draw up a notice of the next committee meeting and include the agenda.   (*R.S.A.*)

7. (*a*) Give *three* items which must always appear on an agenda.

(*b*) Who signs the notice of a meeting?   (*R.S.A.*)

8. In a business meeting what is the correct way for a member

(*a*) to address the chair, (*b*) to present a motion to the meeting, (*c*) to move an amendment to a motion? (*R.S.A.*)

9. (*a*) What do you understand by an amendment to a motion?

(*b*) For what reasons might a member of an organisation be co-opted on to a committee?

(*c*) Give one reason why a meeting might be adjourned for a few days.

(*d*) What is an "ex officio" member of a committee?

(*e*) What is the purpose of a quorum? (*R.S.A.*)

10. What is:

(*a*) a quorum, (*b*) the meaning of "*ad hoc*," (*c*) a casting vote? (*R.S.A.*)

CHAPTER 9

SOURCES OF INFORMATION
AND REFERENCE

IT is not possible, nor indeed is it desirable, to clutter up one's mind with masses of detail which could be easily found in a reference book. Every good secretary should have one or two reference books which are like old friends to her—the pages well thumbed and thoroughly familiar—books which will serve a multitude of reference purposes. A Secretary's Desk Book, a Typist's Desk Book or better still *Pears Cyclopaedia*—these contain enough information on a variety of subjects to meet the general needs of the secretary. For example, *Pears Cyclopaedia* contains information classified under *The Wider World*, which includes such matters as the Law of England, Background to Public Affairs, Education and Careers; *Home and Social*, which includes medical matters, human relations; and *General Reference*, which includes a Gazetteer of the World, an Atlas of the World, General Information, Literary Companion and General Compendium. In the Gazetteer information is to be found on the population of a town, its main industries, the names of rivers, where they flow, etc. In the Literary section, the secretary can look up the meanings of common foreign phrases and classical quotations; here also are to be found abbreviations and their meanings. The General Compendium shows, among a wealth of information, modes of address to persons of rank, weights and measures, correction of printers' proofs, Roman numerals and thermometer reading comparisons between Centigrade and Fahrenheit scales.

For reference on more specialised subjects, the following list will prove useful.

Reference Book	*Information*
A.A. or R.A.C. members' handbook	Motoring information, maps, distances between towns, accommodation, early closing days, breakdown services.
A.B.C. Travel Guides (rail, sea, air)	Travel times, accommodation offered, fares.

Reference Book	*Information*
Black's Titles and Forms of Address	Very comprehensive information on modes of address.
Crockford's Directory	A clerical directory for the Church of England.
Directory of Directors	Particulars of Directors, showing the companies in which they hold directorships.
English Dictionary	Meaning of words, pronunciation, parts of speech, derivations.
Hansard	Verbatim report of proceedings in Parliament.
Kelly's Directory	Manufacturers and suppliers of goods and services in particular towns.
Post Office Guide	Regulations regarding inland and overseas mail. Postage, special declarations, prohibitions. Telephone and telegraph services.
Post Office Street Directory	Names of streets, showing occupiers of offices, shops and houses.
Ready Reckoner	Calculations, percentages, etc.
Roget's Thesaurus of English Words	Words classified by meaning.
Special dictionaries	A variety of special dictionaries are available, *e.g.* technical terms, medical terms, legal terms, etc.
Stock Exchange Yearbook	Full details of quoted companies, *e.g.* address of registered office, capital of the company, directors, company secretary, etc.
Whitaker's Almanack	World affairs, the royal family, the law courts, statistical information on a variety of matters, *e.g.* population, crime, etc.
Who's Who	Particulars of prominent people may be looked up in this book. There are many specialist *Who's Who* volumes, *e.g. Who's Who in the Theatre, in Art*, etc.

The following lists have been arranged to show the minimum number of reference books to which it is recommended the secretary should have ready access.

Books to be kept close at hand, e.g. *in the desk drawer*	*Books to be kept within easy reach*, e.g. *in a cabinet or on a shelf*	*Other useful books*
English Dictionary	A.B.C. Travel Guides	A.A. or R.A.C.
Ready Reckoner	Classified Directories	members' handbook
Secretary's Desk Book	*Pears Cyclopaedia*	*Directory of*
Special dictionary (of	*Post Office Guide*	*Directors*
terms used in the	Telephone/Telex	*Stock Exchange*
employer's line of	directories	*Yearbook*
business)	*Whitaker's Almanack*	*Who's Who*
Street maps		

SOME USEFUL ORGANISATIONS

The British Medical Association,
B.M.A. House, Tavistock Square, London,
WC1 9JP — Medical matters

The Law Society,
113 Chancery Lane, London, WC2A 1PL

Legal matters

The General Council of the Bar,
Fountain Court, Temple, London, EC4Y 9PQ

Her Majesty's Stationery Office,
PO Box 569, Stamford Street, London,
SE1 9NY — Government publications

The British Library,
(Newspaper Library), Colindale Avenue,
London, NW9 5EH — Newspapers, etc.

The Department of Trade
1 Victoria Street, London SW1H 0ET

London Chamber of Commerce and Industry,
69–75 Cannon Street, London, EC4N 5AB

Trade matters

Short-answer Questions

1. Name three reference books which a secretary should keep in her desk drawer.

2. Where would you find the registered office of a quoted company?

3. What information would you expect to find in *Whitaker's Almanack*?

4. What is a classified directory?

5. How would you find out the correct pronunciation of a word?

6. In what reference book would you find out whether Pullman accommodation is offered on a train?

7. What is the difference between a Directory of Directors and a Stock Exchange Yearbook?

8. Name three kinds of special dictionaries.

9. Where would you find out the location of a town?

10. What is *Crockford's Directory*?

Past Examination Questions

1. List six main items of information provided by an A.A. or R.A.C. Members' Handbook.   (*R.S.A.*)

2. List four reference books which contain information about professional or well-known people.   (*R.S.A.*)

3. For each of the following, give the name of one reference book which would be required for: (*a*) travel by train; (*b*) travel by car; (*c*) travel by air; (*d*) travel by sea.   (*R.S.A.*)

4. For what purposes would you use the following books of reference:

(*a*) *Roget's Thesaurus*; (*b*) a classified trade directory; (*c*) A.B.C. railway guide; (*d*) The Law List.   (*R.S.A.*)

5. In which reference books would you look to find the following:

(*a*) whether or not the word "parochial" is a noun;

(*b*) how to pronounce the word "jalousie";

(*c*) a word similar to "nice," but which would better express your meaning;

(*d*) the population of Harrogate;

(*e*) if there is a three-star hotel at Warminster;

(*f*) how long it would normally take an airmail letter to reach New Zealand?   (*R.S.A.*)

6. What information would you find in: (*a*) a ready reckoner; (*b*) *Who's Who*?   (*R.S.A.*)

7. List four well-known reference books and explain some of the circumstances in which you might wish to refer to these books.   (*R.S.A.*)

8. In what reference books would you find: (*a*) information about the Telex system; (*b*) air services between London and Scotland; (*c*) a

list of members of Parliament; (*d*) an abbreviation such as "*et seq.*"?   (*R.S.A.*)

9. Where would you look for information about: (*i*) a qualified medical practitioner; (*ii*) a solicitor; (*iii*) a clergyman of the Church of England; (*iv*) the population of a town; (*v*) a company; (*vi*) the road mileage between two towns?   (*R.S.A.*)

10. From where could the following information be obtained: (*a*) the cost of an air fare to Paris; (*b*) the signs to be used in proof correcting; (*c*) the current cost of an insurance stamp; (*d*) the decorations of a well-known parliamentary figure who will speak at your firm's annual dinner; (*e*) the name of a good hotel in London; (*f*) a speech made by a Member in the House of Commons?   (*R.S.A.*)

CHAPTER 10

FILING

WHY ARE PAPERS FILED?

SURPRISINGLY, people file papers for a variety of reasons: to make the "In Tray" tidier, to look busy when the boss is around, to be able to refer to these papers at a later date, and because they haven't the courage to throw some papers where they belong—in the waste paper basket! As you can see, not all filing is necessary: pieces of paper confirming an appointment could easily be discarded after the date of the appointment; duplicate copies of internal memos are "*de trop*" when the original is returned for filing—literally hundreds of papers could fill the waste paper baskets and free the filing cabinets if only someone had the sense and the courage to relegate them to the waste paper basket.

The purpose of filing is to place documents, letters, etc., where they may be found with the minimum of trouble and delay at a future date. The key phrases are "where they may be found" and "minimum trouble and delay." The first essential is therefore that once filed away the papers should be found: it is less than useless to put a letter in the wrong file because it may never be found when wanted. Every letter should have a subject—after all it must be about something!—and even if the subject is not shown as a heading this should be easily discovered by reading the letter; the subject should then be matched to the title of one of the files. "Minimum trouble and delay" means that although it may be known where the paper required is filed, the file itself should be reasonably accessible. Current files (*i.e.*, those in constant use) should be close at hand, possibly in the secretary's own room if there is no central registry—older files (*e.g.*, for the last two years) may be located in a slightly less accessible place, since they will not be referred to as often as the current files, and "dead" files (*i.e.*, those not likely to be wanted at all—possibly those containing papers over six years old) may be parcelled up, labelled and placed wherever you like—in the loft or the basement for a year or so prior to being burnt, shredded or otherwise disposed of.

1. THE SYSTEM

Although there are many systems of filing in existence it is not always the most up-to-date or the most expensive system that is the best. *The system should suit the requirements* and it is conceivable that in some cases a mere spike would suit the purpose, while at the other extreme elaborate and expensive equipment might be justified.

In just the same way, the method of classifying files should suit the requirements of the office. If the sales office deals with representatives, each of whom is allocated a certain area of the country, then the *geographical* method would be appropriate; if there is some secrecy about the subject titles of the files, then the *numerical* method might be appropriate; if the office is concerned with customers it might be appropriate to file *alphabetically* under their respective names and of course many aspects lend themselves to filing under *subject heading*.

Each system has its advantages and its disadvantages, and it is impossible categorically to state that one is better than another. It would be more sensible to state that one is more *suitable to the particular requirements* than another.

The *alphabetical* method of classifying files is simple to understand (it is assumed that most clerks know how to spell—though it is surprising how many do not!) therefore little training is necessary; it expands to accommodate additional files without any trouble: a new file may be inserted in its correct alphabetical position between two other files without any difficulty. This system is suitable for subject titles, or names of customers, personnel, etc. Difficulties may however arise in misplacing files because of spelling errors, *e.g.* Browne, Clarke, etc. may be spelled with or without an "e" and in deciding where to place files named with prefixes such as Mc, Mac, St, O', d', etc. definite rules must be made and adhered to rigidly.

The *numerical* method of classifying files is also simple to understand and operate, since once again it may be assumed that even the most junior clerk knows how to count. Once again therefore little training is necessary. This method is suitable where there is some secrecy about the titles of the files or where the subject itself is numerical, *e.g.* numbers allocated by the Department of Trade to registered companies, or the registration numbers of a firm's taxis or service vans. The disadvantages lie in the fact that a separate index must usually be maintained in alphabetical (subject or name) order since the files themselves only bear an identifying number, not a title, and this is time-consuming. Expansion is easy so long as it is effected from the last number (it is only possible to add files with higher numbers as it makes for complications to insert a new file *between* existing files. The only possible identification to give a file which had to be placed between files 3 and 4 would be 3a, but what number could be given to a subsequent file which had to be placed between files 3 and 3a?

The *geographical* method of filing is particularly suitable where distinction must be made between areas, towns, countries, and so on. Sales departments may find it useful to file geographically, since each salesman will normally be allocated a territory (say, part of the country). Estate agents may file geographically since they would find if necessary to locate quickly and easily houses for sale in certain areas.

Geographical filing must nevertheless be combined with alphabetical classification, since each area would be placed in alphabetical order in relation to other areas.

Like other methods, the geographical system is capable of easy expansion, but the difficulty in operating it lies in acquainting clerks with the geography of towns, areas, etc.

Subject filing lends itself to great use in most offices, as matter to be filed is often referred to (and therefore best classified) under subjects. Examples are: Minutes of Meetings, Social Club, Pensions, Salaries, etc. Subjects must of course be filed alphabetically and the system therefore expands without any trouble. The difficulty lies in that it is sometimes hard to ascertain *exactly* what subject a letter refers to—it may deal mainly with one subject but also touch on another and while one person might look for such a letter in one file, another person might think it belonged under another title.

It will be seen that no one system is absolutely perfect and it can only be repeated that a good system of filing is one which best suits the requirements of the business.

It will be appreciated that sometimes a combination of methods is necessary: thus files classified under subject title would be placed in alphabetical order in the filing cabinet. Similarly, files classified geographically would also be filed in alphabetical order, the file for Birmingham, for example, being placed in front of that for Brighton.

Sometimes indexing is necessary. If the files are given numbers instead of subject titles, it would be necessary to maintain an index (which need be no more elaborate than a number of small cards kept in alphabetical order in a box) under subject title, indicating the number which a certain subject has been allocated. This of course facilitates finding a file without resorting to the memory or searching through the complete set of files. The filing clerk who becomes thoroughly familiar with the numbers and the subjects to which they refer is an invaluable member of the office staff, but it should be possible for the employer or any other clerk not connected with filing to look up the index card under *subject* and find on that card the *number* of the file in which papers relating to the particular subject are filed.

2. FOLLOW-UP SYSTEMS

It is often necessary in the office to "bring forward" or "follow up" a letter some time after it has been filed. To take a simple example, a letter containing the following sentence is sent to a customer on 1st January: "I am unable to let you have the information at the moment but I have requested our Scottish representative to furnish me with full details and I will write to you again shortly." It is expected that the information will be forthcoming from the Scottish representative in three or four days and it would be wise therefore to "bring forward" the carbon copy of the letter to the customer on the 7th January as a reminder to transmit the information to him. This may be done in several ways:

1. The pending file. Work not yet completed, or which needs to be referred to within a short time, is placed in a "pending file" which is referred to daily. All letters which have to be "actioned" on that day are extracted, dealt with and finally filed away in the proper file or brought forward at a later date. Apart from its simplicity, an advantage of this method is that all unfinished work is kept in one folder; a disadvantage is that the whole contents of the folder have to be looked through to find those letters requiring action on a specified day; another disadvantage is that the subject file does not contain all the relevant papers unless a duplicate copy is taken and placed in it.

2. The diary. Before being filed away in their appropriate files, all letters requiring further action at a later date are marked with the date on which they should be brought forward (*e.g.*, "B/F 7 Jan."), and a corresponding entry is made in the

diary on the 7th January (*e.g.*, "B/F letter to customer"). As soon as the entry is made in the diary, a tick is placed on the letter itself as an indication that the "reminder" has been recorded, and it may then be filed away. This method is also relatively simple and has the advantage that no papers are kept out of their files for any length of time, therefore the complete history is to be found in the file at any time. The disadvantages lie in the time consumed in making the entries by hand in the diary and in cluttering up the diary with "B/F" entries. This latter point is hardly a valid disadvantage since a separate diary may be kept specifically for the purpose if a large number of reminder entries are to be made.

3. *The reminder or tickler method.* This consists of thirty-one cards or folders (one for each day of the month), each card roughly the size of a file and being numbered 1–31. Letters to be brought forward on the first day of the current month are placed behind the first card, those to be brought forward on the fifteenth day are placed behind the fifteenth card and those to be brought forward the next month are placed behind the thirty-first card, to be arranged in the correct order on the last day of the current month. All the cards or folders are placed vertically in a drawer or filing cabinet and each day's folder is referred to once a day. The advantage of this method lies in the fact that no entries need to be recorded, but against that must be weighed the fact that once again letters are not in their respective subject files, so that the complete history is not immediately available in the file; also the special cards or folders have to be bought. Both these disadvantages may be offset by taking an extra carbon copy of the letter to be actioned or by making a separate note of the particulars of the letter and placing that in the folder instead of the carbon copy itself and by making one's own cards or folders or by using a "concertina" type folder with thirty-one divisions.

3. TRACING FILES

It should be a rule of the house that letters, documents, etc., should not be removed from a file: where necessary the complete file should be taken from the cabinet—never a single piece of paper from the file as it could easily be mislaid and any person subsequently looking through the file would not have a complete history and might be unaware that some papers had been removed. If a letter must be removed from a file, a note should be inserted in the place from which the letter has been taken, but this is really second best, and should not be encouraged.

It now becomes necessary to institute a system whereby a file which has been removed from its place in the filing cabinet can be traced to the person who borrowed it. A very simple and effective system is to place "OUT" cards (preferably, but not necessarily of an outstanding colour), in the place from which the file has been removed. Such a card may be pre-printed so that the name of the person who extracted the file and the date on which this was done might be inserted. A further column is also useful to show the date on which the file was returned. Thus if A borrows a file from the central registry on 1st January and B wants it urgently on 2nd January, B will refer to the filing cabinet, find an "OUT" card in place of the file he wants and discover easily from the "OUT" card who has taken the file.

This system relies on individuals returning the files promptly after use. If required, the person in charge of the files may operate a "follow-up" system for the return of files, *e.g.* by making an entry in a diary, say, a week after the file has been booked out, or by referring daily to any "OUT" cards in the cabinets (these cards would be easily seen if they were of an outstanding colour) and checking that the dates showing when the files were borrowed were not more than a week or so old.

4. SECURITY AND SECRECY

Documents and the files in which they are contained must be made secure from a number of hazards—theft, fire, damp, heat, light, publicity and even rodents! Loss and/or damage through theft and fire is obvious but the other hazards could cause just as much damage, depending on the quality of paper filed. Thus damp could cause eventual rotting or might cause two pieces of paper to stick together so firmly as to make it impossible to separate them without tearing. Exposure to heat and/or light could cause curling at the edges, discolouration and fading to such an extent as to make a document illegible. Mice often like a little paper mixed with their cheese, so be careful that the paper they eat does not come from your files!

Documents may also have to be protected from prying eyes. There is much confidential documentation in any office. The degree of restriction will of course vary from office to office, but such matters as salaries, personnel records, minutes of Board meetings are not generally open to inspection. Arrangements must therefore be made to ensure that files containing restricted information are accessible only to authorised personnel. This may be done either by removing them completely from the central registry or by allowing them to remain there but keeping the cabinets locked, the keys being in the possession of a responsible person in charge.

5. STORAGE

If all the papers in a file and all the files in a filing cabinet were retained indefinitely, there would soon be a thousand times more paper than personnel and a tremendous amount of office space (quite costly in this day and age) would be taken up for storage space.

One method of "making room" is known as "thinning." Literally, it consists of reducing the size of a file—thinning it—by leafing through the papers in it and discarding those not likely to be referred to again. This is conveniently done once a year or every other year, depending on the rate at which a file fills up. Thinning should not normally be undertaken more often than once a year as there is a likelihood that some letters might be referred to within that space of time, and it would be dangerous to destroy them. The advocates of thinning claim the following advantages:

1. It may be undertaken at any time convenient to the secretary, *i.e.* when there is a slack period in the office.
2. It keeps files within a reasonable size—exceptionally thick files are awkward to handle.
3. It is methodical and safe, *i.e.* each letter is read through before the decision to discard it is made.

Such a method, although still used in many offices, has some serious disadvantages which are not obvious at first glance:

(*a*) A responsible person (*i.e.*, a senior member of staff) must do this work, as only such a person could decide whether or not to destroy certain papers. This represents a real cost (in terms of salary) for non-productive work.

(*b*) The work is time-consuming and boring.

(*c*) Slack periods in the office could be put to better use.

Another method of releasing filing space is to keep only "current" files in the filing cabinet close at hand. Files over two or three years old are transferred to cabinets or cupboards or shelves in a somewhat less accessible place; files containing general correspondence over six years old may usually be safely bundled up and placed out of the way prior to being completely destroyed. Assuming that no title deeds or other very important documents are kept in general files, the chances that a file might be required after it has been destroyed are quite small, and the inconvenience of having to reconstruct the file or document required or of having to make do without it must be weighed against the value of the time and space gained under this method.

6. RETENTION

(*a*) Some papers do not need to be filed at all; acknowledgments, duplicate copies of correspondence, receipts of small payments made by cheque and such like, could be destroyed before they ever found a place in the files.

(*b*) Most general correspondence is not referred to a year or eighteen months after it has been dealt with, and may conveniently be destroyed or (for those too cautious to do this) transferred to another location for a further short period before destruction.

(*c*) Invoices should normally be retained for a period of three years and those recording items of a capital nature should be retained for six years as they might have to be produced for inspection purposes under the Value Added Tax regulations.

(*d*) Some papers, *e.g.* those evidencing a debt, should be kept for at least six years, since under the Statute of Limitations they do not become statute-barred until after that length of time has elapsed. (Specialty debts, *e.g.* dividends, do not become statute-barred until twelve years have elapsed, and such evidence should be retained for twelve or thirteen years.)

(*e*) Title deeds, insurance policies, minute books and other important documents must be kept indefinitely (or in the case of insurance policies so long as the policy is in force).

7. SORTING AND IDENTIFYING

(a) *Aids to identification*. Filing is not an end in itself—it is a means of classifying and storing material for future reference. Therefore, the filing system must be simple and quick to operate. Any aids to sorting and identifying the papers to be filed or the files themselves should be used; compare the time taken by a filing clerk in sorting a pile of papers into two—export matters and home sales. Each letter must be read, understood and placed in the "export" pile or the "home" pile. If it were a rule that all export letters should have pink flimsy copies, all the internal correspondence could be sorted at a glance merely by extracting the pink "flimsies" from the whole pile of letters, thus reducing the time taken in sorting. Colour in fact should play a much more important part in office systems than it does at present and although most manufacturers do make full use of colour, *e.g.* action tags, guide clips, etc. individual clerks have yet to appreciate how much simpler the work might be if more thought were given to ease of identification. To take another simple example: The mail room in a large company contains a large rack divided into numerous "pigeon holes," each compartment designed to hold correspondence for sales representatives. All the mail for the representatives is placed in the respective compartments and at the end of the day one envelope is typed for each representative, and all his mail is removed from the pigeon hole and inserted in the envelope. Complaints were constantly being received that some mail was being inserted in the wrong envelopes, causing delay due to re-routing and inefficiency. The company decided to allocate a different colour to each representative. Internal memos were written on pink, green, blue, etc. paper. Each pigeon hole in the rack was identified by a small strip of coloured paper corresponding to that allocated to him. At the end of the day when it was time to insert each representative's mail in the envelope, any papers of a different colour were seen immediately to be in the wrong compartment and were removed. Errors dropped to nil.

Many forms could easily bear an identifying mark on the top right hand corner, so that by merely flicking over a pile of papers, sorting is facilitated. In some firms, the files themselves bear distinctive colours, *e.g.* export files—pink; home files—blue; confidential files—red, and so on.

(b) *Punched card hand sorting*. This term refers to sorting

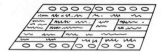

Fig. 10.—An edge-punched card.

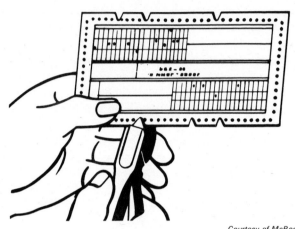

Courtesy of McBee Systems

(*a*) Notching a card.

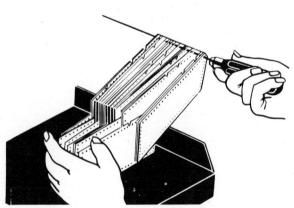

Courtesy of McBee Systems

(*b*) Sorting the cards.

Fig. 11.—Punched card hand sorting.

papers, or more usually cards, which are punched around the edges. Each hole represents coded information, *e.g.* number of personnel under eighteen years, number of personnel with various qualifications, etc. In processing the information, some of the holes are clipped right through to the edge (Figs. 10 and 11(*a*)).

When it is required to sort out those cards which contain certain information as indicated by the clipped edges a small rod, rather like a knitting needle, is inserted, and the cards are then shaken. Obviously those cards which have been punched will remain hanging on the needle, while those whose holes have been clipped through to the edge will fall on the table. Sorting is thus effected simply and quickly (Fig. 11(*b*)).

CENTRALISATION OF FILING SERVICES

In some organisations it is convenient for each department to maintain its own set of files and the filing is undertaken either by the secretary or by a filing clerk, depending on the volume of work. In other organisations, a central registry or filing department is set up, and individual departments send their work down to the Filing Department for filing. When a file is required, a requisition is made out for the Filing Department to supply the file. It is difficult to say which of the two systems is the better. The important point is that the system should suit the requirements of the firm and whichever way makes for less effort, speedier retrieval of files and fewer staff is obviously the better.

1. ADVANTAGES OF CENTRALISATION

1. Since a complete department is devoted to filing, it becomes possible to employ specialised staff, with consequent greater efficiency.
2. Similarly, it is easier to train junior staff; as all personnel in the department are employed on filing, it is easy to demonstrate the various stages of the work, etc.
3. Uniformity of method is ensured, since all the filing is under the supervision of one person.
4. A saving in staff and equipment becomes possible as there is sufficient volume of work for maximum utilisation of resources.

2. ADVANTAGES OF DEPARTMENTAL FILING

1. The secretary who does her own filing naturally becomes intimately familiar with the system, can file and retrieve papers with greater speed and fewer errors.
2. The filing cabinets are close at hand in the department itself and files can therefore be taken to the employer for use with less loss of time than if they were accommodated in a large and possibly remote central filing department.
3. Where there is insufficient work of another nature, *e.g.* short-hand-typing, the secretary may conveniently be employed on filing, thus reducing idle time.
4. It follows from 3 above that departmental filing introduces greater variety in the clerk's routine.
5. As departmental filing implies smaller units, it is not necessary to make and adhere rigidly to such rules and regulations as would be necessary in a large unit.

SOME TERMS AND FILING EQUIPMENT IN COMMON USE

1. CARD INDEX

This is nothing more complicated than a number of cards which are maintained in cross-reference to the files themselves. Thus, if the files are kept in numerical order, there is no clue as to which number refers to a customer's papers. It is necessary therefore to maintain an index in alphabetical order (under customers' names) and these cards would show the number allocated to the file for a particular customer (Fig. 12). It now becomes possible to find the file without further search. The cards may of course bear other information such as the customer's address, details of his latest order, etc.

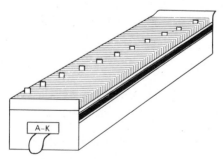

Fig. 12.—A card index. In the box are cards arranged alphabetically (for use in a filing system where the files themselves are arranged in numerical order).

2. STRIP INDEX

This is a form of visible index where a small amount of important information is recorded on a single strip. The information is therefore visible at a glance. As these strips may be easily moved, the index is maintained in the required order, *e.g.* alphabetical, without difficulty (Figs. 13 and 14).

Individual strips easily removed and inserted

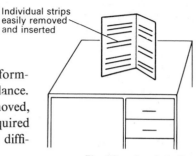

Fig. 13.—A strip index.

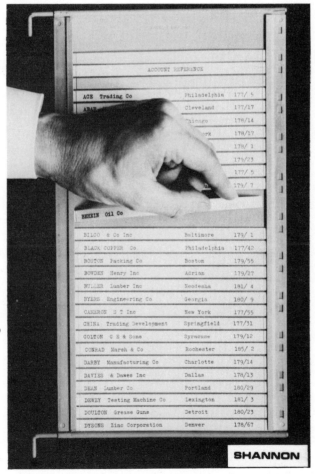

Fig. 14.—Shannostrip one line records.

Courtesy of The Shannon Limited

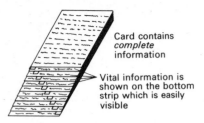

Card contains *complete* information

Vital information is shown on the bottom strip which is easily visible

Fig. 15.—Visible records. The cards contain complete information, but the vital information is shown on the bottom strips, which are easily visible.

3. VISIBLE INDEX

As on the strip index, vital information is shown on a strip, but this strip is merely the visible bottom part of a whole card which bears much more complete information (Figs. 15 and 16).

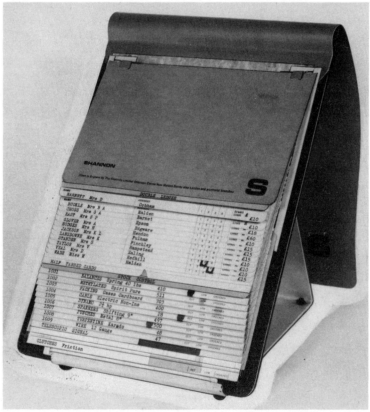

Courtesy of The Shannon Limited

Fig. 16.—Shannovue visible records.

4. ROTARY OR WHEEL INDEX

Where a large number of cards are to be accommodated, these may be attached around a central spindle (Fig. 17). Cards may be revolved to present that section which contains the required card. As can be seen, several tiers of cards may be accommodated, if necessary. (Fig. 18.)

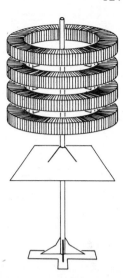

Fig. 17.—Rotary filing. The cards revolve round a central spindle.

Courtesy of Frank Wilson (Filing) Ltd.

Fig. 18.—Railex Rotalink filing.

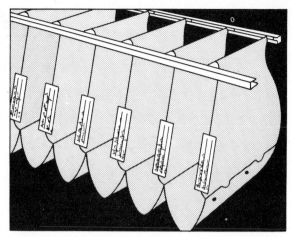

Courtesy of Frank Wilson (Filing) Ltd.

Fig. 19.—Suspension pockets.

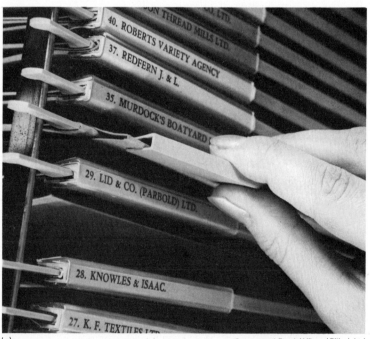

(a)

Courtesy of Frank Wilson (Filing) Ltd.

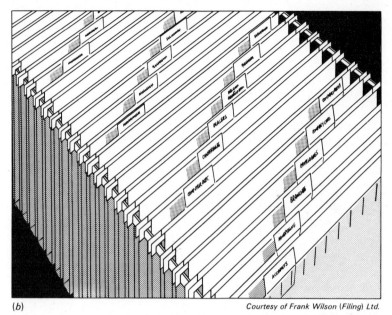

(b)   *Courtesy of Frank Wilson (Filing) Ltd.*

(a) Railex Spendafile Drawer suspension filing. A tab being attached to a pocket.

(b) Suspended filing.

Fig. 20.—Types of suspension filing.

5. HORIZONTAL FILING

This term is reserved for the storing of files horizontally (one on top of the other) as on a shelf. It will be appreciated that this method is not convenient for the average filing, but it is suitable for certain papers, *e.g.* maps or plans which are better stored flat on a shelf or in drawers.

6. VERTICAL FILING

This term is applied to the majority of filing systems which allow the files to be stored vertically (one behind the other) as in a filing cabinet drawer.

7. SUSPENDED FILING

Here the files or papers are accommodated vertically in pocket folders suspended in the cabinet drawer (Figs. 19 and 20).

Courtesy of Frank Wilson (Filing) Ltd.

Fig. 21.—Railex lateral filing.

8. LATERAL FILING

This term is usually applied to files suspended tier upon tier (or shelf upon shelf) in a cabinet or cupboard (Figs. 21 and 22). Sometimes called "floor-to-ceiling filing," this method has the space-saving advantage that drawers do not have to be pulled out.

Courtesy of The Shannon Limited

Fig. 22.—Lateral filing.

9. BOX FILES (sometimes called "LEVER ARCH FILES")

These are box-like containers in which papers may be filed. The boxes may be stored horizontally or vertically on shelves.

10. SPRING CLIP FILES

These are similar to the box files, but contain a spring clip which holds the papers securely.

11. CONCERTINA FOLDER

This is a wallet-type file, with a number of divisions, giving it the appearance of a concertina. It is sometimes used for sorting the papers into alphabetical order before actually putting them in their proper files, thus saving time and reducing the need to handle a file several times in the course of filing the day's papers.

12. SIGNALS, TAGS, GUIDES, TABS AND FLAGS

A variety of names are attached to what might come under the broad umbrella of "indicators." An indicator is intended to point to or draw attention to something. For example, it would be used to pinpoint the separation between the various letters in an alphabetical system of filing.

It might also be used to draw attention to a letter within a file (Fig. 23).

13. CROSS-REFERENCE

This term is used to indicate that material and/or information is to be found not only in the file being consulted but elsewhere also, *i.e.* there is a cross-reference to that other file, each file being marked (or cross-referenced) with the other file's title:

> 1. Correspondence dealing with a company's product may be filed not only in the file bearing the name of the product, but possibly in another file under the name of a customer who has bought this product. To save duplicating all the letters (one copy for each file), both files would be cross-referenced with each other's title. In the Product file would appear: "See also correspondence under customer's file" and in the customer's file would appear: "See also correspondence under Product file."

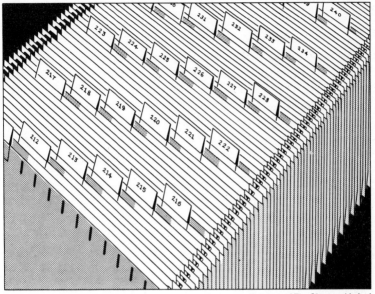

(*a*) Filing guides

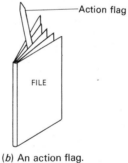

(*b*) An action flag.

Fig. 23.—Types of filing guides.

2. Where the files are kept numerically and it is necessary to keep a card index alphabetically arranged, each card would bear the cross-reference: "See file No. ...."

14. MISCELLANEOUS FILE

Some employers would not have such a thing in their filing system! It is of course a file designed to accommodate all those papers for which a home cannot be found among the files, as where there is insufficient correspondence to warrant the opening of a new file. The reason for some employers denying the value of a miscellaneous file is that they feel too much correspondence might find its way into such a file with consequent difficulty in finding papers at some future date.

15. CHRONOLOGICAL ORDER

It is usual to file the most recently dated papers in the front of the file, *i.e.* on top of the papers already filed, so that an up-to-date picture is seen at a glance; also this is the simplest and quickest way to file papers without removing earlier correspondence. When all correspondence is kept in strict chronological order (date order), it is relatively easy to find a letter by its date.

HOW TO FILE

The overriding rule in any filing system is CONSISTENCY. It does not really matter whether the telephone directory method is used or whether the chief prefers some peculiar method of his own; it makes no difference if all the Mac's and Mc's are placed in front of the letter M, or at the back of the files under M or in their alphabetical place under Mac so long as all clerks using the filing system know the rules and adhere to them rigidly.

Since the aim of any filing system is quick retrieval, time spent in searching should be reduced to the absolute minimum and a clerk should know where to look before even opening the filing cabinet drawer.

Some commonly accepted rules are:

1. File all names with the prefix Mc or Mac in the proper alphabetical order under Mac (*i.e.*, even Mc is filed as though it were Mac). Thus McIntosh is filed after MacBride because I comes after B in the alphabet.
2. File all names with the prefix St. or Saint in the proper alphabetical order under Saint (*e.g.*, St. John is filed after Saint Augustine because J comes after A in the alphabet).
3. Surnames (not Christian names or initials) determine the place of a file, *e.g.* a file on Mary Brown would be placed under Brown, Mary.
4. Surnames with no initials or Christian names are filed in

front of similar names with identifying initials or Christian names, *e.g.* Brown

> Brown, M.
>
> Brown, Mary

5. Names such as D'Arcy, Du Cane, Le Blanc, Van Homer are all filed as though they were a complete word, *e.g.*

> D'Arcy
>
> Debussy
>
> Delaney
>
> Du Cane
>
> Duncan
>
> Le Blanc
>
> Levasseur
>
> Van Homer
>
> Vassalo

6. Ignore titles and "The" when deciding the place for a file, thus Sir John Brown would be filed under Brown, Sir John and The Typewriter Company Ltd. would be filed under Typewriter Company Ltd., The.

Short-answer Questions

1. Explain why it is necessary to file papers.
2. Name three methods of classification.
3. Why is indexing necessary with some systems of filing?
4. How can you ensure that a missing file is traced to the borrower?
5. What do you understand by "thinning" files?
6. How long should you retain general correspondence in a file?
7. Give three advantages for centralised filing.
8. What protection should files be given?
9. What is a "cross-reference"?
10. Explain "horizontal" filing.

Past Examination Questions

1. What is the purpose of filing papers? If carrying out your department's filing were one of your responsibilities would you consider it important or unimportant? Give your reasons.

(R.S.A.)

2. Devise a scheme which deals adequately with the accessibility, retention and destruction of records, where there is limited accommodation for storage. (*L.C.C.*)

3. Give three examples to show how colour may be used to aid identification in clerical work. (*L.C.C.*)

4. (*a*) What is a visible card index? (*b*) What are its advantages? (*R.S.A.*)

5. (*a*) What is the main disadvantage of alphabetical filing?

(*b*) When is an alphabetical card index essential in a filing system?

(*c*) What is a "pending" file?

(*d*) What is a "cross-reference" in filing? (*R.S.A.*)

6. In the head office of a large manufacturing organisation, in what circumstances would you expect the following methods of filing to be used:

(*a*) alphabetical; (*b*) numerical; (*c*) geographical; (*d*) chronological; (*e*) by subject? (*R.S.A.*)

7. How would you indicate in your filing system (*a*) that you had removed a file from the filing cabinet, (*b*) that a letter filed in file 77 also referred to the subject matter dealt with in file 88?

(*R.S.A.*)

8. (*a*) What are strip index cards?

(*b*) For what purposes are signals used on index cards?

(*R.S.A.*)

9. In what circumstances would you recommend the following types of filing:

(*a*) alphabetical; (*b*) geographical; (*c*) numerical; (*d*) departmental; (*e*) central? (*R.S.A.*)

10. (*a*) With which system of filing is it necessary to use an index? What information would you need to obtain from the index?

(*b*) If you frequently have occasion to use a card index system to select groups of staff (for example, all men with an engineering qualification who have been with the firm for five or more years), what system of indexing will you use? (*R.S.A.*)

CHAPTER 11

CONTROL AND ORDERING OF CONSUMABLE OFFICE STORES

INTRODUCTION

HEADED letter paper, carbon paper, bank or other flimsy copy paper, internal memo paper, bond (or other good quality) continuation sheet paper, together with pins, staples, clips, coloured tags and guides or other signals, manilla folders, wallet files, box files, bound books or ledgers with special rulings, form the bulk of "consumable office stores" or, more simply, "stationery." Under this title may be listed any materials which are necessary to clerical work. Thus pens, and pencils, erasers and shorthand notebooks, rubber bands, envelopes and a number of other items legitimately come under this heading.

While there are often elaborate methods in use for the issue and control of other stores or stock maintained by a company (*e.g.*, screws, nails, components used in manufacture or assembly of goods), since these are recognised as stock and therefore part of the assets of the company, it is surprising that office stationery is sometimes dealt with in a haphazard way, clerical staff demanding or helping themselves to whatever items they need, with little control over indiscriminate use or waste. Yet these items are also assets of the company, and taking home a ball point pen or an eraser, or shorthand notebook for private use is just as bad as helping oneself to valuable machine spare parts. The clerical or administrative worker who can honestly say that he or she has never taken home anything belonging to the office is honest indeed.

AN EFFICIENT SYSTEM

The administration of stationery is a responsible task, and may be divided into four main sections:

1. Devising and establishing an efficient system for issue.
2. Controlling issue.

3. Storage.

4. Ordering and re-ordering.

1. DEVISING AN EFFICIENT SYSTEM FOR THE ISSUE OF STATIONERY

In most offices, there is a central place for the storage of office stationery and other supplies, and a responsible person is generally placed in charge. If the organisation is a large one, the central stationery office may be open all day, and each department is allocated a different period of time during which someone may be sent to collect items required for the department. Thus, Sales Department may send a junior to collect their requirements from 9 a.m. to 9.30 a.m., the Company Secretarial Department may send someone between 9.30 a.m. and 10 a.m., the Accounts Department may be served between 10 a.m. and 10.30 a.m., and so on. This avoids queueing in the central stationery office and places the responsibility for departmental requirements on someone within the department who has knowledge of requirements and rate of consumption.

Where the company is not so large, it is often a rule that stationery will only be issued (to all departments) at certain times, *e.g.* between 9 a.m. and 11 a.m. each day. Anyone may call for stationery at these times, but at 11 a.m. the stationery clerk locks up the store and attends to other duties. She may not be prevailed upon to make issues at any other time of day.

It is a wise plan for one person to be put in charge of stationery, and for all departments to be made aware of this person's identity. This not only ensures the advantages of central control, *e.g.* special requirements as well as complaints are made known to the clerk responsible, but also fixes the responsibility for ordering, re-ordering and the general arrangement of the stationery store squarely on one person.

2. CONTROLLING THE ISSUE OF STATIONERY

The clerk in charge should also be made responsible for controlling the issue of stationery. It is her duty to note and report whether any department's consumption is exceptionally large.

Stationery should only be issued against a signed requisition. This method serves several purposes: it is a check against pilfering from the central store since at any time it is possible to verify that the remaining stock plus the signed requisitions together add up to the maximum stock to be held. The requisition slips also serve to analyse the consumption of stationery into the various departments; thus it becomes possible to ascertain *where* the items are being consumed. An analysis could easily show up the fact that one department was ordering an excessive number of shorthand notebooks within a short space of time, while in fact only one shorthand typist was employed in that department. Excessive use of any item could be traced directly to the department responsible. Such control of course also acts as a deterrent against indiscriminate use of stationery. A third use for the requisition slips may be found when the time comes for re-ordering: by analysing the requisitions into the various items ordered, it becomes an easy matter to see what quantities are used within a certain period and this should help in deciding the maximum and minimum levels of stock to be held.

Requisition slips should show the item ordered, the quantity ordered, the department making out the requisition, the signature of the person collecting the stationery and the date on which the stationery was issued. A simple requisition form is shown in Fig. 24.

STATIONERY REQUISITION

Item	Quantity	Department
....	....	....
....	....	....
....	....	....
....	....	....
....	....	....
....	....	....
....	....	....
....	....	....
....	....	....
....	....	....
....	....	....

Date: . . . .   Signature: . . . .

Fig. 24.—A stationery requisition form.

3. STORAGE

If possible, each item should be given a place on a shelf. A neat arrangement will not only look efficient, but will save time and energy in locating items of stationery. Items used most frequently should of course be more readily accessible, the highest shelves being reserved for slow-moving stores. Packed stationery should be easily identified from the outer wrapping—the supplier often does this himself, but if he does not, time is well spent in clear labelling of packages.

Consideration should also be given to the accommodation allocated to items not only in relation to frequency of use, but also in relation to deterioration. Thus heat would damage certain photocopying paper which should not therefore be stored too close to a central heating radiator. Again, direct sunlight could damage rubber bands—a cool, dark cupboard is the best place for these.

Finally, new stores should be placed behind or below existing stock so that the old stock is used up before the new supplies.

4. ORDERING AND RE-ORDERING STATIONERY

The person in charge of stationery must take into consideration:

(*a*) *Quality of the material.* Certain carbons may be cheaper than others but may not last so well or give such clear copies; certain notepaper may be cheaper than others but may not stand up to erasing.

(*b*) *Delivery dates.* This is important, as a supplier who is unreliable may cause serious inconvenience when stocks are low in the office and delivery dates are not met.

(*c*) *Cost.* Some suppliers offer attractive discounts for bulk buying and it may be well worthwhile buying large quantities of fast-moving items in order to take advantage of the discount. On the other hand, items which are slow-moving (*i.e.*, not in great demand in the office) should not be ordered in bulk as the discount gained would soon be lost in the cost of storage space taken up in the stationery office, as well as in the deterioration which would inevitably take place if certain items were stored for very lengthy periods. It is sometimes possible to effect economies by buying cheaper quality stationery which would serve the purpose just as well as a more expensive sort. For example, internal memos may be typed on cheaper quality paper with no loss of prestige but it would be a false economy to buy a cheap quality letterheading paper. The person in charge of ordering stationery must consult senior executives on matters of policy and must use her discretion on minor decisions to be made. Papers most commonly used for general correspondence are:

(*i*) *Bond:* Good texture and durable. Suitable for letter-heading, compliment slips, and general outgoing mail.

(*ii*) *Bank:* Flimsier than bond, but still very durable. Suitable for carbon copies and internal correspondence, *e.g.* memos.

(*iii*) *Other types:* For duplicating, semi-absorbent paper is suitable for ink (stencil) processes and a calendered paper (*i.e.*, smooth-pressed) is suitable for the hectograph (spirit) process. For offset lithography, there is a wider choice available.

(*d*) *Suppliers, including alternative suppliers.* Against the eventuality that the regular supplier may at some time be unable to supply or deliver as required, it would be wise to have at least one reserve supplier on whom one could rely in an emergency. The secretary may try out several, select the best two or three and use them in rotation for the more standard items.

Re-ordering stationery should be done systematically. If minimum and maximum quantities of stock are fixed, it becomes a simple matter to re-order when the minimum level is reached, and the quantity to be re-ordered is easily determined by subtracting the minimum amount from the maximum to be held. The balance is what must be ordered to make up the stock to the maximum level.

One method is to maintain a stock card for each item of stationery. This card should show the item of stationery it represents, the supplier of this item, the minimum and maximum levels to be held in the central store, the date and quantity on which the order (making the stock up to maximum level) was received, the dates and quantities on which issues (to the various departments) were made, the balance in hand and if required, the departments to which the issues were made. An example of a stock record card is shown in Fig. 25.

STOCK RECORD CARD

A4 letterheaded paper

Minimum level: 10 reams   Maximum level: 50 reams

Date	Quantity received	Date	Quantity issued	Department	Balance
...	....	....	....	....	...
...	....	....	....	....	...
...	....	....	....	....	...
...	....	.....	....	....	...

Supplier: ....
....
....

Fig. 25.—A stock record card.

A very simple method which shows at a glance the stock position is to display all the items on shelves and to separate the minimum level from the rest of the stock by placing a brightly coloured marker (Fig. 26) at the appropriate level. When the stock is reduced to the level of the mark, the clerk knows that minimum level has been reached and it is time to re-order.

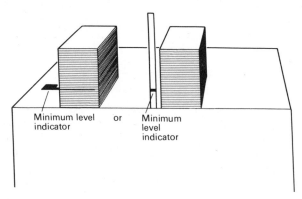

Minimum level indicator   or   Minimum level indicator

Fig. 26.—Stock level indicators.

A further method commonly used is for a wall chart to be kept of all stationery received and issued, as illustrated in Fig. 27.

So far as the re-ordering of printed business letterheading and order forms (and indeed, the overprinting of existing stocks of these items) are concerned, the secretary should take into account the requirements of the *European Communities Act*. Briefly, these requirements are to show on business letterheading and order forms

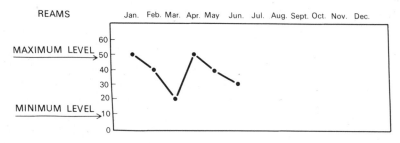

Fig. 27.—A wall chart showing record of A4 letterheading stock.

(*in addition* to the *existing* legal requirements of name of company and, if the company was registered after November 1916, the names and nationalities of any directors who are not British) the following information:

(*a*) The place where the company was registered (*e.g.*, England or Scotland).

(*b*) The registered number of the company (as allocated by the Department of Trade).

(*c*) The registered address of the company.

This additional information must be shown in "legible characters."

Short-answer Questions

1. Why is it important to keep strict control over the issue of office stationery?

2. Name twelve items which might come under the heading of "consumable office stores."

3. There is an easy way of finding out what quantity to re-order; how is this amount arrived at?

4. What is a requisition slip?

5. What is the difference between a requisition slip and a stock record card?

6. What information is normally shown on a stock record card?

7. What information is normally shown on a requisition slip?

8. How can queueing or "bottlenecks" be avoided at times when stationery is issued?

9. Mention a quick method of ascertaining when minimum level of stock has been reached.

10. How can it be discovered whether one department in a company is using an excessive amount of stationery?

Past Examination Questions

1. You have been put in charge of stationery stock and its issue to various departments. Draw up a scheme to ensure that stores are maintained at an adequate level and that the issue of stationery is well regulated and controlled.   (*L.C.C.*)

2. Your employer has drafted the following notes to show possible ways of reducing the cost of stationery as this has been rather high in

your office recently. Amplify these notes by replying in memo form:

(*i*) Printing costs might be reduced if we did our own letter-heads, memos, etc. Do we need to buy any new equipment or can we manage with our existing machines?

(*ii*) I am sure there is much wastage in the internal issue of such items as shorthand notebooks, ball point pens, etc. Can we tighten up here?

(*iii*) It might be possible to obtain better rates from our suppliers. Please see what you can find out about bulk buying and cash discounts. (*L.C.C.*)

3. The stationery cupboard for your department is kept locked, but everyone knows where the key is kept, and staff help themselves. The result is that stationery gets muddled up and supplies of items often run out without being re-ordered. You are asked to take charge. What would you do? (*R.S.A.*)

4. In a medium-sized office you are responsible for the control and supply of consumable office stores.

(*a*) Design an office requisition form which has to be completed before stores are issued to members of the staff.

(*b*) Design a stock card to control and maintain the levels of the stores. (*R.S.A.*)

5. You work for a small firm and one of your responsibilities is to hand out and order stationery. An urgent duplicating job has to be done which requires 50 stencils. You find you have only about 20 left. The following week, you discover that you have let the stock of the firm's notepaper get so low that it is uncertain whether you can have more printed before it runs out. The owner of the firm is extremely annoyed. Suggest what means you would employ to make sure that such a situation did not recur. (*R.S.A.*)

6. Draw up a stock record card for envelopes which are kept in boxes of 1,000 and banded in bundles of 250.

7. Explain briefly what you understand by "consumable office stores." Give three examples. (*R.S.A.*)

8. The printed notepaper of most business firms gives much useful information. What information might you expect to find? (*R.S.A.*)

CHAPTER 12

OFFICE METHODS

INTRODUCTION

METHODS, systems and procedures—these words are often used synonymously. In fact they may be likened to ripples over a surface of water. Thus the complete system or procedure is made up of a network of methods employed to achieve the object of the procedure and each method is often made up of a number of simple operations. This can best be illustrated by example—filing, for instance. The filing *system* is arrived at by centralising the service. The files are kept in a large registry and are suspended vertically in a filing cabinet or drawer; guide tags are used within the drawers for quick location; the files are classified under subject titles in alphabetical order. These are the *methods* employed. The letters and documents to be filed are probably marked with the title of the file into which they are to be placed, as well as with the date (if any) on which they are to be brought forward for further action. The papers are then sorted, those requiring further action are placed in a separate pile and subsequently entered into the diary or other means kept for the purpose. Probably, a tick is placed beside the entry on the letter to show that the date for further action has been recorded. Finally the letters are sorted into alphabetical order and all the papers which are to be accommodated in one file are then put into chronological order before being finally placed in the file. A number of simple *operations* have just been described.

Clerical operations—indeed, methods and systems as well—need periodic review. Conditions in the office change—nothing remains static for long—requirements change and new techniques are invented. These reasons make it desirable for a responsible person in the office—sometimes the office manager, sometimes the secretary—deliberately to question whether the work is being done in the most efficient way. What was efficient a year ago may not only be out of date now, but worse (or better) still, not required at all! The questions to be asked are:

1. Why are we doing it at all? What would happen if we stopped doing it?	The answers to these questions will show whether a procedure may now be discarded, or whether it is still required.
2. Who is at present doing this work? Why must it be this particular person? Who else could do the job? What would happen if someone else did it?	These questions are designed to show whether the person actually doing the work is in fact the best person to do it.
3. Why is it done in this way? Is there any other way of doing it? What would happen if we did it in another way?	The answers to these questions will show whether it is worth looking into other ways of doing the work.

It is not, of course, suggested that the secretary should undertake work best left to trained and experienced O. & M. officers. What *is* suggested is that the secretary (and indeed any other office worker) should be on the lookout for more efficient ways of getting her work done. "More efficient" in this context means:

(*a*) more quickly; and/or
(*b*) more accurately; and/or
(*c*) with less effort; and/or
(*d*) at lower cost; and/or
(*e*) by employing fewer staff.

If the secretary were alert enough, interested enough and sufficiently O. & M.-minded, she might find that some of her tasks were unnecessary; that others could be handed over to a junior after only a little training; and that the remaining tasks could be done in a more efficient way (Fig. 28). To implement changes as required might leave the secretary free to:

(*a*) undertake more work which only she is capable of doing; and/or

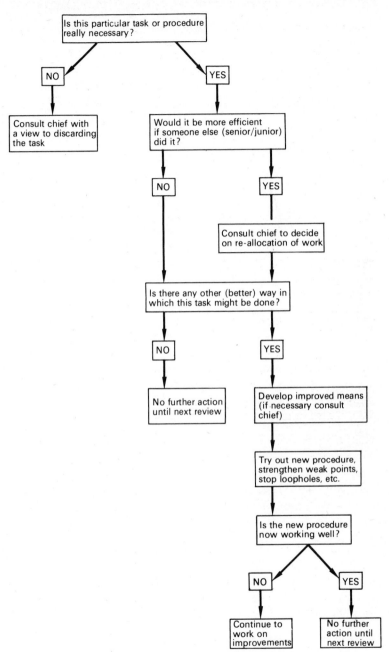

Fig. 28.—Flow chart reviewing a task or procedure.

(*b*) learn new work with which to be of greater assistance to her chief; and/or

(*c*) learn new higher-grade work which will increase her chances of promotion.

Where systematic review of procedures is undertaken, it should be a firm rule that no changes are to be made without proper consultation. Members of staff often think they have found a better way of doing the work when in fact they may not realise the far-reaching consequences of making an alternation, since, as explained at the beginning of this Chapter, the whole network of functions within a firm is inter-related. By all means everyone in the office should be encouraged to think of improved methods, but no changes should be implemented without consulting the chief. *If, however, the idea is a good one, due credit should be given to the clerk who originated it.*

SECURITY IN THE OFFICE

There are a variety of articles which must be made secure in an office.

1. PERSONAL BELONGINGS OF STAFF

A cupboard, locker or even a drawer which is fitted with a lock should be available for members of staff. The secretary, her junior assistant and other workers will almost certainly want to place handbag, cosmetics, etc., in a safe and easily accessible place.

2. STAMPS, REGISTERED ENVELOPES, ETC.

These are items which are sometimes required by members of staff for personal use and it can be very tempting to take a stamp or two if they are left lying around. Many secretaries like to keep a "stamp book" (rather on the lines of a petty cash book), in which the number of stamps purchased is entered, and a record kept of the letters for which stamps were used, as well as the date the letter was sent. A check is thus kept on the stamps in hand.

3. PETTY CASH

Most offices keep a petty cash box for small day-to-day items of expenditure. Whether the "float" (the amount to which the petty cash is always made up) is small (£5; £10; £25) or large (£50; £100) meticulous care should always be taken both in making payments— the petty cashier should invariably require a duly authorised petty cash voucher—and in keeping the box itself secure. Thus, it is most unwise to leave the box on the desk and go out of the room, even for only a few minutes. The correct procedure would be to lock the box itself and then put it away in the safe or other place where it is kept, locking that also before leaving the room.

If more than one person occupies the room, then of course it is permissible to ask the other occupant to keep an eye on the petty cash for a few minutes, but this procedure is really second best as it throws undue responsibility on another clerk.

4. WAGES

Although many offices now pay wages by methods which do not involve handling of notes and coins, it still happens that a wages cheque is made out for cash, the cheque is cashed at the bank and the money brought back to the office for distribution into the staff wage-packets. The precautions to be taken here start with signing the cheque. As this cheque must be "opened" (signed a second time against the words "please pay cash") before it can be cashed, it is wise to have the cheque signed just prior to going to the bank as it could be dangerous to leave an "open" cheque lying around. The wages clerk should not be allowed to go to the bank alone—many insurance companies insist that two persons should go together. A stout bag or case is usually provided by the company and this should be fitted with a lock and key. Whether the trip to and from the bank is made by car (which is usual) or on foot, both the time and the route should be varied from week to week. Finally, when the cash is brought back to the office, every precaution should be taken for its safety until distribution to the staff. It is preferable for the wage packets to be made up straight away (sometimes the door is locked while the cash is being divided, sometimes it is a rule that two trusted persons should do the work together). A procedure must then be followed to get the pay into the hands of the staff. Sometimes the rule is made that members of staff call at the wages office at staggered times; sometimes the pay clerk distributes the pay-packets by visiting the various departments. In both cases it is advisable that the pay clerk have an assistant present and that a signature be obtained from staff receiving their wages.

5. CONFIDENTIAL CORRESPONDENCE, LEDGERS, MINUTE BOOKS, ETC.

Every office has its confidential material. Personnel records, staff salaries, minute books of Board Meetings, private ledgers and any ·correspondence of a confidential nature must be safeguarded from unauthorised inspection.

The secretary will find that confidential records are usually kept in a cabinet or cupboard fitted with lock and key, and that there is a place for the key—on the chief's keyring, in his desk drawer or in her own custody. Before long, the secretary will know which persons are authorised to require production of these records. Possibly, her chief will give her a list of names: if he does not, she is entitled to ask him. When faced with a request by an unauthorised person for the production of a confidential file, the secretary should temper her refusal with tact.

> "I'm afraid I haven't got the key to the cabinet where it is kept. I'll ask my chief for it and bring the file to you later if that's all right." (This will usually produce an answer of "I really need it now, so I'll have to manage without it.")
>
> "I'm so sorry, I just don't know where this file is kept. Perhaps you would like to ask my chief?" (The answer to this one is likely to be a mumbled retort of "I'll see him later" accompanied by an embarrassed retreat.)
>
> "The ... file, you say? We haven't got such a file in our office. Try the Managing Director's secretary" (or other formidable person). (There is no other reply to this one than "Yes, I suppose I'll have to do that.")

It sometimes happens that confidential work is actually in progress when an inquisitive person enters the room and tries to obtain information. If the secretary is in the course of typing confidential work when the office gossip comes in there are several ways out of the situation without being hurtful or impolite.

1. She may turn down the paper in the typewriter so that it is hidden from view before dealing with the enquirer.
2. She may place a blank sheet of paper over the typescript so as to hide it from view.
3. She may remove the typescript from the typewriter and place it face down on the desk or in a drawer.

If you are asked for information which you are not authorised to publicise it is an easy matter to appear ignorant and to resist the temptation to show that you are one of the privileged few who "knows the secret."

"I'm afraid I don't know" is an answer which is face-saving for the enquirer. "I'm not allowed to say" is the sort of answer which sounds boastful and could be very hurtful. It can only be justified by very persistent questioning.

THE O. & M. OF SECRETARIAL DUTIES

Every secretary with some practical experience behind her will have discovered some "short cuts" in her duties. The following "tips" are merely a few examples intended to indicate how much room exists for improvement.

1. INSERTING CARBONS

Interleaving carbons is commonly done by laying the top copy face down on the desk, placing a sheet of carbon paper coated side up on top of it, and continuing the process with flimsy paper and further carbon paper, until the required number of "copies" is reached. The whole set is then picked up, straightened by tapping the edge of the sheets smartly on the desk and finally inserted in the typewriter. Compare the following operations;

Method A
1. Select top copy, say, two sheets of flimsy paper and two sheets of carbon paper.
2. Place top copy face down on desk.
3. Place one sheet of carbon paper (coated side up) over the top copy.
4. Place first sheet of copy paper over the carbon paper.
5. Place second sheet of carbon paper over the copy paper.
6. Place second sheet of copy paper over the carbon paper.
7. Gather up the complete "set."
8. Tap edges of the "set" smartly on the desk to obtain straight edges.
9. Insert in typewriter.

Method B
1. Select top copy, say, two sheets of flimsy paper and two sheets of carbon paper.

2. Tap the edges of top copy and flimsies smartly on the desk to obtain straight edges.
3. Insert in typewriter.
4. Turn the platen up about two or three lines (just enough to grip the papers).
5. Interleave each sheet with carbon paper (coated side facing you) (two operations, *i.e.* two sheets of carbon to be interleaved).

You will note that not only is the *number of operations reduced,* but the method is *neater* (there is no risk of marking the top copy by laying it face down on the desk), and when the letter has been typed and taken out of the typewriter, it will be found that there is just enough space at the top of the set to grip the papers (but not the carbons) between the finger and thumb of the left hand while smartly pulling out all the carbons together from the bottom of the set with the right hand. (The carbons will protrude slightly since the letter paper was inserted in the machine and the platen turned up before the carbons were inserted.)

If you don't think this is a quicker method than the one you use at present, give it a try and think again.

2. MULTI-SET FORMS

It is often possible to economise on writing and checking time by the use of a set of forms. These may be partially carbon-backed, so that although a number of entries are made on the top copy (required for department A), only a few of these entries are duplicated on the first copy (required for department B) and only those entries required by department C appear on the second copy. For example, a despatch note, advice note, invoice and copy invoice may all be prepared in one operation. N.C.R. ("No carbon required") paper saves time in handling and inserting carbons (the reverse of the sheet of paper is treated to produce a copy when pressure is applied, *e.g.* by writing or typing).

3. CONTINUOUS STATIONERY

Inserting and removing the paper from the typewriter can take up disproportionate time and effort when the typescript itself consists of only a few lines. Continuous stationery, which may be N.C.R. or interleaved with carbon, is put to excellent use in such work as invoice typing.

4. STANDARD LETTERS

Many letters are of a routine nature and contain only a small amount of variable material. Where such letters can be pre-printed or duplicated, the time taken in composing the letter afresh each time it is written is completely eliminated, and the time taken in typing it is drastically reduced since only the name and address and other variable information need to be typed. An example of the use to which this idea might be put is writing reminder letters to debtors (only the name of the debtor and the amount of the debt varies).

5. HECTOGRAPH RIBBON

Where numerous spirit masters are to be typed, it is possible to fit a hectograph ribbon to the typewriter, thus saving time and effort in collating master/transfer sheets.

6. CHAIN TYPING ENVELOPES

Where a large number of envelopes have to be typed, much time and effort can be saved by placing the blank envelopes in a pile ready beside the typewriter (all with the flap facing in the same direction). The first envelope is inserted in the typewriter, the margin adjusted and the name and address typed. Before taking the envelope out of the machine, have the next one ready for insertion behind the platen so that the same twist of the wrist turning up the platen to remove the first envelope performs the work of inserting the second envelope which is ready to be typed immediately the first is removed.

7. GUMMED STRIP ADDRESSING

Another quick way of getting envelopes addressed without the aid of an addressing machine, is by using a roll of gummed paper which is perforated every two inches or so. Each address is typed within the space allowed by the perforations and when all the addresses are completed, the gummed side of the roll is damped with a sponge and the sections are detached and stuck on the envelopes. The saving of time and effort here is in inserting and removing the envelopes from the typewriter (the same idea as continuous stationery). A further advantage is that if required, one or more carbon copies may be taken of the addresses in the same operation and then stored for later use.

SYSTEMS ADAPTATION

New requirements may often be satisfied by adaptation of an existing system. Did you know, for example, that it was possible to make a master for spirit duplicating, on a heat (or thermal) copier? When the original together with the master sheet and special hectograph carbon paper are put through the copier, the heat causes the "carbon" to dissolve and adhere to the master paper, thereby producing a master ready for duplicating. This is particularly useful where the original contains material, *e.g.* diagrams, not easily copied by hand or on the typewriter.

Where a spirit master has been stored and is required for re-use it may be put through the heat copier which will activate the carbon, thus rejuvenating the master for a limited number of additional copies.

Dyeline masters may be produced particularly well on a reflex (wet) copier since these give a very sharp black and white contrast.

Masters for offset duplicating are easily produced from an electrostatic copier.

The above examples illustrate how it is possible to "cash in" on existing systems without buying new equipment.

THE WORKING AREA

1. POINTS TO NOTE

The secretary's desk should be laid out with an eye to ease and economy of movement. For example, a stationery rack is invaluable as it will save opening the desk drawer each time notepaper, envelopes, etc. are required, but much of the benefit will be lost if this rack is placed immediately behind the typewriter so that the typist has to stand up before she can reach the papers. Similarly the "In" and "Out" trays should be arranged in the most convenient position, *e.g.* to the left and right of the desk. Drawers which afford the easiest access should be reserved for items which are most often required. This idea can of course be carried further: the arrangement of furniture and equipment in a room should be so designed as to take account of the flow of work and to eliminate unnecessary walking and movement. Compare the two layouts in Fig. 29.

Note that in arrangement B, the furniture and equipment is so situated, that the working surface (which is used to sort/collate

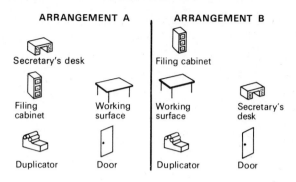

Fig. 29.—Arrangements of the working space.

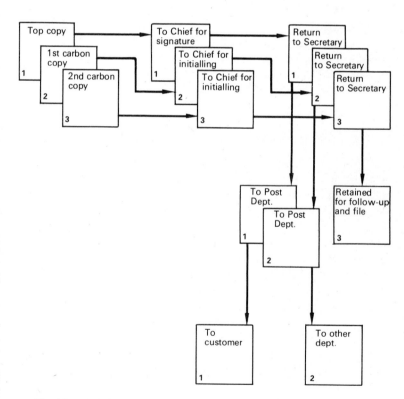

Fig. 30.—A simple flow chart showing the routing of a letter after typing.

papers for filing and duplicating) is located *between* the filing cabinet and the duplicator. Can you see how much "travel" is saved if the secretary gets up from her desk, goes to the duplicator and then walks over to the working surface to collate the duplicated copies?

Fig. 30 shows how much "travel" can be involved in routing letters after typing.

2. THE OPEN PLAN OFFICE
This idea is said to have many advantages.

1. Supervision is easier (the supervisor can survey a wider area).
2. More economic use of space and equipment (*e.g.*, two persons may share a telephone whereas two instruments would be required if the clerks were in separate rooms).
3. Possible saving in heating, lighting and general maintenance costs.
4. Easier to arrange the positioning of clerks and equipment to suit the flow of work.
5. Clerks are able to see a wider area of the work and therefore gain a better understanding of the part they play in the "whole."
6. Time spent in locating people is reduced (there is no need to walk into an office partitioned by a closed door to see if a member of staff is available; nor is there any need to locate him by telephone if he can be seen instantly in the open plan office).

The opponents of the open plan are able to suggest as many disadvantages:

1. The noise can detract from the efficiency of the staff. Not only are machines noisy, *e.g.* typewriters, adding machines, telephones, etc., but inconsequential chatter, clicking heels, etc. also disturb concentration. To some extent this disadvantage can be minimised (but not eliminated) by improved acoustics, felt pads under machines, carpeting, buzzers or lights on telephones instead of bells.
2. The larger the number of people accommodated in one room, the harder it is to satisfy them all with regard to heating and ventilation. The amount of heat which barely warms one

person will send another off to sleep! The amount of fresh air let in to keep one person breathing happily will cause another to complain of draughts and colds!

3. Germs from colds and 'flu may spread more rapidly in the open plan office.

4. There is a loss of individuality—the clerk sees himself as one among many.

5. Loss of privacy—reprimand, even commendation, is best effected in private.

6. Can be inhibiting to some clerks who get the feeling of being "on display."

The open plan layout need not portray rows of desks arranged one behind the other as in a classroom. A better plan is to divide the area into sections or units, the divisions being effected by the judicious positioning of furniture and equipment. The idea here is to arrange a view of the room which is pleasing to the eye (or workers and visitors) and to preserve the sense of "belonging" by clearly marking out the various sections. A few plants, which secretaries love to tend, enhance the picture. Such an arrangement is sometimes called the *panoramic* office.

Short-answer Questions

1. Why is it necessary to review clerical methods and routines periodically?

2. Name four general office items which should be made secure.

3. Give four ideas which can help to make the cash payment of wages safer.

4. What do you understand by the O. & M. of secretarial work?

5. Why is it important to pay attention to the layout of office furniture and equipment?

6. Give four advantages and four disadvantages of the open plan office.

7. What saving is effected by gummed strip addressing?

8. For what sort of typing work might you use continuous stationery?

9. What would you reply to an enquiry by an unauthorised person about confidential work?

10. What purpose does a hectograph ribbon serve?

Past Examination Questions

1. (*a*) What is continuous stationery and for which purposes is it most suitable?

(*b*) Explain briefly the difference between "bank" and "bond" quality paper. Give examples to show when you would use either paper. Give reasons for your answer. (*L.C.C.*)

2. What precautions should be taken to safeguard wages money? Your answer should start with the cashing of the wages cheque and end with the distribution of the pay packets. (*L.C.C.*)

3. Various methods are used in offices for answering letters. List four and discuss the advantages and disadvantages, if any, of each method. (*L.C.C.*)

4. In your work as a private secretary you sometimes deal with very confidential matters. How can you: (*a*) ensure that persons who come into your office do not see this confidential work while it is being typed; (*b*) ensure that filed copies of this work remain inaccessible to unauthorised persons; (*c*) deal with colleagues who ask you direct questions about this work. (*L.C.C.*)

5. What are the advantages and disadvantages of the modern method of open-plan offices? (*L.C.C.*)

6. Discuss the ways in which the mechanisation of offices today is affecting secretarial staff. (*L.C.C.*)

7. (*a*) Describe the main features of an open-plan office.

(*b*) What are the advantages and disadvantages of such an office to:

(*i*) the executives of a firm,
(*ii*) other office staff? (*R.S.A.*)

CHAPTER 13

SERVICE DEPARTMENTS

CENTRALISATION

THERE are some general office services which have to be used by any department within an organisation, no matter how specialised that particular department may be. For example, the Design and Development Department, the Accounts Department, the Personnel Department—all these receive incoming mail and send out correspondence (mail handling); all must get their correspondence typed using shorthand, audio-typing or copy-typing methods (typing and secretarial pools); all must have their copy letters filed (central filing); the copying and duplicating needs of each department must be met (reprography); computer and switchboard installations are invariably used by all the departments, as it would be absolutely impracticable to duplicate the equipment, staff and special accommodation required; stores and stationery may be conveniently centralised; and finally it is usually convenient to receive visitors at one central point, *e.g.* the office entrance, and subsequently route them to the particular department concerned (reception).

By establishing service departments it becomes possible to benefit from all the advantages of centralisation.

1. ADVANTAGES OF CENTRALISATION

1. Saving of space and equipment (no duplication in the individual departments).
2. Training of staff is easier—the whole system may be viewed —and a better understanding is gained.
3. Uniformity of method (which makes for simplicity) and standardisation of equipment is easier to achieve.
4. Volume of work usually permits specialisation (division of labour) with the attendant advantages of speed, accuracy, etc.
5. It follows from 4 above that specialist staff—experts in their field—may be employed.

6. Quicker results may be obtained, *e.g.* in a secretarial pool, the first available typist handles the job.
7. The work load can be spread more equally among the staff of a central unit than among departmental clerks.
8. It follows that absenteeism is a smaller problem when work is centralised.

2. DISADVANTAGES OF CENTRALISATION

1. The large volume of work implies a large department to cope with the work and any large unit necessitates the making of rules and regulations and rigid adherence to them.
2. Strick adherence to the rules may mean delays—"red tape."
3. The confidential nature of some work does not lend itself readily to a centralised system.
4. Staff who do not wish to specialise may find that work which is all related to one service is boring.
5. If the central unit is very large, an impersonal atmosphere may prevail—no sense of "belonging" exists.

SERVICE DEPARTMENTS

Some of the services (mail handling, typing/secretarial pools, filing, stationery, reprography, computer, switchboard and reception) which are often centralised are dealt with elsewhere in some detail in this book, but it is convenient to note certain aspects at this stage.

1. MAIL HANDLING

In all but the smallest organisations the incoming and outgoing mail is centralised. Equipment is not duplicated in the various departments; the mailing clerks acquire specialised knowledge and experience and are therefore able to deal more efficiently with the work; large savings may be effected in postage and stationery (*e.g.*, one large envelope can be used for *all* mail to a branch office); and it is possible to keep a close check on incoming cash, cheques, etc. (It is usual to record these in a book kept for the purpose before passing to the cashier for banking.) *See* also Chapter 14 on Mailroom Procedure.

2. TYPING AND SECRETARIAL POOLS

The employer has a choice between drafting letters by hand for subsequent copy-typing, using a dictating machine for subsequent audio-typing, and using the services of a "live" stenographer from whose shorthand notes a transcription will subsequently be typed. Each of these methods has its own merits and disadvantages.

With handwritten drafts there is always the danger that the typist may be unable to read badly written, technical words and the method is time-consuming for the executive. On the other hand, where the executive exercises some care in printing clearly difficult names, or words or special instructions, this method is easy for the typist who need not worry about punctuation, paragraphing or other display if this is already indicated in the draft. Thus junior staff who are less expensive to remunerate may be employed.

With audio dictation, the equipment is of course costly in initial capital outlay and where the executive uses this method he should be trained to forsee the pitfalls: difficult words must be spelled out, if necessary punctuation should be indicated, special instructions should always be given at the beginning of the letter, not at the end ("let me have three extra copies, please"—this at the end of a lengthy report!), the microphone should be held at the correct distance from the mouth (a few inches), speech should be clear and full use should be made of the indicator strip which is designed to show the length of dictation for each letter, the position of corrections, insertions, etc. especially where non-magnetic media is used. On the positive side, this method is quicker than writing by hand and the typist does not have to worry over deciphering poor handwriting. Another advantage is that the executive may dictate outside office hours or while he is away from the office, *e.g.* travelling on business. This latter advantage also applies of course to manuscript work which can be mailed to the typist.

In spite of increased and improved mechanisation in dictating methods, however, the girl who is able to take shorthand notes is still in great demand. This is so:

1. because some executives resent the implied loss of status if their correspondence has to be relegated to a machine. This may not be a valid argument but it is nevertheless a real one;
2. because many executives like to dictate to a "live" person who is able to supply the right phrase he may be looking for; to supply information or to take instructions which a machine cannot do;
3. because shorthand notes are rather more "coded" than tapes

or belts and therefore confidential work is better entrusted to a stenographer;

4. because there is always the danger that mechanical and electrical equipment may be subject to breakdown or to power cuts;

5. because a stenographer may be called upon to undertake other work which an audio machine is incapable of doing (switchboard relief, filing, etc.);

6. because there is that personal relationship which cannot be created with a machine.

However, it can be very wasteful of a stenographer's time to sit, and wait, and think about other duties waiting to be done while the executive hum's and ha's about his dictation.

In conclusion, it should be mentioned that copy typists are more easily trained for audio-typing than for shorthand-typing; transcription difficulties may occur with a shorthand writer (they shouldn't but they sometimes do!) and this cannot arise with audio dictation (although it must be admitted that mumbling or incoherent recording is just as bad).

Although from the employee's point of view there appears to be some stigma in being attached to a shorthand or typing pool, the advantages are many and the disadvantages few.

(a) *Advantages to the typist/stenographer.*

(i) The pool is a good starting point. There is usually a helpful supervisor or other senior person in charge to whom the young typist may turn for help. Much of the responsibility is shouldered by the supervisor, not the typist.

(ii) Since all the typing work is centralised, there is more scope for proper training in all aspects, *e.g.* stencil cutting, tabular display, typing from manuscript.

(iii) As a number of girls are all employed on similar work, there is a greater likelihood of meeting colleagues in a similar age-group, with similar interests, than if the typist worked for in a small office for one man.

(iv) As it is the large companies which normally have sufficient volume of work to justify centralisation, all the advantages of working for a large organisation accrue: systematic salary increases, staff welfare schemes, opportunities for specialisation, etc.

(*v*) As a variety of executives draw on the services of the pool, the employee gains a wealth of experience—this would be impossible if she worked for one man.

(*vi*) Many companies draw on the resources of the pool when seeking to fill secretarial vacancies; the girls from the pool are already "company-orientated" and need less time to "settle in." Promotion prospects are therefore good for such employees.

(*b*) *Disadvantages to the typist/stenographer.*

(*i*) It may be harder to convince *another* employer that she is ready for a secretarial post if *all* her previous experience has been of typing pools.

(*ii*) There seems to be a persistent "stigma"—a sense of inferior status.

(*iii*) The lack of variety (no duties other than typing correspondence) can induce monotony.

3. FILING

This is dealt with fully in Chapter 10 on Filing, and it is sufficient to enumerate here the benefits that a clerk might gain from being attached to a central registry:

(*a*) All aspects of the work are seen—from the initial receipt of papers through the various stages of sorting, classifying and eventual filing.

(*b*) Vertical promotion (*i.e.*, in the same line of work) is simple: indeed, it may be automatic.

(*c*) The organisation of a central registry is a responsible post: suitable equipment must be selected, methods must be devised, a routine must be established and maintained. A clerk who is responsible for this level of work will command a salary commensurate with the responsibility it carries.

4. STATIONERY AND OFFICE STORES

This subject is dealt with fully in Chapter 11 on control and ordering of consumable stores.

5. REPROGRAPHY

Modern methods of copying and duplicating have made big business of this aspect of office work. Indeed, where the volume of work permits, a whole department may be given over to reproduction. The specialist operator is thus able to select the machine most appropriate to the purpose, taking into consideration speed, quality of reproduction, quantity required. As this type of work involves working with machines and relies to a large extent on the skill of the operator, it is often a rule of the firm that only specialist staff may operate the machines and all copying and duplicating is routed to the Reprography Department. Where a large installation exists which involves the use of a variety of machines, a great saving may be gained by judicious selection of equipment. Photocopying costs vary with the type of paper and chemicals used; even a simple duplicating job can involve tremendous waste of paper if the operator is not trained to observe and make all adjustments from the first copy which is "run off." This subject merits special treatment and is dealt with fully in Chapter 21 on Office Machines.

6. COMPUTER SERVICES

A computer installation may need special accommodation (*e.g.*, dust-free, air-conditioned); it will certainly need specialist staff (*e.g.*, systems analysts, programmers, machine operators); the capital outlay may be large both in hardware (actual machinery) and software (input and out media). These reasons justify the use of computer bureaux (computer time is paid for by a number of companies each requiring computer services but not able or willing to have an installation of its own). It goes without saying that where an organisation has its own computer installation the services offered by the computer section are utilised by a number of internal departments. *See also* Chapter 22 on Office Machines.

7. SWITCHBOARD AND RECEPTION SERVICES

Sometimes the two are combined, the operator of a small switchboard performing reception duties at the entrance of the office. Where this is the case, regard should be had to the accommodation required to house the switchboard equipment—at the very least a cupboard or screening will be required apart from the switchboard itself. If neither telephone calls nor visitors are likely to arrive in great numbers, then one person can conveniently combine both duties. After all, there is a common element: telephone calls and visitors are both *received*; the switchboard operator and the receptionist both make a first impression on callers. If, however, there is a danger that the switchboard may become busy and that visitors may have to be kept waiting, there is much to be said for employing a trained telephone operator and for allowing visitors to make their own way up to the office, perhaps by following suitable indicator signs, to be met by a receptionist who, if not employed solely on reception duties, can at least put down her other work to attend to the requirements of visitors.

It is money well spent to make the reception area pleasant. The chairs should be comfortable, the plants, if any, should be well tended (there is nothing more depressing than a jaded-looking pot plant), a supply of light reading material should be available and the whole area should be meticulously clean. The receptionist herself should be pleasant and helpful and make every effort to route the visitor to his destination efficiently. Preferably he should be escorted to his destination (not by the receptionist, but by someone whom she has contacted for the purpose); if this is not possible, then very clear instructions should be given to him, unless he is not a new visitor. In any event, the person he is going to see should be alerted that the visitor has arrived, so that the whole sequence of events, from the time the visitor arrives up to the time he is shown out of the building, gives an impression of orderly and efficient organisation. *See also* Chapter 4 on Communication and Chapter 23 on The Daily Routine.

CONCLUSION

In most offices of course, even where certain services are centralised, there is still a small amount of departmental work undertaken. Thus, an executive may make use of the typing pool, but may still have a secretary allocated to him for confidential work; most of the filing may be sent to the central registry but there is still at least one filing cabinet to house those papers which only the department concerned is likely to require, or which are of a confidential nature. All mail will of course go to the central post room for despatch, but the secretary probably has a few stamps to use for letters which have missed the last office collection; and finally some companies which have a central copying and duplicating department nevertheless allow individual departments to purchase a small photocopier or a spirit duplicator for instant use.

Short-answer Questions

1. Name four services which are often centralised.

2. Why do organisations make use of service departments?

3. Mention four advantages of centralisation, and three disadvantages.

4. It is sometimes claimed that the employee in a central department has better prospects of promotion than if he/she were in a decentralised unit. Why is this so?

5. What do you understand by the phrase "company-orientated"?

6. Are there any advantages for a girl who finds work in a secretarial pool as compared with working for one man?

7. Do you think there is a sort of "stigma" attached to "pools"? If so, why?

8. In view of the advantages which may be gained from centralising work, why do some executives prefer a private secretary?

9. In what circumstances might you advise a young school leaver to seek employment in a "pool"?

10. How do you see the role of a supervisor of a secretarial pool?

Past Examination Questions

1. The eight departments in your firm each keep their own files under different systems. A central filing system has been suggested. Draw up lists, in two columns, setting out the arguments for and against a central filing system.   (L.C.C.)

2. Your firm endeavours to promote shorthand-typists to junior secretaries. The Sales Manager's secretary is leaving next month and as a shorthand-typist in the pool, you are very keen to be considered for this post. Write the letter of application to the Personnel Manager.   (L.C.C.)

3. Give your opinion on the centralisation of office services, with special reference to typing pools, including audio-typing.

(L.C.C.)

4. List the responsibilities you consider the supervisor of a typing pool has:

   (a) to her employers,
   (b) to her typists.   (R.S.A.)

5. What is the value, to a large business organisation, of a centralised dictating system?   (R.S.A.)

6. In your firm, secretaries are appointed from among the short-hand-typists in the pool in which you work. The Sales Manager's secretary is leaving, and you are among those invited to apply for the post. Write this letter of application, addressed to the Personnel Manager. *(R.S.A.)*

7. State three functions of a central filing system. *(R.S.A.)*

8. Explain what is meant by a centralised dictating system and give the advantages and disadvantages of such a system to the executive and to the audio-typist. *(R.S.A.)*

9. Discuss the advantages and disadvantages of a centralised audio-typing section for (*a*) the typist, and (*b*) the executive.

(R.S.A.)

10. Your firm is having great difficulty in obtaining competent shorthand-typists and your employer, the Personnel Manager, is considering the introduction of audio-typing. He has asked you to express your views on this, setting out clearly what would be involved and what are the advantages and disadvantages.

(L.C.C.)

CHAPTER 14

MAILROOM PROCEDURE

INCOMING MAIL

In the majority of large offices, the postal department is a central unit serving the various departments of the firm. There is therefore a large amount of incoming mail to be dealt with before distribution.

It is usual for a senior member of staff to be in charge of a number of junior clerks detailed to open the envelopes and carry out simple sorting. The staff in this section are expected to arrive about half an hour before the rest of the office staff so that the mail may be distributed in good time. They may be compensated by being given time off on a rota system, by being allowed to leave earlier in the evening, or by being given a longer lunch hour.

The first essential is to ensure that no enclosures remain in the envelopes before they are discarded. A variety of methods may be employed to this end.

1. Open out the envelopes flat on the table (effective but time-consuming).
2. Hold the envelopes up to the light and pass your hand behind it (not effective where stout envelopes are used).
3. Fit a lighted panel to a small section of the table (*e.g.*, a translucent panel with an electric light bulb underneath) and slide the envelopes over the panel (rather more effective than 2 above).
4. Read each letter to see if an enclosure was inserted before discarding the envelope (time-consuming, especially where the junior opens the envelopes and a senior clerk reads the contents and sorts into departments).

It will be seen that no method is perfect and try as one may, it does occasionally happen that a complaint will be received from one of the departments that a letter has arrived without its enclosure. For this reason, it is wise to retain the contents of the waste paper basket (the envelopes) for at least one day before burning, shredding or other-wise disposing of them. If such a complaint is received, it is a simple (but tedious) matter to go through the old envelopes to see if the enclosure has remained inside. To get through this task quicker, a little detective work may be used:

(a) If the enclosure is large, e.g. a booklet, there is no need to look into any of the small envelopes.

(b) Note the town from which the letter was sent and look for the postmark on the envelopes, only taking the trouble to look inside those which bear the appropriate postmark.

(c) Note whether the letter shows any mark of a clip or pin—if it does this could be an indication that the enclosure became detached after sorting in the postroom, especially if the envelope is found to be empty.

The usual procedure is for the sorting staff to work around a large table which is marked out into the various departments of the firm or which has a number of labelled trays set out on it, e.g. Accounts, Sales, Production, Export, Advertising, Company Secretarial, etc. The juniors remove the contents from the envelopes, stamp each letter with a rubber stamp showing the date of receipt and pass the letters on to more senior staff for sorting. Those documents which are easily identified, e.g. invoices, statements, letters accompanied by remittances, share certificates and stock transfer forms, etc. may be put into the appropriate tray by the juniors, but correspondence which has to be read through before a decision is made as to which department should receive it, is best handled by a senior member of staff.

When all the letters have been sorted into their appropriate piles, they are inserted into folders and distributed to the departments. There will probably be two piles left on the sorting table: remittances (which, in some offices, have to be recorded in a book before being passed over to the cashier for banking) and letters which require the attention of more than one person or department. In the former case, the entries are made in the remittance book and the cash, or cheques, are then taken to the cashier, who will make out receipts where necessary, notify the Accounts Department to credit debtors' accounts and then bank the money. In the case of letters which require the attention of more than one person, the problem may be dealt with in several ways:

1. CIRCULATION LIST

The names ot those concerned are listed on a small sheet of paper which is pinned or stapled to the letter. The letter is then passed to the first named person for attention. When that person has dealt with the letter, he crosses his name off the list, enters the date beside his name and sends the letter to the second person named on the list. This procedure is then repeated until all those concerned have seen and dealt with the letter. The disadvantage of this method is obvious: it may take a long time before each successive person gets a sight of the letter, and the method relies on each individual dealing with his part of the letter promptly and then not forgetting to pass it on to the next person.

2. PHOTOCOPIES

The postal department is equipped with a photocopier and a number of copies are made of the original, each copy being marked with the name of the person whose attention is required. This method is of course quick, it can cope with matter not easily copied by hand, *e.g.* maps, charts, etc. and ensures that each person receives a copy of the letter at the same time.

3. COPYTYPING

Where no photocopier is available, copies may be taken on the typewriter. Apart from the length of time taken in actual copytyping, more time must be spent in checking over the typing and in correcting any errors found.

The actual distribution of the incoming mail may safely be undertaken by a junior member of the postal department, so long as she understands that it is quite a responsible task. Much inconvenience can be caused if the mail gets taken to the wrong department or if a letter is dropped on the way. A route should be planned which avoids unnecessary back-tracking and which takes account of any special order of distribution (*e.g.*, Managing Director first).

It is important to deal promptly with all incoming mail as every department in the company will probably want to see its mail before planning the day's work.

OUTGOING MAIL

Where a central postal department exists, it is usual for that department to take charge of all outgoing mail. In some companies each department sends its outgoing correspondence to the postal department for despatch, in other companies a post messenger goes round the various departments to collect the mail. Whichever method is employed, a few rules are usually necessary:

1. Outgoing post should be ready for collection at stated times, e.g. 12 noon and 4 p.m. The postal department cannot accept responsibility to despatch letters which are not ready for collection at 4 p.m., and these would have to await the following day's despatch or alternatively be sent off by other means, *e.g.* by the secretarial staff of the department concerned. Sometimes, of course, it is possible for one or two members of the postal department to stay late and deal with last-minute outgoing mail. Mail for internal distribution should of course be collected and delivered at shorter intervals throughout the day.

2. Special requirements should be clearly indicated, *e.g.* first class mail, recorded delivery, certificate of posting, etc. This may be done by a pencil note on the envelope itself or by special verbal request or by attaching a written instruction to the envelope. If the volume of special instructions warrants it, a good plan is to have separate trays for first class mail, second class mail and "special" letters which require recorded delivery or other procedure.

3. A routine should be established for dealing with outgoing correspondence in the postal department itself. After collection from the various departments, all the envelopes for customers and other outside addresses should be sealed, weighed and marked with the postage required. They should then be sorted according to size and passed through the franking machine (Fig. 31). Very large packets or envelopes which cannot be accepted by the franking machine may have a gummed strip which has been franked stuck on them.

Where arrangements have been made with the Post Office to collect the mail from the company's premises, the envelopes should be tied in bundles of a convenient size (*e.g.*, twenty enveloes) and placed in the mail bag to await collection.

Outgoing mail does not consist only of letters and packets addressed to customers and others outside the firm. A large proportion of the mail will probably be made up of letters and memoranda addressed to Branch Offices, Sales and/or Area representatives and to persons in other departments on the premises. Post for Branch Offices, etc. is best dealt with by sorting into flap sorters or, preferably, pigeon holes, each marked with the name of the Branch Office. When the time comes to post this correspondence, all the letters intended for one Branch Office are inserted in one large envelope (which has been previously addressed by a junior), thus saving stationery, postage and writing time on individual envelopes.

Correspondence for internal delivery can be dealt with in one of two ways. Either it is collected by the messenger, brought back to the postal department and dealt with as described for Branch Office correspondence (with the addition of more frequent distribution), or, better still, it may be collected by the messenger and distributed directly (*i.e.*, without being taken to the postal room for sorting). If this latter method is adopted, a well-planned route should be established for the messenger to follow and it may be necessary to provide a trolley fitted with sorting devices, *e.g.* flap sorters or individual folders, so that the mail may be collected from the "OUT" trays of the various departments, placed in the appropriate folder on the trolley and the round continued to the next department where correspondence already collected from other departments may be offloaded from the trolley to the "IN" tray, and the "OUT" tray emptied into the folders carried on the trolley, and so on. Mailroom courses are run at most Head Post Offices for firms' mailroom staff.

Figs. 32–34 show some of the mailroom equipment which can be installed to increase the efficiency of a mailroom.

Finally, it is well worth investigating the arrangements which may

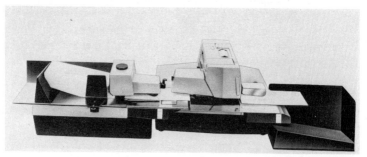

Courtesy of Roneo Vickers Limited

Fig. 31.—A franking machine.

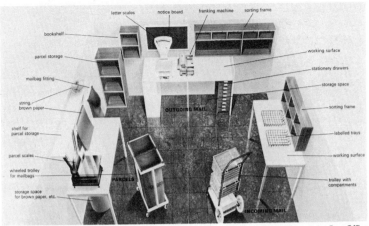

Courtesy of the Post Office

(*a*) Layout plan of an efficient postroom.

Courtesy of the Post Office

(*b*) Another view of a well-planned postroom.

Fig. 32.—Postroom layout.

(a)   *Courtesy of the Post Office*

(a) Mail bags: a hook fitting will hold mail bags upright and open to receive tied bundles of mail. An alternative is a wheeled trolley frame which will take two bags.

(b) Outgoing mail work surface: modern franking machines have attachments for sealing, stacking and even advertising. The postage impression can be printed on to the envelope or on to gummed paper. There should be room underneath for stationery labels and forms and sorting frames for segregating letters, packets and airmail are useful (*see* Fig. 34).

(c) Bookshelf: small bookshelf for reference books, *Post Office Guide*, postcode directories, etc. is a good idea.

Fig. 33.—Postroom equipment.

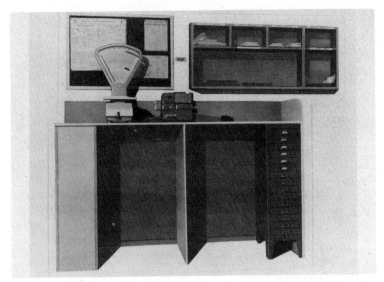

(b)   *Courtesy of the Post Office*

(c)   *Courtesy of the Post Office*

Courtesy of the Post Office

Fig. 34.—A sorting frame.

be made with the Post Office to meet the special requirements of individual companies. The collection of mail from the company's premises mentioned previously is only one such example. Private posting bags, private posting boxes and special messenger services are additional examples. These and other Post Office services are dealt with in greater detail in Chapter 15 on Post Office services.

OTHER WORK

Because the work in a postal department is subject to peak periods of concentrated work at regular times throughout the day and corresponding slack periods, it is often convenient for this department to undertake other work not directly connected with the post. Duplicating and copying, if there is not a separate department for this work, is an example. The machines involved are dealt with in detail in Chapter 21 on Office Machines, as is the equipment usually found in the mailroom of a large organisation. Two points should however be mentioned here in connection with reprography:

1. Specially treated paper used in some photocopying processes can be quite expensive and the operator should avoid waste. As in other skills, practice makes perfect and it is possible to improve one's skill by practising, in slack periods, with small pieces of paper (*e.g.,* using one sheet to make say, four copies). Duplicating paper is not treated in any way and is relatively cheap. However, tremendous quantities may be wasted if great care is not taken against unnecessary "trials." The paper should be fanned to let in some air between the sheets, thus avoiding the tendency for several sheets to be fed through together; too much inking should be avoided and one copy should be run off. This should be examined carefully and all adjustments (*e.g.,*.top, bottom and side margins, inking and registration) should be made. One further copy should be taken to ensure that the adjustments made were adequate. If all is well, "rolling off" may commence.

2. Where several pages are run off, these need to be sorted into numerical order and attached securely. This process is known as *collating*. Equipment is available (manual and power-driven) to cope with this work, and this is covered fully in Chapter 21 on Office Machines, but where no such equipment is available, or where only a few pages need to be collated, this work may be undertaken by hand. The method of placing all sheets in neat piles of page 1, page 2, page 3, etc. alongside one another on a desk is not the quickest way. The piles should be placed within reach of an easy arm movement in the following order:

Page 3	Page 1	Page 2	Page 4
Page 7	Page 5	Page 6	Page 8

Both hands should be used in picking up the papers. Fanning the piles and using rubber "thimbles" on the fingers facilitate picking up single sheets.

EQUIPMENT CHECK LIST

Apart from larger items of equipment and machinery dealt with in Chapter 21, the following smaller items of stationery and equipment are useful in the mailroom:
Weighing machine.
Guillotine.
Punch.
Stapler, including a long arm stapler.
Sponge (or other means of moistening envelopes prior to sealing).
A variety of rubber stamps (date, circulation).
Trays.
Flap sorters.
Letter opener.
String, paper, clips, pins, staples, rubber bands, rubber finger "thimbles."
Sellotape, glue.

Short-answer Questions

1. Mention two methods of ensuring that enclosures do not remain in the envelopes of incoming mail when the accompanying letter is extracted.

2. Name two items which may be received (letters, documents, forms, etc.) and which could be easily identified from their format without thorough reading.

3. Mention one aid to the sorting of correspondence into various departments.

4. Some incoming letters require the attention of more than one person; how can such letters be dealt with?

5. Mention four different kinds of communication which may be received in the incoming mail.

6. Why should a route be planned for the internal messenger who collects and delivers mail on the premises?

7. Why is it necessary for those who deal with incoming mail to attended earlier than the rest of the office staff?

8. How can letters which have missed the last internal collection for the post be despatched without the delay of waiting until the following day?

9. Why do you think it is necessary to date-stamp all incoming mail?

10. Name six departments into which incoming mail might be sorted.

Past Examination Questions

1. List four methods of routing a letter to various persons or departments in a business organisation and state which, in your opinion, is the most satisfactory and for what reasons. (*L.C.C.*)

2. List instructions for a new junior in a small office for dealing with incoming mail. (*L.C.C.*)

3. When sorting the incoming mail, to which departments or sub-divisions of departments would you send the following mail:

(*a*) a statement of account;

(*b*) a complaint that certain goods despatched by your company have arrived in a damaged condition;

(*c*) a cheque in settlement of goods purchased from your company;

(*d*) an enquiry as to the price of a machine manufactured by your company and the date of delivery;

(*e*) a complaint by a shareholder that a divident recently paid by your company has not been received;

(*f*) a letter acknowledging receipt of a quotation for goods;

(*g*) a registered letter stating that unless your company paid a sum of £80 for goods received legal action would be taken;

(*h*) a letter from a firm overseas enquiring whether your company manufactured certain appliances;

(*i*) a letter from one of your commercial travellers asking what discount he might quote to an educational establishment;

(*j*) a letter marked Private and Confidential and addressed to a former commercial traveller of your company (this person left the company's employ two months ago).

Give reasons for your choice in cases (*e*), (*g*) and (*h*), bearing in mind that several different items are involved. (*L.C.C.*)

4. What important points should you bear in mind when you are opening and sorting incoming mail? (*R.S.A.*)

5. List six simple items of equipment or stationery you would need to make up a parcel ready for despatch by registered post.

(*R.S.A.*)

CHAPTER 15

POST OFFICE SERVICES

THE *Post Office Guide* is a book no self-respecting secretary should be without. It contains information on the services offered by the Post Office and charges therefor. The *Post Office Guide* is published annually and supplements are published approximately every two months.

INLAND SERVICES

The following are some, but not all, of the services shown in the *Post Office Guide.*

1. FIRST AND SECOND CLASS MAIL

All envelopes may now be sealed, whether sent by first or second class mail (second class normally takes up to one day longer for delivery than first class mail). This applies to letters and cards.

2. UNSTAMPED LETTERS

Unstamped or understamped letters are treated as second class mail and charged on delivery with double the amount of second class postage or double the amount of the deficit, as the case may be. This is known as *surcharge.*

3. POST OFFICE PREFERRED (POP) ENVELOPES AND CARDS

A scheme for preferred sizes has been postponed (not abandoned). To qualify, letters and cards must be at least 90 mm × 140 mm ($3\frac{1}{2}$ in × $5\frac{1}{2}$ in) and not larger than 120 mm × 235 mm ($4\frac{3}{4}$ in × $9\frac{1}{4}$ in), oblong in shape with the longer side at least 1·414 times the shorter side, and made from paper weighing at least 63 grammes per square metre. Aperture envelopes (with the address panel not covered with transparent material) will not qualify, but window envelopes (with the address panel covered with transparent material) will qualify.

Mail weighing up to 2 oz posted in envelopes outside the preferred sizes will of course still be dealt with by the Post Office but will merely be liable to an additional charge.

4. BUSINESS REPLY SERVICE

This service is particularly suitable for a person or firm who wants to encourage replies to a questionnaire sent out for completion and return, or where a prospective customer is encouraged to send an

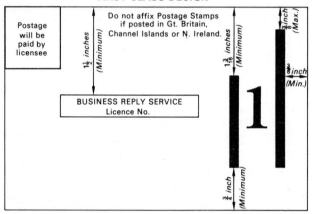

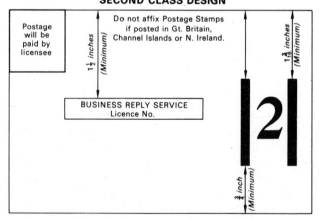

Fig. 35.—Business reply envelopes.

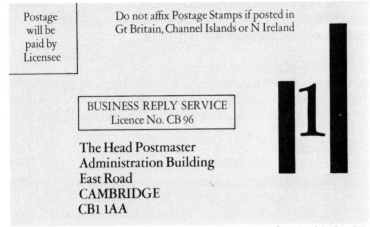

Postage will be paid by Licensee

Do not affix Postage Stamps if posted in Gt Britain, Channel Islands or N Ireland

BUSINESS REPLY SERVICE
Licence No. CB 96

The Head Postmaster
Administration Building
East Road
CAMBRIDGE
CB1 1AA

Courtesy of the Post Office

Fig. 36.—A business reply card.

enquiry to the firm (Figs. 35 and 36). Thus, a card, envelope, label, etc. of the approved design and size, may be posted unstamped and the addressee (the firm or person holding the licence from the Post Office) is charged for all the replies he receives. This method is more economical than sending out *stamped*, self-addressed envelopes, since only those envelopes actually returned are charged for (a small extra charge is made for handling). A licence must be obtained from the local Head Postmaster and there are certain conditions as to size, design and colour. More details are given in the *Post Office Guide*.

5. REBATES OF POSTAGE

This applies only to second class letters posted in bulk, the minimum qualifying number being 4,251. There are certain conditions which posters must comply with, *e.g.* pre-sorting requirements (whereby the number of town and county selections is governed by the size of the posting), presentation with all the addresses facing in the same direction, and arrangement in secure bundles of fifty each (or ten per bundle for bulky items). Special arrangements must be made with the local Head Postmaster, and close liaison between the poster and the Post Office is desirable. Such a service would interest companies concerned with mail advertising, or share registration companies dealing with a large membership. As, however, rebate postings are normally dealt with during off-peak periods, the handling span is normally seven working days: some companies may therefore prefer not to take advantage of the rebate facility, but instead choose to use the quicker second class service.

6. ARTICLES FOR THE BLIND

Specified articles weighing no more than 15 lb may be transmitted by first class letter service free of charge. A packet must show the name and address of the sender and be marked "Articles for the Blind."

7. FREEPOST

A firm, advertiser or other person who wishes to obtain a reply from a client or member of the public without putting him to the expense of paying postage may include in his communication a special address (usually in abbreviated form and bearing the word FREE-POST, *e.g.* A.B. Co. Ltd., FREEPOST, London, EC1 XYZ). The reply bearing this address can then posted without a stamp and the addressee is charged postage plus $\frac{1}{2}$p extra on all the replies received. A licence must be obtained. Replies may only be sent second class.

It will be seen that the difference between Freepost and Business Reply Service is that with Freepost the licenceholder need not go the trouble and expense of printing and he may also save on cost of stationery, leaving it to the sender of the communication to use his own envelope. He may of course send out addressed envelopes if he wishes.

Users of both Freepost and Business Reply Service must tender a deposit against which the cost of postage and handling will be charged.

8. PRE-PAYMENT OF POSTAGE IN MONEY

Subject to certain conditions, *e.g.* minimum numbers, tied in bundles, handed in over the counter and so on, it is possible to pre-pay the postage on postal packets in money at Post Offices. Full particulars may be obtained from the local Postmaster.

9. FRANKING MACHINES

Subject to certain conditions, the use of franking machines is permitted by the Post Office, saving the upkeep of post books and sticking on stamps. Permission must be obtained for each machine and payment for postage must be made in advance. There are two methods of crediting machines: one type must be taken to a Post

Office for resetting; the other uses a card purchased from the Post Office. A control card must be maintained showing meter readings and be sent to the Post Office weekly. The franking machine must be maintained regularly. Franked correspondence should be securely tied in bundles and handed in at a Post Office. Permission can be obtained to use posting boxes when special envelopes are used.

10. ADDRESSING AND COLLECTION

Secretaries will find the Post Office publication *Postal Addresses* very useful. The following information should also be noted: The post towns are key points of the postal system (they act as clearing points for a particular district) and should always be shown in *block capitals*. The name of the county in which the post town is situated is also necessary as this facilitates sorting.

Boundaries and county names have recently been changed. The new county names are:

Avon	Gwent	Salop
Berkshire	Gwynedd	South Glamorgan
Cambridgeshire	Leicestershire	South Humberside
Cheshire	Merseyside	South Yorkshire
Cleveland	Mid-Glamorgan	Tyne and Wear
Clywd	North Humberside	West Glamorgan
Cumbria	North Yorkshire	West Midlands
Dorset	Oxfordshire	West Sussex
Dyfed	Powys	West Yorkshire
East Sussex		

A helpful booklet entitled Addresses have changed has been issued by the Post Office. This lists the post towns affected by changed county names and boundaries, together with the old and new county names.

The *postcode* represents an address in abbreviated form to aid automatic sorting and should be shown in *block capitals* on a separate line, as the last item of information in the address. Postcode Directories are issued by the Post Office and copies are available at local Post Offices.

Postmen are not allowed, in towns, to accept post from the public and all letters must be posted in letterboxes, and parcels handed in over the counter, unless special arrangements are made. Special arrangements may be made for free collection from the premises, for example when the number of letters amounts to 1,000 or more. Again, arrangements may be made (for a fee) for collection to be made from a private posting box. This might prove useful where a firm wishes to provide this facility for a large number of employees.

11. POST RESTANTE

This service is normally provided for the convenience of travellers (*e.g.*, if an address is not available) and may not be used in the same town for more than three months. The Post Office will hold letters awaiting collection but callers for their letters must furnish proof of identity.

12. PRIVATE BOXES AND BAGS

A private box may be rented at the delivery Post Office so that mail may be called for instead of delivered by the postman. This service would be used when it was desired to obtain mail outside normal delivery times. It is also possible to use a lockable private bag for posting and receipt of correspondence. Where a private box is used, the number must be shown as well as full address.

13. SELECTAPOST

It is possible to make arrangements for mail to be subdivided by the Post Office, *e.g.* into the different departments of a firm before delivery. A fee is payable and the address on the envelope must indicate the subdivision.

14. REDIRECTION

Letters, cards and newspapers may be redirected (by the public) free of charge provided they are re-posted not later than the day after delivery, not counting Sundays and Public holidays and have not been opened. Parcels are subject to additional postage unless both the old and new addresses are served by the same delivery office or are within the same local parcel delivery area and are re-posted within a day after delivery.

Letters, parcels, etc. may be redirected by the Post Office. Application must be made to the local delivery office serving the old address and a fee is payable. The service is available for periods of one month, three months or twelve months, and may be renewed.

15. LATE POSTED PACKETS

This service is available for letters paid at first class rate. Posting boxes are provided on all Travelling Post Offices (mail trains to which sorting carriages are attached), and postal packets prepaid with a small additional charge (stamp) will be dealt with. Registered and recorded delivery items are accepted in Travelling Post Offices at railway stations up to five minutes before departure time. Extra postage is required, in addition to the registration or recorded delivery fee and first class postage.

16. EXPRESS SERVICES

(*a*) *Express by P.O. messenger all the way.* This service (chargeable) may be used for the conveyance of urgent letters, goods, etc. (a Post Office Messenger collects and delivers the letter). The word *Express* must be boldly written above the address in the left-hand corner of the cover. Application must be made at the Post Office (telephone applications are accepted) and letters or parcels must not be posted in a letterbox.

(*b*) *Express from office of delivery at request of addressee.* If an addressee requires delivery of his post in advance of ordinary delivery times, he may require express messenger delivery. This service is also chargeable and application by telephone is accepted.

(*c*) *Railex.* This service is available between specified railway stations. Unregistered items are accepted by the Post Office for conveyance to the appropriate railway station for transmission to the station of destination. A messenger collects it from that station for delivery to the addressee.

17. RAILWAY AND AIRWAY LETTERS

Special arrangements between the Post Office and railways and airways concerns make it possible for mail to be accepted at certain railway stations and air terminals.

18. CASH ON DELIVERY

Under this service the amount, called the trade charge, specified by the sender for collection on delivery of a parcel, or a first class letter or packet can, on certain conditions, be collected from the addressee by the Post Office and remitted to the sender by means of a crossed order. No compensation is paid for the loss or damage of an ordinary C.O.D. parcel. The maximum amount of compensation paid for the loss or damage of compensation fee parcels and registered letter packets is determined by the amount of the fee paid.

19. REGISTRATION

First class letters or letter packets may be sent by registered post if it is desired to claim compensation from the Post Office in the event of loss or damage. A fee is payable to cover compensation, which will not be paid by the Post Office on coin, bank notes or other monetary documents, *e.g.* uncrossed warrants, savings stamps, etc. unless enclosed in the special envelopes bearing the familiar horizontal and vertical blue lines sold by the Post Office. Packing must be made secure, if necessary with sealing wax, and must be marked "Registered" in the bottom left-hand corner. A receipt is obtained from the Post Office and for an additional fee the sender may require an "Advice of Delivery" which will be sent to him when delivery has been effected.

20. COMPENSATION FEE PARCEL SERVICE

If a compensation fee is paid at the time of posting, compensation can be claimed for loss or damage to the parcel. A certificate of posting is obtained at time of posting.

(All other parcels are sent at sender's risk, *i.e.* no compensation is payable for loss or damage.)

21. RECORDED DELIVERY

This service provides a record of posting and delivery, as does registration, but only limited compensation in the event of loss or damage. Here also a receipt is obtained, and a special distinguishing (yellow) label affixed to the letter (Fig. 37). As with registered items, "Advice of Delivery" may be requested at the sender's option. This service is useful for transmission of documents, etc. where these are important but not intrinsically valuable.

22. CERTIFICATE OF POSTING OF UNREGISTERED LETTERS

If it is desired to have a record that an item, *e.g.* an unregistered letter, has been posted, a certificate of posting may be obtained by handing the letter in to the Post Office. A small fee is payable, but no compensation is of course payable in the event of loss or damage.

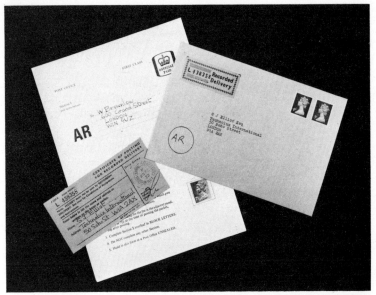

Courtesy of the Post Office

Fig. 37.—A recorded delivery label and certificate of posting.

OVERSEAS SERVICES

Under the "*All-up Service*" letters, etc. for Europe are sent by air at no extra charge and there is no need for special air mail marking. The familiar *blue air mail label* must be affixed in the top left hand corner of the letter or other item, and the specified postage paid, for letters to be sent to countries outside Europe by air mail. Alternatively, the words *By air mail* may be boldly written, instead of affixing the label.

1. AIR LETTER FORMS
These are now available in two sizes and may be sent to all countries. These forms may be obtained from Post Offices and must not, of course, contain any enclosures.

2. REPLY COUPONS
These are exchangeable at Post Offices abroad for postage stamps and thus enable the sender of a letter to a place abroad to pre-pay a reply. Similarly, coupons received from countries abroad may be exchanged for stamps or airletter forms at Post Offices in this

Counter No. ....

Office Stamp

POST OFFICE

INLAND TELEGRAM

FOR POSTAGE STAMPS

Serial No. ....

Charge	Changeable Words	Sent at/by
Tariff excl. RP £		
VAT £		
RP £		Circulation
TOTAL £		

Prefix	Handed in	Service Instructions	Actual Words

If you wish to pay for a reply insert RP here

To

BLOCK LETTERS THROUGHOUT PLEASE

The particulars on the back of this form should be completed.

Courtesy of the Post Office

(*a*) The face of the form.

*NAME AND ADDRESS OF SENDER ....
and telephone number (if any)

....

....

*Note: These particulars will not be telegraphed unless included in the message overleaf.

McC 56–4147

A

Courtesy of the Post Office

(*b*) The reverse of the form.

Fig. 38.—An inland telegram form.

country. Two types of Reply Coupon are available: Commonwealth Reply Coupons and International Reply Coupons.

NOTE: It should be noted that the above information is summarised and basic information only. The overseas service includes some facilities broadly similar to some in the inland service, *e.g.* registration, articles for the blind, pre-payment of postage on money, etc. but the "General Information" section on the overseas post in the *Post Office Guide* should be carefully and regularly consulted for complete details.

OTHER SERVICES

1. INLAND TELEGRAMS

Charges are all subject to value added tax except the Reply Paid Voucher (the charge for the reply telegram will itself attract V.A.T.). A specimen ordinary inland telegram is shown at Fig. 38. In addition, De Luxe or Standard *Greetings* telegrams are available on attractively designed forms. Greetings telegrams may be handed over in advance and a request made for subsequent delivery on a specified day. *Overnight* telegrams may be sent between 8 a.m. and 10.30 p.m. for delivery the following morning (usually by first post). These are cheaper. *Priority* telegrams are those which receive priority in transmission and delivery during normal scheduled delivery hours over other rate telegrams. An extra fee is payable. Telegrams are delivered by hand, by telephone, by telex or by post.

2. MULTIPLE ADDRESS TELEGRAMS

A telegram may be sent to two or more addresses in the same delivery area at a reduced charge.

3. TELEGRAPHIC ADDRESS

Persons and business firms who receive a large number of telegrams may register with the Post Office an abbreviated telegraphic address (usually two words). These addresses are useful because they save cost on a number of words in the name and address.

4. WEATHER INFORMATION AND FORECASTS

This may be obtained by sending a reply-paid telegram to the Meteorological Office (telegraphic address WEATHER BRACKNELL TELEX).

5. CERTIFIED COPIES OF TELEGRAMS

These may be obtained within three months of the date of sending.

Telegrams may be written in plain language or may be coded. They may be handed in over the counter at the Post Office and should be written in *block capitals*. Telegrams may also be dictated by telephone to the Telegrams Service. Such telegrams should be dictated very clearly, two or three words at a time.

6. TELEX

Telex may also be used to hand in a message for transmission as a telegram. The telex numbers of telegraph offices are shown on the dialling code cards supplied to telex subscribers, and under the Telexogram service a telegram may be delivered from a public telegraph office in one country to the telex machine of a telex subscriber in another. Only certain European countries participate.

7. DATEL SERVICES

These provide facilities for digital data transmission both inland and overseas. Certain datel users are also enabled to gain access to a remote computer centre by means of a local fee telephone call.

8. PHOTOTELEGRAPH SERVICE

Pictures, photographs, drawings, etc. may be telegraphed in facsimile to and from many places in the world. Black printing on a white background is best for reproduction; photographic tone can be satisfactorily reproduced but coloured printing, faint or indistinct pictures are not suitable for transmission. The matter to be transmitted should be on one side of the paper only, and the paper should be pliable enough to be rolled. Phototelegrams are accepted at the more important offices, including the Post Office International Telegraph Offices. Pictures may also be sent by subscribers who have their own equipment to private stations overseas (countries to which this service is available are shown in the *Post Office Guide*). Finally, pictures may be sent from the Post Office in London (if the subscriber has no equipment of his own) to private stations abroad.

9. SAVINGS, REMITTANCES AND OTHER SERVICES

The Post Office offers of course the telephone service, a number of savings and investment account services, the National Giro service and remittance services. In addition, a number of other services are available, for example National Insurance and Industrial Insurance stamps may be purchased at Post Offices, pensions and allowances may be paid at Post Offices, licences may be issued from Post Offices, and so on. Some of these facilities are dealt with elsewhere in this book. For National Giro *see* Methods of Payment, Chapter 17.

Short-answer Questions

1. What is the Business Reply Service?

2. What is the Express All The Way Service?

3. What do you understand by C.O.D.?

4. Explain the difference between Recorded Delivery Service and Registration.

5. What is the difference between an air mail letter and an air letter form?

6. What is an International Reply Coupon?

7. What do you understand by Facsimile Telegraphy?

8. Why do some firms register an abbreviated telegraphic address?

9. What is a multiple address telegram?

10. Name five services offered by the Post Office.

Past Examination Questions

1. (*a*) What advantages are to be gained from the use of a franking machine?

(*b*) Explain the difference between recorded and registered mail.

(*c*) What is a reply paid envelope? Give an example to illustrate its use. (*L.C.C.*)

2. Write fully on the following Post Office services:

(*a*) Railex; (*b*) Express Service; (*c*) Travelling Post Office. (*L.C.C.*)

3. When would you use: (*a*) recorded delivery; (*b*) registered post? (*R.S.A.*)

4. (*a*) Name two express services offered by the Post Office.

(*b*) What is an International Reply Coupon? (*R.S.A.*)

5. In addressing correspondence what is the particular significance of:

(*a*) post town; (*b*) postcode? (*R.S.A.*)

6. Give one advantage of: (*a*) a telegraphic address; (*b*) an air letter form; (*c*) poste restante. (*R.S.A.*)

7. Which Post Office service would you use to send the following:

(*a*) jewellery; (*b*) a summons to appear in Court; (*c*) some proofs which you wish to reach the printer on the day on which you send them; (*d*) money wanted very urgently by a member of your staff who is working temporarily in another town?

(*R.S.A.*)

8. What is a Postcode directory? Where would you find one?

(*R.S.A.*)

9. (*a*) Explain the postal regulations regarding the re-direction, by the public, of letters and parcels. Are re-directed parcels subject to additional postal charges?

(*b*) If your firm is removing to new premises, what arrangements can be made with the Post Office for the re-direction of letters and parcels? Is any charge made for this service?

(*R.S.A.*)

10. (*a*) Which part of an address on an envelope should be typed in capital letters? Why is this?

(*b*) The Post Office Guide gives information about a Business Reply Service. What is this? (*R.S.A.*)

CHAPTER 16

BANKING SERVICES

LOANS AND OVERDRAFTS

THESE two terms are not entirely synonymous; a loan for a *specified* amount of money may be made by a bank to a business firm or to a private person. Such a loan might be subject to varying conditions according to the particular circumstances. For example, the loan might be made for a *fixed term*, *i.e.* repayment to be made on an agreed date, or it could be made for an *indefinite period*—the rate of interest paid by the borrower would of course vary. Another factor which might affect the conditions of the loan is the *security* or collateral offered by the borrower. If shares are tendered as security, this gives the bank a *lien* (a hold) over the shares.

An overdraft can be described as the amount which the bank has agreed the client may overdraw on his account. To the extent agreed, the bank will honour the client's cheques even though his account is overdrawn. Again, the figure agreed upon and the conditions of the overdraft will depend upon the particular circumstances and the security offered by the client. Firms often make use of this service: although they have to pay interest on the overdraft, it may be more profitable to do that and to use their liquid resources (ready cash) in other ways, *e.g.* as an investment which will earn a higher interest than that paid to the bank or to buy fast-moving stock which sells at a high profit, and so on. The security which firms offer may of course vary but a common one is to give the bank a "fixed and floating charge" on the assets of the undertaking. This term means that the bank is given rights over the property charged (or pledged): the *fixed* charge is over definite assets which are named, *e.g.* a freehold building or certain plant and equipment and the *floating* charge is over assets which the client has the right to deal with even though they have been pledged; such assets may change in form and in value, as for example stocks of goods which are sold at a profit for cash therefore turn into cash (a change in form), or stocks of goods which are sold on credit and turn into debts, many of which remain unpaid and become bad debts (a change in form and in value (now decreased)). It will be seen that if the firm manages the assets subject to a floating charge well, or if trading conditions flourish, the bank's security is enhanced; if the assets are imprudently managed, or for some other reason fall in value, the value of the bank's security may be considerably reduced. If the client makes default, *e.g.* in paying interest to the bank, or in repaying the principal borrowed, the charge is said to "crystallise," and the bank may look to the assets which are available at that moment in time.

DEPOSITING SECURITIES

Many firms (and private persons) find it convenient to deposit important documents with their banks. Two examples of documents commonly deposited are title deeds to property and share certificates, both of which would cause great concern and inconvenience if lost or stolen and which are not used often enough to warrant putting in a safe on the premises.

FOREIGN CURRENCY AND TRAVELLERS' CHEQUES

Banks will, of course, obtain and issue both foreign currency and travellers' cheques and the secretary whose chief travels much will probably need to order both. Some currency will be essential to meet his immediate needs on arriving in the foreign country (to pay for newspapers, taxi fares, meals, tips) and the rest of his money should be in the form of travellers' cheques which are available in a variety of denominations.

ACCOUNTS

By far the best known activity of banks is the handling of accounts. Firms and private individuals alike make use of this service. Deposit accounts may require prior notice of withdrawals or minimum term deposits, and offer interest in return; current accounts offer no interest but require no prior notice of withdrawal. Cash, cheques, warrants, etc. may be paid into an account together with a paying-in slip (which shows the details of the total deposited, *e.g.* notes, cheques, etc. and also shows the date of deposit, to whose account the deposit was made, and by whom the deposit was made). Drawings from an account are most often made by cheque, but there are other methods, *e.g.* standing orders, traders' credits and direct debits which are dealt with in detail in Chapter 17 on Methods of Payment.

CHEQUES

A cheque is really an instruction by the account holder to his bank to pay out of his account a specified sum of money to the person named on the cheque. A cheque may bear a *general crossing* (two bold lines across the face of the cheque, possibly with the words & Co. written inside the crossing). This is a safety precaution and means that the cheque can only be paid into a bank account and cannot be cashed over the counter. Thus a person who finds or steals a crossed cheque will derive little value from it since it can only be paid into the bank account of the payee (the person named on the cheque)—unless of course the thief forges an endorsement! A crossing on a cheque may also be *specific*, *i.e.* the name of the account into which it is to be paid is written within the two lines, for example, a cheque made payable to "The Post Office" and crossed "Telephone Account." An *open cheque* is one which has the words "please pay cash" over an additional signature written within the crossing. Such a cheque may be made out to "self," "bearer," or, to an indication of the account to which it will be debited, *e.g.* to "wages." An open cheque attracts great risk in the event of loss since it is the equivalent of an uncrossed cheque and is an instruction to the banker to pay cash over the counter. For this reason it is a wise precaution not to open a cheque until just before presenting it to the bank. If a cheque is made out to a named payee and that person does not wish to cash it himself but prefers to offer it in payment to a third party, he may *endorse* the cheque by signing his name on the reverse before handing it to the third party. That person may then pay the cheque into his own bank account. The bank may also require an endorsement on open cheques payable to "self" as an added precaution.

For any one of a number of reasons, it may become necessary for payment on a cheque to be *stopped*. For example, if a cheque has been lost and another one made out in its place, it would be a wise precaution for the account holder to ask the bank to stop payment on the first cheque, should it be presented. Preliminary notice may be given to the bank by telephone, quoting the number and date of the cheque, the amount payable and the name of the payee. The account holder should also give his account number. The telephone request should be followed up immediately by letter so that the bank has a written instruction.

BANK RECONCILIATION STATEMENT

Periodically, the bank will issue to its client a bank statement which shows the balance brought forward from the preceding statement, the credits paid into the account and the debits made from it, ending with a figure which shows the balance in hand or overdrawn (the latter may be shown in red ink, hence the phrase "in the red"). It is important for this final figure to be "reconciled" or agreed with the customer's own record of the balance, which may for a number of reasons differ from the bank's figure.

1. The client may have drawn cheques on his account but such cheques have not yet been presented for payment, therefore his bank statement will include such amounts while his own record (or cash book) will show a reduced balance.
2. Similarly the client may have paid into his account cheques he has recently received but the bank may have sent out the statement before these cheques could be included in it, therefore the bank's figure will be smaller than that shown in the client's cash book.
3. Some transactions of which the client is unaware might be recorded on the bank statement but not in his cash book, *e.g.* standing orders for payment, or bank charges.
4. Finally cheques paid into his account by the client and entered in his cash book might have been dishonoured and therefore not shown to his credit in the bank statement.

In business it is often the bookkeeper's task to make out a Bank Reconciliation Statement, but private persons should also reconcile the bank's statement with their own record and it is useful if the secretary knows how to do this. Very simply, it is headed "Bank Reconciliation Statement" and starts with the balance shown on the bank statement. To this are added all the cheques which the client has recently paid in but the bank has not yet shown on the statement, and from the resulting figure is deducted the amount of any cheques which the client has drawn on his account in order to pay debts but which his creditors have not yet presented for payment. A simple example of a Bank Reconciliation Statement is shown in Fig. 39.

BANK RECONCILIATION STATEMENT

			£
Balance as per pass book			250
		£	
Add: Cheques paid in but not yet credited: Brown	25		
Green	10		
White	15		50
		£	300
Deduct: Cheques drawn but not yet presented: Black	5		
Jones	50		55
Balance as per cash book			245

Fig. 39.—Bank reconciliation statement.

OTHER SERVICES

Banks offer a variety of other services, the following being a few examples.

1. NIGHT SAFE
To safeguard cash (which would otherwise remain on the offices or shop premises after banking hours) from theft or fire, a person or firm may arrange with the bank to make use of its night safe facilities. For a small annual fee the bank issues a wallet fitted with lock and key and the cash is put into the wallet which is locked and deposited into the night safe through the trap door. The wallet drops into the bank's safe. The following day the contents of the wallet may be either paid in or removed according to the client's requirements.

2. ADVICE
This may be given on a variety of matters including financial and business management.

3. SECURITIES
Stocks and shares may be purchased and sold through the bank's brokers, all communication being made through the bank itself. Advice is also available through the bank's brokers.

4. EXECUTOR AND TRUSTEE DEPARTMENT
Banks will act as executors or co-executors of a will, as trustees, and so on.

5. LOANS

Loans may be made to persons with acceptable security to offer (*e.g.*, title deeds to property, securities, etc.), or in some instances to personal customers even without security. Different terms would of course apply according to the special circumstances.

6. SAFE DEPOSIT AND SAFE CUSTODY

According to the customer's requirements, "safe deposits" (private steel safes) may be rented, or alternatively locked deed boxes and sealed packets (envelopes or small parcels distinctively sealed) will be accepted for safe keeping. Valuable papers (*e.g.*, insurance policies, securities, property deeds, etc.) may also be kept in safe custody by the bank for the client.

7. INSURANCE

Some banks will help with advice in choosing the right type of insurance policy for special requirements, in placing it with the right insurance company, in short, acting as insurance brokers.

Short-answer Questions

1. What do you understand by the word "overdraft"?
2. How is a cheque "opened"?
3. What is an endorsement on a cheque?
4. Why are cheques usually crossed?
5. Give two examples of a crossing on a cheque.
6. How can payment on a cheque be stopped?
7. Why is it that the balance shown on the bank statement often differs from that shown in the client's cash book?
8. Give two services, other than the handling of cheque accounts, commonly offered by banks.
9. If you had an account with a bank and wanted to draw some ready cash from it, what would you do?
10. What would you do if you had sent a cheque in payment of services rendered and were subsequently told that the cheque had not been received?

Past Examination Questions

1. Explain the difference between a Crossed Cheque and an Open Cheque. *(L.C.C.)*

2. You receive a telephone call from one of your company's suppliers of raw materials. He tells you that he has not yet received a cheque for £28 which your company owes him. Two weeks ago you had made out a list of creditors showing their names, addresses and the amounts due to them. From that list you had prepared the cheques which your employer signed and these had been sent out in the normal way.

(a) How would you deal with the telephone call?
(b) What subsequent action would you take?

3. Explain how the following banking documents are used:
(a) pay-in-book; (b) deposit book; (c) cheque counterfoil.

(R.S.A.)*

4. What is:

(a) a bank statement; (b) a paying-in book; (c) a standing order?
(R.S.A.)

5. State four circumstances when a cheque drawn by a customer in favour of a person to whom he owes money would not be paid by that customer's bank. (R.S.A.)

6. What services would the office of a retailer normally require from a bank? (R.S.A.)*

7. How would you turn the following into cash: an open cheque?
(R.S.A.)*

8. You work personally for Mr. X who is in Paris on holiday. During Mr. X's absence you receive a telephone call from Mr. Y (to whom you posted a cheque last week), who says that he has not yet received the £10 promised before Mr. X left. What action would you take? (R.S.A.)

* Only part of a longer question included.

CHAPTER 17

METHODS OF PAYMENT

THROUGHOUT the ages payment for goods supplied or services rendered has been made in a variety of ways: barter, beads, precious stones and precious metals, and cash (in the shape of coin and paper), to name but a few.

CASH

Coin and bank notes need no description, but few business concerns and a decreasing number of private individuals now make extensive use of this commodity. It is bulky to carry around and to store; it is easily lost and not so easily recovered, and because of its negotiable character and the difficulty in tracing it, it is a temptation to theft.

Notes and coin, uncrossed cheques and warrants payable to bearer, unobliterated postage stamps, and the like may of course be sent through the post, but no compensation will normally be paid unless they are enclosed in one of the registered letter envelopes sold by the post office *and* are sent by registered letter post. Coin (not exceeding £5) so sent must be packed in such a way that it cannot move about.

The minimum registration fee is 20p rising through $22\frac{1}{2}$p to 25p for which maximum compensation of £150, £300 and £500 may be paid respectively.

Money may also be sent (inland) by Post Office express messenger all the way at sender's risk without being registered.

Money sent overseas (where this is allowed) may be insured for compensation beyond that covered by registration up to a maximum of £500.

CHEQUES

Cheques are still commonly used as a method of payment for all but the smallest amounts. The use of a cheque eliminates handling actual cash—hence loss and theft are eliminated: after all, if you lose a cheque you have only lost a piece of paper; you may draw on your bank account by cheque to its full extent (and even beyond in the case of business firms working on an overdraft), and if you wish to stop payment on one of your cheques all that is necessary is an instruction to the bank, quoting details of the particular cheque: number, date, name of payee, amount payable and account number.

One of the effects of the *Cheques Act* 1957, has been to reduce the number of receipts issued since a cheque processed through a bank now provides evidence of payment. It is common practice therefore not to issue receipts for payments made by cheque unless a specific request is made.

BANKER'S ORDER

This is a signed instruction to the bank to make regular payments of a fixed amount to a named payee on specific dates. Examples when banker's orders might be used are mortgage repayments, subscription fees to clubs or professional associations, regular donations to charitable institutions, and so on. It will be noticed that the banker's order is a suitable method of payment when it is desired to ensure that payments will not be forgotten (the bank acts on the initial instruction to pay monthly, annually, etc. *until further notice*, or until a *specified number of payments have been made*); when the payee remains constant; when the amount to be paid is not subject to constant change; and when the dates for payment are fixed in advance. A banker's order may of course be revoked at any time at the instance of the account holder. Banker's orders are sometimes called Standing Orders because the instruction to the bank is indeed an order which is likely to be long-standing (not subject to continual change), hence *Standing Order*.

TRADER'S CREDIT

This is a service offered by banks to persons and business concerns who have opened accounts with them. By this service, a bank account holder may instruct his bank to make transfers from his own account to the credit of other bank accounts (not necessarily the same bank). The agreement of the other account holders must first be obtained by the person wishing to make the payments, but these days when most people have bank accounts, this agreement is usually readily forthcoming. The advantages of this system are that a single instruction is made out to the bank with an accompanying list of the accounts to be credited and a saving is thus effected in stationery costs, postage and time. The bank makes a single debit entry in the account holder's account and arranges for the various amounts to be credited to the other bank accounts, under advice to the payee.

It will be seen that where a businessman has to pay, say, ten suppliers £5 each, he may either write a single instruction to his bank to debit his own account with a total amount of £50 and credit ten other (named) accounts with £5 each, or he may himself write out ten cheques and post these to his ten suppliers. As each supplier receives his cheque and presents it for payment, a credit entry must be effected in his account and a debit entry must be effected in the businessman's account. The neatness of the Trader's Credit system is thus easily seen.

Persons who do not themselves have bank accounts may still make use of the system if they wish to make payments direct into the bank account of another person or business concern. This is done by merely completing a trader's credit form (sometimes called a credit transfer form) indicating the amount to be paid, the account to be credited, and the identity of the person making the payment, and presenting it to the bank clerk over the counter, together with the *cash* to be paid. A small fee is charged by the bank if no account is held at the bank.

As this system is concerned with making transfers of funds, it is sometimes known as *credit transfer, banker's transfer, bank transfer* or *trader's credit*.

Many large organisations are now taking full advantage of this system by not only paying their creditors by credit transfer, but by encouraging their employees to accept salary payments transferred directly into their bank accounts (Fig. 40). This of course eliminates the handling of cash quite apart from the saving in time and stationery costs outlined above. Figure 40(*a*) is the credit slip used when it is desired to credit an account at another branch or bank; (*b*) is the form used to credit an account at the same bank.

DIRECT DEBIT

This is rather like the automatic debit transfer described under the services offered by the National Giro system. The person who wants to make the payment gives his permission for the person who has to

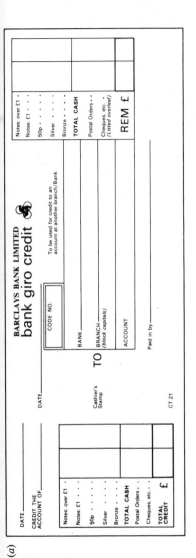

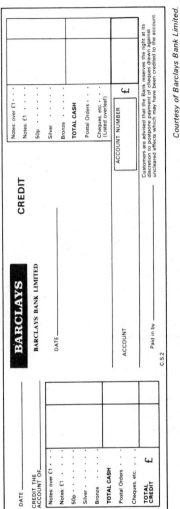

Fig. 40.—Bank Giro credit forms.

Courtesy of Barclays Bank Limited.

receive the payment to take the amount due by having the account of the former debited. The bank is instructed to permit this procedure. It really means that whereas with a standing order the instruction is to the debtor's bank to make the payment to the creditor, with a direct debit, the creditor (with the debtor's prior permission) credits his own account and advises the debtor's bank that this has been done so that the debtor's account may be debited by his bank.

As with standing orders, the system is suitable for regular payments of a fixed amount made at specified dates. It is comparatively new and at present only such organisations as are regularly owed fixed amounts are making use of the system, and of course the prior agreement of the account holder must be obtained. Examples of the type of organisation most likely to benefit from this system are building societies, professional associations and insurance companies. The great advantage is of course that reminder correspondence about overdue subscriptions, premiums, etc. is eliminated, and the creditor does not have to rely on a standing order for payment being placed (or forgotten to be placed) by the debtor with his bank.

CREDIT CARDS

Payment by credit card is also a relatively new method; Barclaycard (Fig. 41) appeared a few years ago and in 1972 Access Cards (Fig. 43(a)). These two are not of course the only credit cards in use, *e.g.* diners cards, etc. are also credit cards. Agreement is reached as to the amount of credit the client is to be allowed and the client may shop up to that extent at those establishments which indicate that they participate in the scheme. The client does not pay in cash nor by cheque but merely signs the sales voucher and hands his credit card to the trader who extracts the particulars and returns the card to the client. The trader recovers the sum due (less a small discount) from a branch of the client's bank (which has undertaken to meet all expenses properly incurred by its client under the scheme) and the client eventually (once a month) receives a statement from the Card Centre, showing the total amount which it has paid on his behalf (Figs. 42 and 43(b)).

If the client settles the complete amount outstanding on his statement within an agreed period (usually twenty-five or twenty-eight days), no interest accrues, but if the client prefers to pay only a proportion of the outstanding amount, then interest is charged on the

Courtesy of Barclaycard

Fig. 41.—A Barclaycard.

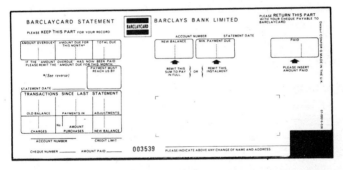

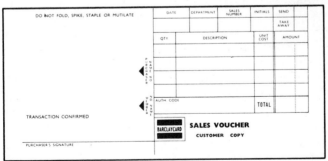

Courtesy of Barclaycard

Fig. 42.—Statement sent by credit card centre to client. At the bottom of the statement is the sales voucher sent by the credit card centre to the client (one copy of this was given to the client by the trader at the time of purchase).

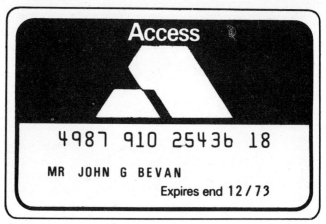

Courtesy of "Access"

(*a*) Credit card.

Courtesy of "Access"

(*b*) Statement sent by card centre to client.

Fig. 43.—The Access card system.

amount left outstanding. To the client, this system offers a sort of "shopping on credit" scheme and allows him to spread his expenses over a longer period instead of paying them in full on the day they are incurred. The scheme is an improvement on hire purchase buying because the client only pays interest if he chooses to leave a sum outstanding on his account with the Card Centre and only on such balance as he chooses to leave outstanding. Traders are induced to participate because, although it may cost them a small discount on the amount credited by the bank, they are at least assured that the bank will meet the expenses of their clients, and this is of course safer than accepting a cheque (which might not be honoured) from a shopper. The Card Centre's benefit arises from the discount which they deduct from the trader's account when they credit him with the total amount due from shoppers and from the interest charged to clients who choose not to settle the complete amount within the agreed time.

Barclaycard facilities are of course offered by Barclays Bank Ltd., and the banks participating in the Access Card scheme are Lloyds Bank Ltd., Midland Bank Ltd., National Westminster Bank Ltd. and Williams and Glyns Bank Ltd.

It is not essential for cardholders to have a bank account with a particular bank, although in many cases they do in fact have an account with the bank which is connected with the particular scheme. However, it is quite possible for a responsible person who can show a steady income (*e.g.*, salary) to apply for and be given a credit card. If the card holder has no bank account at all he may settle his account with the Card Centre by some means other than cheque, *e.g.* cash, postal order, etc.

CHEQUE CARDS

Some banks issue a cheque card to their client so that when the client wishes to pay by cheque for his shopping, he may display his cheque card to the trader (who compares the signature on the cheque card with that on the cheque and extracts certain information, *e.g.* number) before returning the card to the client. The client is assured that the trader will not hesitate to accept his cheque in payment. On his part, the trader has the bank's assurance that it will honour any cheques offered in payment by its client (up to an agreed amount shown on the cheque card, usually £30).

Both credit and cheque card schemes offer the facility of immediate withdrawal of a limited amount of cash from any branch of the bank participating in the scheme.

CASH CARDS

These are not really a method of payment in themselves but enable a client of a bank to obtain cash at a time when he cannot cash a cheque over the counter at the bank itself, *e.g.* after office hours or if there is a queue at the counter and the client is unwilling to wait. The bank issues a card to the client and, separately, he is given a personal number. If the client should urgently require limited cash (£10 per day) he may obtain this from the dispensing machine in the outer wall of the bank by inserting the card in the machine and pressing the correct digits of the personal number. The card is then taken back by the client and the cash is received in much the same way as goods from a vending machine or stamps from the outer wall of some Post Offices. In due course the client's account with the bank is debited with the amount withdrawn from the dispensing machine.

Not all branches have installed these automatic cash dispensing machines but where they are installed, the machines operate for twenty-four hours a day, seven days a week.

A slight variation of the system described above is for the account holder to be supplied with a number of vouchers instead of a cash card. After the personal code number is tapped out on the machine, the special voucher is inserted. These vouchers are then debited by the bank to the client's account as and when used.

It is of course most important to keep the personal code number secret and to carry the vouchers or the cash card in a safe place, *e.g.* the purse or wallet.

Barclays introduced the world's first automatic cash dispenser, but the system is now available with other banks also.

MONEY ORDER

A money order may be obtained from the Post Office for any sum which does not exceed £50 and does not contain a fraction of 1p. This method of payment is therefore not suitable for very small sums but it offers a safety precaution and might be used where the payee has no bank account and it is desirable that he should cash the money at a Post Office.

To buy a money order a requisition form has to be obtained from the Post Office and completed by the sender. On the requisition form should be entered the full name, title or designation of the payee and of the remitter, as well as the amount payable and the Post Office at which it is to be paid (unless payable through a bank). A money order may be crossed or uncrossed; if crossed it can only be paid through a bank. If the money order is uncrossed, an advice is sent from the issuing office to the paying office and when it is presented at the Post Office for payment, the payee will have to sign his name and give the remitter's name (as indicated on the requisition form by the sender). Payment will not be made unless this is done accurately.

It will be seen that although complete information is shown on the requisition form and that such information is transmitted to the paying office, the money order itself discloses neither the remitter's identity nor that of the payee. This information will be requested by the paying office from the person presenting the money order (he must sign his name on the money order and state the name of the remitter), before payment will be made. If therefore the money order should fall into the wrong person's hands it is unlikely that the correct information will be given and the cash will not be paid over.

Payment on a money order may be deferred for a period not exceeding ten days and if this is required, the sender should complete and sign the request on the requisition form and also draw the attention of the issuing officer to this fact at the time of purchase.

It is also possible to transfer payment of a money order from one Post Office to another and to obtain refund of a money order not presented. Both services are chargeable. If it should be necessary to alter the name of the payee or the sender, this may also be done by application to the issuing office.

To stop payment of a money order, application should be made to the paying office or, if the order is crossed, to the Giro and Remittance Services Department (M.O.B.), Post Office, Chetwynd House, Chesterfield, Derbyshire, S49 1PF.

Finally, if the sender so wishes, he will be furnished with an "advice of payment" showing the date on which the payment was made.

TELEGRAPH MONEY ORDER

Inland money orders may be transmitted to the payee by telegraph. A charge is made for the telegraph money order plus a further fixed charge for the standard telegram of advice. For an additional charge per word a private message may be sent with the order. The words "By Telegraph" must be written across the completed requisition form and if the order is to be delivered at the payee's address this should also be given in the space provided on the requisition form. As in the case of an ordinary money order, the telegraph money order may be crossed for payment through a bank and may likewise be stopped—if required the stop notice may be sent by telegram. Similarly, advice of payment will be sent by post on payment of a small fee.

If the order is left until called for at the Post Office, evidence of identity must be produced by the payee. (In the Irish Republic, the payee must either be known to the paying officer or bring some person known at the paying office to prove his identity.) Inland money orders are valid for six months (but may be renewed on payment of a fee).

Money orders may be sent to and received from many countries abroad by post or telegraph, but there may of course be special conditions affecting the various countries and Exchange Control Regulations must be observed. The period of validity for overseas money orders varies between one and twelve months, depending on the country concerned.

POSTAL ORDER

This may be purchased at most Post Offices in the country and is available in certain fixed values as follows:

5p to 25p by $2\frac{1}{2}$p steps $\Big\}$ 3p fee charged on orders up to £1.
30p to £1 by 5p steps
£2, £3, £4, £5: 6p fee charged on each order.
£6, £7, £8, £9 and £10: 8p fee charged on each order.

If it is desired to increase the value of a postal order, postage stamps may be affixed in the space provided (not more than two stamps up to the value of $4\frac{1}{2}$p).

Each postal order is provided with a counterfoil, which should be retained by the sender for his own records.

The sender should enter the payee's name on the postal order and may also indicate the office of payment or the town where the payee lives when the postal order will be paid at any Post Office in that town.

If the postal order is crossed, it may only be paid through a bank.

Payment may of course also be made at Post Offices if the order is not crossed. The payee must sign the postal order as indicated, as a form of receipt.

A postal order is normally valid for six months.

OVERSEAS POSTAL ORDERS

British postal orders are issued and paid in the Irish Republic and most countries within the British Commonwealth but may not under the current Exchange Control Regulations be sent to any place outside the Scheduled Territories (formerly known as the Sterling Area).

NATIONAL GIRO SERVICE

This is a simple, inexpensive, money transfer banking system run by the Post Office (the National Giro Centre was opened in 1968). Among the benefits offered are current account facilities, with standing order, bill paying and automatic debit transfer services between Giro accounts. Money can be paid in and taken out at some 22,000 Post Offices in the United Kingdom, but all Giro accounts are kept centrally at the National Giro Centre.

1. TRANSFERS

An account may be opened with a small initial deposit (£1) by any person over the age of fifteen years, either in a private capacity or in the name of a business. Such an account enables *transfers* to be made to other individuals or businesses who hold accounts (Fig. 44). Thus as an alternative to paying by cheque a transfer of funds is effected by the Giro centre debiting one account and crediting another on the instruction of the transferor. This instruction is given by the account holder who wishes to pay sending a transfer form (which is overprinted with his name, address and Giro account number) to the National Giro Centre. Before sending off the form he must of course insert the amount he wishes to be transferred out of his account and the Giro account number of the person into whose account the amount is to be transferred. If required, he may also add a message to the payee. The account holder is supplied with transfer forms, Giro cheques and pre-paid envelopes. There is no charge for the transfer.

2. DEPOSITS

These may also be made by an account holder into his own account free of charge. The account holder may either pay in cash at a Post Office or by cheque or warrant sent to the Giro centre for credit of his account. A completed deposit form must accompany his payment. An account holder may withdraw (by cashing cheques) up to £20 from his own account on demand at either of two Post Offices nominated by him. If an account holder has his salary paid directly into his Giro account, he may apply for a Gold Card which will enable him to draw up to £30 in cash at *any* Post Office, on alternate days, free of charge. For larger amounts, he can send a Giro cheque to the Giro centre indicating the amount he wishes to withdraw and when this is returned to him (after authentication at the Giro Centre) he may take it to any Post Office for a cash withdrawal. A small charge is made.

(a)

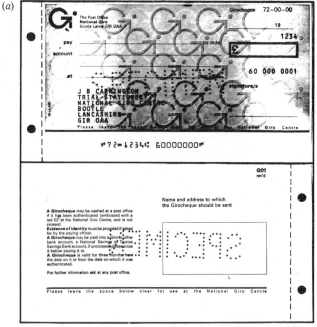

Courtesy of the Post Office

(b)

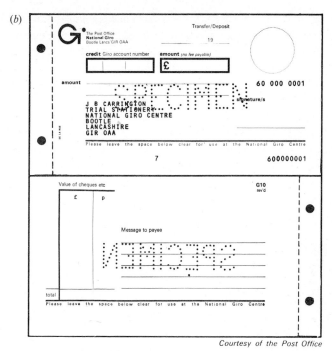

Courtesy of the Post Office

(a) Girocheque and reverse.

(b) Transfer deposit form and reverse.

Fig. 44.—The National Giro system.

3. INPAYMENTS

Anyone without a Giro account may make payments of not less than 25p to an account holder. This may be done at most Post Offices by completing the standard inpayment form (available at the Post Office) or by completing a Giro form included by many organisations as part of their bill. The payment may then be effected over the counter at the Post Office, but it must be made in cash and a charge of 10p is payable, except where the billing organisation has contracted to pay the fee. If required, a message to the payee (the account holder) may be written on the back of an inpayment form.

4. OUTPAYMENTS

If an account holder wishes to make a payment from his account to a person who does not have a Giro account he may do so on payment of a small fee. He must complete a Giro cheque and either send this direct to the payee like any other cheque (in which case it can only be paid through a bank) or he can send it to the Giro centre for authentication and onward transmission to the payee (who can then present it to any Post Office for a cash payment over the counter).

5. STANDING ORDERS

As with banks, an account holder may instruct the Giro centre to make regular payments (at fixed dates) of a specified amount to another Giro account holder until further notice is given.

6. AUTOMATIC DEBIT TRANSFER

This is a sort of direct debit not unlike that described elsewhere in this chapter under the heading of direct debit. It would be particularly useful where, for example, a business concern wished to ensure receipt of payments owed to him by other persons or business concerns. Both the debtor and the creditor must be Giro account holders and the creditor must obtain prior agreement of his debtor to the automatic debit transfer, which operates as follows: when the creditor (*e.g.*, a shopkeeper) sends a bill to his customer, he also notifies the Giro centre which (after an agreed period) automatically effects a transfer from the debtor's account to that of the creditor.

Account holders receive frequent statements showing all transactions.

Giro transfers may be made to Giro account holders in many European countries and Japan, but as with any overseas transactions involving money, Exchange Control Regulations must of course be complied with.

7. OTHER ADVANTAGES

There are two further advantages of having a Giro account:

(*a*) *Loans through Giro.* Account holders can borrow money from Mercantile Credit, a large finance house. Such loans take the form of revolving credit, under which the customer is allowed a credit limit of thirty-six times the amount of his monthly repayments, or a fixed term loan for a large sum over an agreed period.

(*b*) *Pay through Giro.* Account holders who have their pay credited directly into their accounts are given special cheap terms and facilities for a fee of £1 per half year:

(*i*) they may apply for a Gold Card with which they may cash cheques for up to £30 at any Post Office in the U.K. on alternate days six days a week;

(*ii*) they may obtain loans (*see* Loans through Giro *above*) at better terms than ordinary account holders (*i.e.*, those who do not have their pay credited direct into their account);

(*iii*) they are not charged for cashing cheques or for the supply of stationery, *e.g.* cheques, transfers and postage-paid envelopes.

A *National Giro Handbook* may be inspected at any Post Office or may be obtained free of charge on application to the Accounts Manager, National Giro Centre, Bootle, Lancs. G1R 0AA.

MAKING PAYMENTS ABROAD

Subject to current Exchange Control Regulations it is of course possible to obtain currency abroad. It is always advisable to have one's passport readily available in case it is necessary to have it endorsed with the amount of currency provided. The bank, the travel agency and/or the foreign embassy should be consulted to ascertain the currency regulations.

1. TRAVELLERS' CHEQUES

At present, more people use these than any other means of payment abroad. Travellers' cheques may be obtained in a variety of denominations, in sterling, dollars or most of the popular foreign currencies. They are signed once at the time of purchase and again at the time of payment (to shopkeeper, etc.). If lost or stolen, the value may be refunded.

2. FOREIGN CURRENCY

It is essential to have some foreign currency, if only to meet small expenses until a travellers' cheque can be changed. Regulations as to the limit (if any) imposed on the amount of cash brought into the foreign country must be ascertained from the bank or from the embassy concerned. At least a week's notice should be given to the bank, as not all branches can make foreign currency available immediately on demand.

3. EUROCHEQUE

Certain credit card holders, *e.g.* Barclaycard holders, who are also the holders of a bank account, may present their personal cheque book, together with their credit card, to any bank in Western Europe which is a member of the Eurocheque scheme (indicated by the distinctive Eurocheque sign (Fig. 45)) and cash a cheque of up to £30 sterling to be debited to the account at home in Britain. No prior arrangements are necessary, but the limit is £30 on the cheque, and the whole chequebook, not merely a single cheque, must be presented. It will of course be returned, only the cheque to be cashed being retained.

Courtesy of Barclays Bank Limited

Fig. 45.—The Eurocheque symbol.

4. MAIL OR TELEGRAPHIC TRANSFER

Whether or not a person is a customer of the bank, it is possible to ask the bank to transfer funds to a bank abroad. The foreign branch must be specified. Telegraphic transfers involve the cost of cable charge, but the transaction may be completed within a few hours.

5. OPEN CREDIT

A specific branch of the bank is instructed by the home bank to allow the customer to make withdrawals from that bank in the same way as from his own home account. For persons who are touring, it may be difficult to specify a particular branch, so open credits are less popular for overseas visits than for home travel.

6. LETTER OF CREDIT

This is an identification card and an open letter to the Bank's agents abroad, stating the limit of credit allowed to the customer (usually

£2,500 maximum £50 minimum). As withdrawals are made from various branches in various countries, the figures are entered on the letter of credit until the maximum figure is reached. As a precaution against loss or theft, it is wise to keep the two parts of the letter of credit separately, except of course when making withdrawals. This method is useful if more cash is needed than can conveniently be obtained another way, *e.g.* by carrying travellers' cheques.

7. CASH ADVANCE ON CREDIT CARD

Cash advances (usually up to £25) may be made in some overseas countries against the cardholder's account with the Card centre.

Short-answer Questions

1. What is a standing order? For what purposes is it a suitable method of payment?

2. What is the maximum amount for which a money order may be obtained?

3. Explain why a money order may be safer to post than a postal order.

4. If you wanted to send cash to someone, which postal service would you use?

5. May persons who do not have a National Giro account, nevertheless make payments to a Giro account holder, using the Giro system?

6. Why is the trader's credit (or credit transfer) method said to save time, stationery and postage costs?

7. How does the credit card system work?

8. Why are some shopkeepers reluctant to accept cheques not accompanied by a cheque card?

9. Indicate two methods whereby a person may obtain cash from a bank.

10. Is it necessary to have a bank account before applying for a credit card?

Past Examination Questions

1. Suggest two methods (other than cash) of paying salaries and indicate what advantages might be gained (*i*) by employers and (*ii*) by employees from the adoption of such methods. (*L.C.C.*)

2. Explain the difference between:

(*a*) Banker's Order and Trader's Credit;
(*b*) Crossed cheque and Open cheque;
(*c*) Money Order and Postal Order;

and give an example to show when each might be used. (*L.C.C.*)

3. State one advantage and one disadvantage to employees in being paid by each of the following methods:

(*a*) credit transfer;
(*b*) cash.   (*R.S.A.*)

4. Your offices are situated in a house which has a garden at the back. A gardener works at the weekends when the office is closed. He has no bank account. Give three ways in which his wages of £3 a week could be sent to him. State which method you consider the best and why.   (*R.S.A.*)

5. (*a*) What is a Giro cheque?

(*b*) What is the main difference between a Giro cheque and an ordinary bank cheque?   (*R.S.A.*)

6. Explain how the following banking documents are used: (*a*) credit transfer, (*b*) credit card.   (*R.S.A.*)*

7. State two advantages of using the National Giro.(*R.S.A.*)

8. Your employer wishes to introduce payment of office staff through National Giro and asks you to draft a circular letter which explains the method and suggests its advantages to the individual employee. Draft the letter.   (*R.S.A.*)

9. What is the maximum value of: (*a*) a money order; (*b*) a postal order?   (*R.S.A.*)*

10. (*a*) How much money is needed to open a National Giro account?

(*b*) What period of notice, if any, is needed to withdraw £10 from such an account.   (*R.S.A.*)

* Only part of longer question included.

CHAPTER 18

PAYMENT OF WAGES

THE SECRETARY'S ROLE IN THE PREPARATION OF WAGES

IN large organisations there is sufficient work to warrant the employment of full-time specialist staff on each aspect of wages payment, and it is unlikely that a secretary would be called upon to do the work of a specialist wages clerk. However, such division of work is not always possible—nor indeed is it always desirable—and it does often happen in practice that the secretary has to prepare the wages: either in order to help out in the wages office, or as part of her regular duties. Whatever the reason, it is as well to learn something of the procedure (and in any case, examiners in secretarial subjects are fond of inserting in their papers a question or two on this aspect).

1. THE WAGES OFFICE

Even in very small offices, it is desirable that there should be more than one person involved in the preparation of wages, and the office itself must be made secure (*a*) from theft if wages are being paid in cash and (*b*) from inquisitive persons. Some managements feel that there is security if the office is "on view," *e.g.* surrounded by transparent glass partitions; thus if any unauthorised person is in the office he is easily seen and this acts as a deterrent. Others hold the view that security is better achieved if the wages are prepared behind closed doors so that all and sundry are not tempted by tantalising glimpses of cash and/or wages sheets.

2. CONFIDENTIALITY

Whatever arrangement is chosen, it goes without saying that those involved in the preparation of wages must be trusted employees, not only because they may be handling cash but also because they are in a position to know the wages earned by a number of employees and will possibly be questioned by the office gossip or other inquisitive persons. Under no circumstances should such information be disclosed by anyone dealing with wages: if an employee does not mind other people knowing what he earns, then it is for him to tell, not anyone else.

Inquisitive people may approach the secretary in a variety of ways:

"What an interesting/difficult/important job you have—do you really prepare the wages for everyone in the office?"
"Mary was saying the other day that she earns £X per week, but I don't believe her."
"I think I ought to ask for a rise; other girls are earning more than I am, aren't they?"

It should be possible to give tactful but unrevealing answers; a poor memory, pressure of work, disinterest—all these may account for lack of information!

METHODS OF PAYING WAGES

Under the *Truck Acts* certain employees were unable to receive their wages in any form other than cash. This aspect of the Act is now outdated: few employers today would attempt to take advantage of their employees by paying them (short measure) in kind, and most employees have personal bank accounts. *The Payment of Wages Act 1960* is a permissive Act, allowing payment of wages to be made in other ways than cash with the *agreement of both employer and employee*. Thus wages may now be paid by cheque, bank transfer, National Giro, money order, etc. as well as in cash.

At the request of the employee (such request must be in writing, and must specify precisely and fully the method required), the employer may start paying in the new way as from the next pay day; or he may, in writing to the employee, agree to the request but state that he will not start paying in the new way until some future date; or he may, in writing to the employee, refuse the request. If the employer ignores the request for more than a fortnight, then it automatically lapses and the employee must make a further written request. If however the employer agrees to the request for payment of wages other than in cash, he must at or before each wage payment, give the employee a statement which shows the gross wages earned, the amount of each deduction, specifying the purpose of such deduction, and the net amount payable. The employer may not charge the employee for any new arrangement. The new arrangement now continues until either the employee or the employer gives notice to the other party that he wishes to revert to payment in cash. Four weeks' notice in writing must be given, unless both parties agree in writing to waive this period of notice. The Act makes special provisions for persons who are sick or away from work and who are being paid in cash: they may be paid by postal order or money order (without any special request on their part) unless they give written notice that they do not wish to be paid in either of these ways.

It will be seen that payment in any way other than cash is now permitted, but *only at the request of the employee*, and for more than a decade now many employees, including manual workers, have agreed to receive their wages by cheque or, more popularly, by bank transfer or, more recently, through the National Giro service. The advantages to both employer and employee are certainly worth having:

To the Employee:
> (a) He des not receive the whole of his wages in one cash sum, hence the fear of loss or theft is eliminated.
> (b) If wages are paid into his account he may draw only such amount as he requires at any time, thus only smaller sums of cash are handled (and this may be an inducement to save).
> (c) Having a bank account, he may make use of other banking facilities, *e.g.* payment of bills, subscriptions, etc.

To the Employer:
> (a) Large sums of cash need no longer be carried from the bank to the office, with consequent risk of loss, theft and possible injury to employees.
> (b) Security firms are not required and insurance terms are more beneficial.
> (c) Time is saved because individual pay-packets do not have to be made up.

1. CASH

Where wages are paid in cash, the wages cheque must be cashed at the bank, and it has been suggested (on p. 149) that arrangements for the security of the cash and the safety of the clerks must be made. Varying the time and route for collection of the cash and return to the office; sending two clerks together, one at least preferably being male; sending the employees in the office car; these are necessary and basic precautions. In addition, employers will take out "cash in transit" insurance. When the cash is brought back to the office, it must be checked (it is unlikely that time will be wasted at the bank doing this), and then it must be divided up into individual pay packets as indicated by the net amounts shown on the wages sheets. The wages cheque will of course have been "coined" (an indication shown on the back of the cheque as to how many notes and coins of each denomination are required), and when the work has been completed, all the cash should be accounted for exactly in the pay packets. Some offices use coin dispensing machines; otherwise, the pay clerk will stack the notes and coins manually, ready for use. A system must then be devised for getting the pay to the employees: either a clerk goes round to the various employees handing out the pay packets, or an arrangement is made for them to come to the wages office for collection of their pay. Some offices ask for the employee's signature on receipt of his pay. The advantage of cash payment to the employee is that he has immediately available to him the whole of his wages in cash to dispose of in any way he wishes. The disadvantages are of course the danger of loss, or of theft, not forgetting the temptation to spend!

2. CHEQUE

No handling of cash is required here. When the wages sheets have been prepared, a cheque for the net amount payable to each employee is made out. As such cheques are invariably crossed, there is little danger of theft, and they may be handed out to or collected by the employee with little additional safety precautions. The advantages to the employee are that he does not have to carry home a large sum of cash, he is not tempted to spend any of it since it is not in the form of ready cash, and he can make full use of other banking services if he opens a bank account to cash his cheques. The disadvantages are that without a bank account, he has to find someone to change his cheque into cash, and he does not have available on pay day the whole of his wages in ready cash to dispose of as he wishes. There is always the risk of loss, and finally from the employer's point of view cheques which are not presented promptly have to be accounted for in the bank reconciliation statement.

3. BANK TRANSFER AND NATIONAL GIRO

When the wages sheets have been prepared, the employer (or his wages clerk) makes out an instruction to the Bank, or to the Giro centre. This instruction is for one composite amount to be debited to the employer's account and a number of individual credits to be made to the named accounts of the employees. The great advantage to the employer is in the saving of time and stationery in making out individual cheques and in the days when stamp duty was payable on cheques, the saving effected was greater still. Bank transfer is today much favoured by employers: a single instruction to the bank is all that is required to effect payment into the account of individual employees. It is of course a requirement of the *Payment of Wages Act* 1960 that the employer should give a statement of pay to the employee, but these "payslips" need be no more than a carbon copy of the entry on the wages sheet and need not therefore involve the employer in much additional work.

The advantages to the employee are similar to those he would enjoy if he were paid by cheque: he does not have to carry large sums of money home on pay day; he is not tempted to spend his pay since he does not have it in his pocket, and he may make full use of the numerous banking services if he opens a bank account (or a National Giro account). In addition, as it is a pre-requisite that he should name an account into which his wages are to be paid, the employee does not have to find someone to cash his cheque as he would if he were paid by cheque but had no bank or Giro account.

WAGES CALCULATIONS

An employee's net wages are calculated by deducting from the gross wages all compulsory and voluntary deductions. Income tax, national insurance contributions and graduated contributions are compulsory deductions, while personal savings schemes and private hospitalisation schemes are examples of voluntary deductions which the employee may ask his employer to deduct from his pay.

1. P.A.Y.E.

The present scheme in this country for collecting income tax payable by an employee is known as P.A.Y.E. (Pay As You Earn). The amount of tax due is calculated and must be deducted by the employer *at source* (*i.e.*, before the pay reaches the employee's hands). The advantages of this system go to the employee and to the Inland Revenue, rather than to the employer, who is put in the position of having to deduct the employee's tax from his pay, and then having to remit such sums to the Inland Revenue, with all the attendant clerical work which this system necessitates. The employer is accountable to the Inland Revenue for income tax deducted. The benefit to the employee lies in the fact that he does not have to meet a large fiscal bill once or twice in the year, but merely contributes small sums weekly or monthly over the year, and even then his contributions do not have to be saved and paid by him, but are deducted by his employer before the employee has a chance to spend the money! The Inland Revenue receive monthly remittances from the employer, and do not have to collect from individual employees, thus remittances are received from a smaller number of people (one employer remits for several employees) and there is of course much less risk of bad debts arising since the employer deducts the amount due before the employee can otherwise dispose of the money.

The P.A.Y.E. method of deducting income tax applies (with very few isolated exceptions) to all income derived from offices or employments and this includes not only weekly wages and monthly salaries, but income earned by way of commission, annual bonus, etc. It should be noted that it is the employer's duty to deduct income tax from the pay of his employees and if he does not do so he may incur liability to penalties and may be required to pay over to the Inland Revenue the amount of tax which he should have deducted.

The income tax due is ascertained by reference to the employee's code number (allocated by the Inland Revenue) and to tax tables A and B–D (issued to the employer by the Inland Revenue). *Table A deals with free pay to which the employee is entitled* and *Tables B–D deal with taxable pay*—these tables may be likened to a sort of ready reckoner. The employer must account for tax deducted from the pay of his employees, and he is required to make entries on a *Deduction Card* to be kept for each employee. On this card must be included, separately, National Insurance graduated contributions. (Exceptionally, *e.g.* where a mechanised system is in operation, the employer may keep other records than the official deduction cards, provided agreement is obtained from the Tax Office.) The entries made on the deduction cards must be agreed with the amount of tax collected by the employer, and the cards must be returned to the Collector of Taxes at the end of the income tax year. (The tax year ends on 5th April and the latest date for returning the cards is the 19th April.)

Under P.A.Y.E., the amount of tax which the employer must deduct on any pay day depends on (*a*) the employee's total gross pay less any superannuation contributions for which he is entitled to tax relief, since the beginning of the income tax year, (*b*) his tax allowances (or free pay) for the same period (this is determined by his code number) and (*c*) the total tax deducted on previous pay days. Thus for each pay day, the employer first calculates the pay due to the employee and then adds to that figure the total of all previous payments made to the employee from 6th April (the beginning of the income tax year) up to date. He has now arrived at the employee's total gross pay—*see* (*a*) *above*. The employer now finds in the Free Pay Tables (Table A) for the employee's code number the proportion of the employee's allowances from 6th April up to date (*see* (*b*) *above*) and subtracts this figure from the total gross pay to date. The resulting figure is the employee's taxable pay to date. The employer now looks up this last figure in the Taxable Pay Tables (Tables B–D) to find out the total tax due to date on the employee's taxable pay. From that figure of total tax due to date the employer deducts the tax already deducted and the remainder is of course the amount of tax to be deducted from the employee's pay on the pay day in question.

This may sound complicated, but could be simply summarised as follows:

1. Find out the employee's total pay to date (since the beginning of the tax year).
2. Find out the employee's free pay entitlement (by referring to Table A).
3. Deduct the free pay from the total pay to find the employee's taxable pay.
4. Look up the figure of taxable pay in Table B to discover the total tax due.
5. Deduct from the total tax due (as shown in Table B) the tax already deducted in previous weeks, thus arriving at the tax to be deducted on the pay day in question.

If it should happen that the figure of total tax shown by the Tax Tables is less than the tax already deducted, then of course the employer must *refund* tax to the employee instead of making a deduction.

The employer must keep records of the figures of pay and tax at each pay day.

Copies of the Tax Tables should be made available by the employer to any employee who wishes to check the deductions made from his pay. Tax Tables are also available at public libraries and, of course, Tax Offices.

The employer is informed by the Tax Office of the code number that has been allocated to the employee (and similarly any future changes in an employee's code number are notified to the employer by the Tax Office), but if for any reason this information is not received in time to make the correct deduction of tax, then *a code specified for emergency use* is allocated (this is code 59L—in place of code E which was used up to 1972/73 and must be applied on a week 1 or month 1 basis). The allocation of such a code may well mean that more tax than necessary is being deducted but an adjustment and refund, if necessary, will be made when the proper code number is notified to the employer.

A code specified for emergency use (Code 59L) will be necessary:

(*a*) when no notification of code has been received for an employee on whose earnings tax is payable; or

(*b*) when form P.45 is not produced by a new employee on whose earnings tax is payable.

Form P.45 should be given to an employee by the employer when the employee leaves the employment. This is a three-part form: among the details required to be shown are the name and address of the employee, the date of leaving, his code number, including prefix or suffix, and particulars of entries made on his deduction card, *e.g.* total net pay to date (*i.e.*, gross pay less any superannuation contributions for which he is entitled to tax relief) and total tax paid to date. Part 1 of the form P.45 must be sent by the employer to the Tax Office immediately the employee leaves and parts 2 and 3 must be given to the employee. When the employee joins his new employer, he must hand parts 2 and 3 to his new employer. The latter retains part 2 (from which he is able to ascertain the tax position of his new employee) and sends part 3 to the Income Tax Office. The new employer is thus able to start making correct deductions of tax from the new employee's pay without delay. If the new employer happens to be the first employer (*e.g.*, of a school leaver), there is obviously no P.45 prepared by a former employer and until instructions are received from the Tax Office, the employer is bound to deduct tax in accordance with a code specified for emergency use. Where the new employee is liable to pay tax but has not produced a P.45, the employer should notify the Tax Office on Form P.46.

The employer should also give Form P.50 to an employee who leaves his employ unless it is known that the employee is going straight to a new employer. This form P.50 would be used to claim any refund of income tax which may be due to the employee through unemployment.

Monthly remittances (of tax deducted less tax refunded and of National Insurance graduated contributions) must be made to the Collector of Taxes by the employer. A single remittance for the total amount is sufficient but the accompanying remittance card should show how the amount is made up between income tax and national insurance graduated contributions.

As previously mentioned, at the end of the income tax year the employer must send all Deduction Cards duly agreed and completed to the Collector of Taxes. These must be accompanied by a covering certificate on Form P.35 (Employer's Annual Declaration and Certificate) and must be sent off not later than the 19th April of the year to which they relate.

Once a year (at the end of the income tax year), the employer is required to give to each employee a Certificate of Pay and Tax Deducted for the preceding year. Form P.60 is supplied for this purpose but an employer may (with Tax Office approval) use a substitute form.

An employer is required to keep records of employees' earnings for at least three years after the end of the income tax year to which the earnings relate.

There are of course many practical instances which may occur and which have not been covered by the above summary of P.A.Y.E. procedure. The Tax Office may be approached for advice and, if a secretary is actively engaged in the preparation of wages and salaries, she should obtain and make herself thoroughly familiar with the booklet entitled *The Employer's Guide to P. A.Y. E.* which is issued by the Board of Inland Revenue and is obtainable free of charge from local Tax Offices.

NOTE. It is expected that the National Insurance scheme will be radically altered in April 1975. All contributions for *employed* persons will be earnings-related and recorded on the Deduction Card. The employer will therefore no longer have to maintain National Insurance cards, nor will he have to affix National Insurance stamps thereto. Self-employed and non-employed persons will continue to keep and stamp their own cards.

2. NATIONAL INSURANCE CONTRIBUTIONS

In addition to income tax and graduated National Insurance contributions, the employer also deducts from his employees' pay their share of the flat rate National Insurance contribution. This contribution, supplemented by the employer's own contribution on behalf of his employees, and supported by the State, provides insurance cover against unemployment, sickness, industrial injury, retirement pension and a few other benefits, *e.g.* maternity and death grants.

There are three classes of contributors:

Class 1 for employed persons;
Class 2 for self-employed persons;
Class 3 for non-employed persons;

each requiring a contribution of a different value.

The employer's and employee's contributions are normally paid together in one lump sum through the purchase, by the employer, of a National Insurance stamp of the appropriate value, and this is affixed each week to the employee's National Insurance card. These stamps must be bought from a Post Office. The value of the stamp includes a separate National Health Service contribution, and, where the employee is eighteen years old or over, the employer's contribution to the Redundancy Fund.

Although it is the employer's responsibility to pay the whole contribution he may (and usually does!) deduct the employee's share from his wages.

The following points should be noted:

1. It is the employer's duty to obtain a card from his new employee and it is the employee's duty to see that a card is produced to his employer. (Cards for young persons under the age of eighteen years are obtainable through Careers Offices and for adults through local Social Security Offices.) If for any reason the employer is unable to obtain a card from his employee, he must apply to the local Social Security Office for one.

2. It is the employer's responsibility to see that his employees' cards are properly stamped. In the first instance it is his responsibility to pay the whole contribution, but he is entitled, with very few exceptions, to deduct the employee's share from the wages paid to the employee.

3. The employer normally pays the contributions by affixing a National Insurance stamp of the correct value (which he has bought from a Post Office) to the employee's insurance card. The stamps must be cancelled forthwith, usually by writing the date across the face of the stamp.

4. The employer is responsible for stamping his employees' cards for each week of employment. He is also responsible to pay for the stamp if the employee has been employed for only part of a week (but two contributions, *i.e.*, from an earlier and a subsequent employer within a week are not required: generally only the first employer is liable).

5. The employer is responsible for the safe custody of his employees' cards and he must immediately report to the local Social Security Office if any are lost, destroyed or defaced.

6. As insurance stamps represent quite a substantial sum of money, especially where cards are held for a large number of employees, some employers prefer to use the alternative methods allowed, rather than the stamping method. The two most commonly used methods are:

   (*a*) *Direct payment—schedule system.* Providing the arrangement applies to at least 100 employees, payment may be made by cheque, supported by detailed schedules.
   (*b*) *Impressed stamping.* Under certain conditions permission is given for the cards to be impressed (as with a franking machine).

   Permission must be obtained from the Department of Health and Social Security before either of these methods are adopted.

7. There are six types of national insurance cards:

   Men aged eighteen and over.
   Boys under eighteen.
   Men (special card).
   Women aged eighteen and over.
   Girls under eighteen.
   Women (special card).

Special cards are used by certain married women and

    widows who have elected not to pay contributions (apart from industrial injuries) and persons over retirement age who are treated as retired.

8. When the currency of a card expires (currency lasts for fifty-two or fifty-three weeks), the employer must surrender it to the local Social Security Office. A fresh card is then issued to him in exchange.

9. Before exchanging the card, the employer must arrange for the employee to sign his card and insert his latest address.

10. The cards may be inspected (*a*) by Inspectors under the *National Insurance Acts* at any time and (*b*) by the employee (but not necessarily more often than once a month).

11. On the termination of employment, the employer must immediately return the card to the employee. If this is not possible, *e.g.* if the employee dies, his card must be surrendered to the local Social Security Office.

12. The employer has a special duty under the Industrial Injuries Scheme to investigate any accidents occurring to his employees during the course of their employment, and (subject to minor exceptions) to keep an accident book in which employees or persons acting on their behalf may record details of such accidents.

13. Penalties may be imposed on the employer for default in complying with the above requirements.

The Employer's Guide to National Insurance Flat Rate Contributions is available, free of charge, from the Department of Health and Social Security.

3. NATIONAL INSURANCE GRADUATED CONTRIBUTIONS

Graduated National Insurance contributions came into effect in April 1961 and are designed to supplement the retirement pension with benefits graduated in relation to the payments credited: for every £7·50 (men) or £9·50 (women) which has been credited, an additional pension of $2\frac{1}{2}$p will be paid on retirement. These contributions must normally be paid for any employee aged eighteen years or over whose pay exceeds £9 in any income tax week, but there are exceptions, *e.g.* retirement pensioners and employees over sixty-five (women) or seventy (men).

An employer may apply for a Certificate of Non-participation if he wishes his employees to be "contracted out" of the graduated National Insurance scheme; if the certificate is granted, a reduced contribution becomes payable (note that the contribution is not completely eliminated, merely reduced, even if the employee is "contracted out"). This Certificate of Non-participation is not granted automatically on application: it will normally only be granted if the pension scheme offered by the employer is not less beneficial to the employee than the State scheme.

Equal graduated contributions must be made by both employers and employees, and such contributions are additional to and are collected separately from those made through the purchase of National Insurance stamps. The method of collection is through the P.A.Y.E. system. The employee's share of the contribution is entered on his Deduction Card (required under the P.A.Y.E. scheme), and it is the employer's duty to remit the correct amount together with the monthly payments of income tax due under P.A.Y.E. to the Collector of Taxes. A single cheque for the total amount is sufficient, but the remittance card which accompanies the cheque must show how that amount is made up between income tax and graduated national insurance contributions. The employer's contribution is always the same amount as the employee's share, but as only the employee's share is shown on the Deduction Card, the remittance sent to the Collector of Taxes (in respect of the National Insurance graduated contribution) will of course always be twice the amount shown on the Deduction Card.

Just as tax tables are used in the P.A.Y.E. scheme for income tax, so special Graduated Contribution Tables (available from Social Security Offices) are used to read off the correct amount of the graduated National Insurance contribution.

The Employer's Guide to National Insurance Graduated Contributions is available, free of charge, from the Department of Social Security.

Short-answer Questions

1. Give two methods of paying wages to an employee.
2. Give two advantages to the employee of having his wages paid into his bank account.

3. Give two advantages to the employer of paying employees' wages into their bank accounts.

4. What does P.A.Y.E. stand for?

5. What is tax form P.45 used for? How many parts does it have?

6. When should tax form P.46 be sent to the Tax Office?

7. Why is income tax sometimes deducted at emergency rates?

8. What are Tax Tables A and B used for?

9. How may National Insurance contributions be paid for other than by buying stamps and affixing them on the employee's National Insurance card?

10. How are National Insurance graduated contributions paid?

Past Examination Questions

1. Explain briefly the purpose of a code number in connection with P.A.Y.E.   (*R.S.A.*)

2. What does an employer do with the money he collects from his employees for the following:

(*a*) P.A.Y.E.; (*b*) National Insurance contributions; (*c*) Graduated contributions?   (*R.S.A.*)

3. Copy the following passage, filling in the blank spaces with the appropriate words taken from the list given below:

P.A.Y.E. is a tax imposed by the ......, and is a system by which income tax is deducted from ...... and .... It is deducted from any income received from ...... The ...... under this system, pays his income tax as he ...... The amount of tax on the employee's earnings is ascertained from the ...... Each card shows the ...... given to an employee, and is based on the ...... to which he is entitled. ...... are supplied for each week or month in the year, and the ...... refers to these, to the employee's ...... and to his code number, to see how much tax must be deducted.   (*R.S.A.*)

wages	government
employment	[tax] deduction card
code number	salaries
employer	gross earnings
allowances	tax tables
employee	earns

4. What is the difference between P.A.Y.E. and National Insurance? Explain briefly why such deductions are made from your salary. (R.S.A.)

5. When dealing with P.A.Y.E. what do you understand by:

(a) free pay; (b) refund; (c) emergency coding? (R.S.A.)

6. State briefly the advantages and/or the disadvantages of the P.A.Y.E. system of collecting income tax

(a) to the state; (b) to the employer; (c) to the employee. (R.S.A.)

7. What income tax document must a new employee produce on his arrival? What is the purpose of this document and what must be done if the employee does not bring it with him? (R.S.A.)

8. State briefly what is meant by:

(a) P.A.Y.E. code numbers; (b) tax deduction tables. (R.S.A.)

9. Give three examples of statutory deductions from salary and three examples of voluntary deductions. (R.S.A.)

10. What are forms P.45, P.60 and P.46 and what is their purpose? (L.C.C.)*

* Only part of longer question included.

CHAPTER 19

PETTY CASH

USES OF PETTY CASH

IN most offices it is necessary to keep a limited amount of ready cash available to meet small day-to-day expenses. For example, it may be necessary to pay an odd-job man in cash rather than by cheque. If the supply of typewriter ribbons or ball point pens runs out unexpectedly, the secretary may have to purchase one or two immediately and it would be rather ridiculous to offer a cheque or a postal order to a shopkeeper for ten or fifteen pence. Taxi fares, a special newspaper or periodical, stamps, office tea, sugar and milk—all these and many other small expenses may be drawn from the petty cash box.

It is usual to keep such petty cash in a businesslike manner. A petty cash box may be purchased for a small sum at most stationers' and such a box is better than a biscuit tin or some other such container, as it has separate compartments for various denominations of coin, notes and receipted vouchers, and is fitted with a lock and key.

THE PETTY CASH BOOK

A proper petty cash book should always be kept, and this is really part of the double entry book-keeping of the firm. It may, in fact, be regarded as a sub-division of the cash book, recording in full detail the small day-to-day expenses which are too small and numerous to be shown singly in the cash book itself. Therefore, when cash is received by the petty cashier (often the secretary herself) and entered in the petty cash book, she must make a debit entry in the petty cash book and, to complete the double entry, a credit entry in the cash book. We are not here concerned with detailed book-keeping and it will suffice if the secretary realises that in the accounting ledgers of most companies accounts are kept under various titles, including travelling expenses, postage, stationery, general office expenses, etc. Where petty cash is required for expenses under such account titles, they are analysed on the credit side of the petty cash book.

A typical petty cash book ruling might appear as in Fig. 46.

(Debit side)					(Credit side)			
Cash received £	Date	Description	Voucher No.	Total £	Travelling Expenses £	Postage £	Stationery £	General Office Expenses £

Fig. 46.—Petty cash book rulings.

The amount of cash which has been decided on as the "float" (the amount required for the week or month until a further drawing of cash is made) is received by the petty cashier and entered on the debit side of the petty cash book, together with the date (Fig. 47).

Cash Received £	Date	Description
	19.. Jan.	
10	1	To Cash(CB)

Fig. 47.—Petty cash book rulings: cash received.

As expenses are incurred, the petty cashier uses the cash from her petty cash box (which it can be seen, contained £10) and replaces such cash with receipts or petty cash vouchers, so that at any one time the total float is represented in the petty cash box by cash and/or vouchers. Periodically, she will clear the box of vouchers by first entering them in the petty cash box, ticking (or otherwise marking) them to indicate that this has been done, and then filing them away in numerical order. Expenses entered on the credit side of the petty cash book might appear as in Fig. 48.

It will be noted that the date on which the expense was incurred is shown; under the heading of "description" is an indication of what the expense was for; this is analysed further along into the various account titles; the voucher is given a consecutive number which is also entered in the appropriate column; and finally the total amount spent as shown on the voucher is reproduced in the "total" column.

Date	Description	Voucher No.	Total £	Travelling Expenses £	Postage £	Stationery £	General Office Expenses £
Jan. 3	Taxi to Old Broad Street (for Board Meeting)	1	1.25	1.25			
4	Biro; milk	2	0.15			0.10	0.05
15	Recorded delivery to Mr. Brown	3	0.07		0.07		

Fig. 48.—Petty cash book rulings: credit entries.

This will eventually show how much must be credited to the cash book (and debited to the petty cash book) to make up the amount of the float once again.

In Fig. 49 is reproduced the same page from the petty cash book, showing both the original amount received of £10 and the expenses to the 15th of January.

Cash Received £	Date	Description	Voucher No.	Total £	Travelling Expenses £	Postage £	Stationery £	General Office Expenses £
10	19 Jan. 1	To Cash (CB)						
	3	Taxi to Old Broad Street (for Board Meeting)	1	1.25	1.25			
	4	Biro and milk	2	0.15			0.10	0.05
	15	Recorded delivery to Mr. Brown	3	0.07		0.07		

Fig. 49.—Petty cash book rulings: credit and debit entries.

If the petty cash book is to be balanced on the 15th of the month, then the "total" column must be added up and cross-cast with the analysis columns to check the accuracy of the figures. The "total" column will show how much has been spent, and therefore how much must be drawn to make up the total float once again. The double entry is effected (as previously stated) by debiting the petty cash book and crediting the cash book, and this is indicated by cross-referencing each account so that the petty cash book shows the letters CB (cash book) and the cash book shows the letters PCB (petty cash book) against the entries. Our page now looks something like Fig. 50.

Cash Received £	Date	Description	Voucher No.	Total £	Travelling Expenses £	Postage £	Stationery £	General Office Expenses £
	19.. Jan.							
10	1	To Cash (CB)						
	3	Taxi to Old Broad Street (for Board Meeting)	1	1.25	1.25			
	4	Biro and milk	2	0.15			0.10	0.05
	15	Recorded delivery to Mr. Brown	3	0.07		0.07		
1.47	15	To Cash (CB)		1.47	1.25	0.07	0.10	0.05
		Balance c/d		10.00	L1	L3	L5	L7
11.47				11.47				
10.00	15	To Balance b/d						

Fig. 50.—Petty cash rulings: completed entries.

The only items not accounted for are the mysterious L1, L3, L5 and L7, which merely represent the folio numbers of the accounts into which these entries have been posted.

The system just described is known as the *Imprest System*. If it sounds at all complicated, this is possibly because it has been described in great detail. It could be shown in a different formula: imprest system means replenishing the petty cash by drawing from the bank the amount of cash which has been spent in a given period in order to bring back the float to the correct figure. It really is as simple as that!

It is not of course essential to keep petty cash on the imprest system and, if required, sums may be drawn as and when required, without maintaining a float at a constant figure.

Whatever the system used, the person in charge of petty cash should be very careful to keep it in a proper box carefully locked away when not in use. Whenever cash is taken out of the box, something else (voucher or receipt) should be put into the box, so that whenever the box is examined, the total sum originally drawn from the bank can be accounted for. Apart from periodic internal auditing, the auditors of the company will probably examine not only the petty cash book itself, but the supporting vouchers, receipts, etc.

Petty cash should only be given out against a properly authorised petty cash voucher (to which may be attached a supporting receipt); the voucher should indicate the date the expenditure was incurred, the reason for the expenditure, the signature of the person authorising the expenditure, and the signature of the person who has received the cash. It is usual for only one or two responsible members of staff to have the power to authorise petty cash vouchers. When the voucher is entered up in the petty cash book, it will also be given a consecutive number.

Figure 51 is an example of a petty cash voucher.

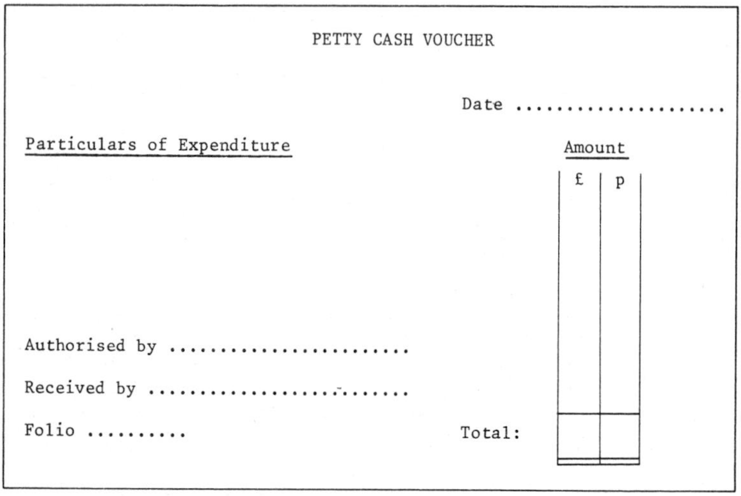
PETTY CASH VOUCHER

Date ....

Particulars of Expenditure

Amount

£ | p

Authorised by ....

Received by ....

Folio ....

Total:

Fig. 51.—A petty cash voucher.

Short-answer Questions

1. Describe two methods of drawing petty cash.
2. What is a "float" in connection with petty cash?
3. Why is it necessary for all petty cash disbursements to be supported by petty cash vouchers?
4. How can you check, at any given time, whether the balance left in your petty cash box is accurate?
5. What information should be shown on a petty cash voucher?
6. Why are items of expenditure usually "analysed" when entered in the petty cash book?
7. Two signatures often appear on a petty cash voucher; whose are these?
8. Suggest three items of expenditure which might be made from

petty cash and give the title of the accounts to which they would eventually be posted.

9. What two entries are made when cash is drawn for petty cash?

10. Why is it necessary to keep petty cash in the office?

Past Examination Questions

1. Consider carefully the extract from a Petty Cash Book on p. 242, and then answer the following questions.

(*a*) What do you call this system of recording petty cash transactions?

(*b*) What is the purpose of this system?

(*c*) What is the purpose of the column headed "Voucher No."?

(*d*) What do you understand by "L93"?

(*e*) On 7th June, £10·27 is shown as cash received. How was this amount determined?   (*R.S.A.*)**

2. The total of petty cash vouchers together with the money remaining in the petty cash box should always equal the petty cash float. Explain this.   (*R.S.A.*)

3. Give the headings of four expenditure columns, other than the total, that you might find in a petty cash book.   (*R.S.A.*)

4. Why would you expect to find two signatures on a completed petty cash voucher?   (*R.S.A.*)

5. Draw up the complete a petty cash voucher.   (*R.S.A.*)

6. You are in charge of the petty cash which is operated on the imprest system, your float being £15. Cash is drawn to restore the float on the last day of each month. Make the following entries:

September 8th   £1·50 is spent on stamps.

September 11th   You pay out £0·75 to the window cleaner.

September 15th   A parcel is delivered C.O.D.; the charge is £2·25.

September 25th   You buy tea and sugar for the office and spend £0·25.

October 3rd   Stamps again cost £1·50.

October 6th   You pay the milkman £0·75.

October 31st   The office boy draws £0·25 for fares for delivering a parcel.   (*R.S.A.*)**

RECEIPTS	1974		Details	VOUCHER NO.	TOTAL	STATIONERY	POSTAGE	OFFICE EXPENSES	TRAVELLING EXPENSES
25	JUN	1	Balance b/d						
		3	Laundry	136	78			78	
			Date stamp & pad	137	74	74			
			Stamps	138	45		45		
		4	Shorthand note books	139	1 18	1 18			
			First aid supplies	140	36			36	
		5	J. Jones - Birmingham	141	2 47				2 47
			Registered Letter	142	19		19		
			Milk	143	54			54	
		6	S. Smith - Manchester	144	3 56				3 56
				CB 21	10 27	1 92	64	1 68	6 03
10 27		7	Cash		25 -				
			Balance c/d		35 27				
£35 27					35 27	£ 93	£ 81	£ 75	£ 95
25 -		8	Balance b/d						

7. You work for a firm where you are in charge of petty cash. The firm has three departments and expenses are allocated accordingly. These departments are Sales, Purchases and Publicity. You are allowed to pay out petty cash up to £1, provided that the voucher is correctly completed.

(*a*) What would you look for before paying money out against a voucher?

(*b*) Draw up a voucher showing the necessary entries.

(*R.S.A.*)

8. What do you understand by: (*i*) petty cash vouchers; (*ii*) an imprest system of petty cash? (*R.S.A.*)*

9. What is the purpose of a Petty Cash Book? Give examples of items of expense which you would expect to find as column headings in a Petty Cash Book. What particulars would you expect to find on the debit side? (*R.S.A.*)

10. (*a*) Draw up a form for use as petty cash voucher.

(*b*) Explain the meaning of imprest system. (*L.C.C.*)

* Only part of a longer question included.
** This question has been decimalised.

CHAPTER 20

PICTORIAL REPRESENTATION OF
INFORMATION

WHY SHOW INFORMATION PICTORIALLY?

IT has already been stated that the *raison d'être* of the office is to deal
with information. The purpose of showing information in graphic or
pictorial form is to make that information more meaningful (to
indicate a comparison or a future trend, for example) and more
quickly understood (a soaring line graph shows a rise more clearly
and emphatically than a written sentence or even tabulated figures).

Diagrams and pictures also overcome language barriers—think
how road signs can be easily understood by foreign motorists (Fig. 52).

 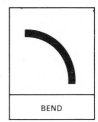 

ROAD
NARROWS

BEND

ROUND
ABOUT

Fig. 52.—Pictorial diagrams.

Finally, a picture or diagram, once seen, is often more readily
recalled to mind than information given to the brain aurally. This is
one of the reasons why so many concerns adopt distinctive trade
marks: their goods are recognised not only by the name of the
company but by the representative symbol. When a decision has to
be reached in the light of certain information, it is important that the
information should be presented in as meaningful a manner as possible. Thus, a review of the sales figures for certain lines of goods
sold might show that line X made a profit of £1,000 in 1965, £1,500
in 1966, £1,750 in 1967, £2,000 in 1968 and £2,250 in 1969, and
line Y made a profit of £1,500 in 1965, £2,000 in 1966, £3,750 in

1967, £3,500 in 1968 and £4,000 in 1969. It would be correct to assume from these figures that both line X and line Y are making a profit for the firm. However, if graphs of these figures are plotted, the picture in Fig. 53 emerges. It now becomes clear at a glance that although both lines are indeed earning a profit, line Y is earning a greater profit than line X and it would therefore pay to increase production of that line rather than of line X. The information depicted is *more meaningful* and the meaning itself can be ascertained *more quickly*.

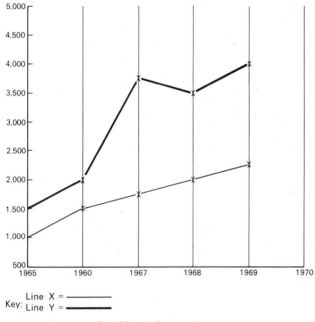

Fig. 53.—A line graph.

Graphs and charts are often used to ascertain *trends* (in the above example there is an upward trend of sales) and for purposes of *comparison* (again, in the above example line X has been compared with line Y).

TYPES OF DIAGRAM

1. BAR GRAPH

A bar graph serves much the same purpose as the line graph, and the figures used in Fig. 53 may be represented as in Fig. 54.

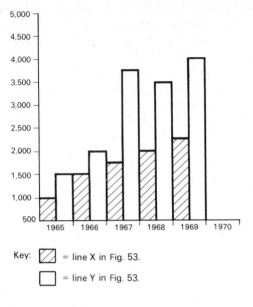

Key: ▨ = line X in Fig. 53.

□ = line Y in Fig. 53.

Fig. 54.—A bar graph.

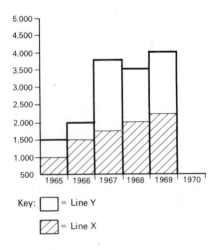

Key: □ = Line Y

▨ = Line X

Fig. 55.—A compound bar graph.

2. COMPOUND BAR GRAPH
This is a variation of the bar graph, showing more than one item plotted within the same area, as in Fig. 55.

3. PIE CHART
In this type of picture, the weight of the figures is represented by the size of a slice of the pie (Fig. 56). It can be seen at a glance that sales

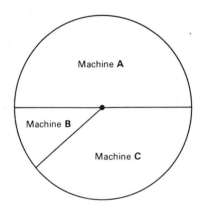

Fig. 56.—A pie chart.

of machine A account for 50 per cent of the total sales; machine B accounts for $12\frac{1}{2}$ per cent and machine C for $37\frac{1}{2}$ per cent of total sales.

4. SIGNALS AND CONTROL CHARTS
Statistical information may also be recorded by coloured signals on a pegboard frame, *e.g.* the graph is plotted by clipping small plastic signals on to a frame on the wall. When the information is no longer required, the signals are easily removed and stored for future use. These are sometimes called visual control charts, as they are used for control purposes.

5. KEY
Whatever type of chart or graph is used, the key to the code or colour should never be omitted; note the prominence given to the key in each of the preceding examples.

Short-answer Questions

1. Name and describe two kinds of graphs.

2. Why are graphs and diagrams sometimes used?

3. What is a pie chart?

4. Which would you choose to compare the sales of two machines: a pie chart or a line graph?

5. What is a compound bar graph?

6. What is a "key" on a chart or graph?

7. Draw a pie chart (freehand) to show that 75 per cent of the funds received by a charitable organisation is applied directly to those whom it is intended to benefit, $12\frac{1}{2}$ per cent to paid workers and $12\frac{1}{2}$ per cent to overheads such as heat, light, rent.

8. Plot a line graph (freehand) to show that in December 1969, 1,000 Christmas trees were sold, in December 1970, 1,500 trees were sold, in December 1971, 3,000 trees were sold and in December 1972, 2,500 trees were sold.

9. Show the same information as in 8 above in the form of a bar graph.

10. Why might you use removable signals on a pegboard instead of a graph plotted in pen and ink?

Past Examination Questions

1. Construct a line graph from the following information to show the comparative sales of a London branch and a provincial branch of a trading concern:

	London	Provincial
1950	£5,000	£20,000
1951	£10,000	£17,000
1952	£12,000	£15,000
1953	£15,000	£10,000
1954	£17,000	£8,000
1955	£12,000	£12,000
1956	£10,000	£20,000
1957	£4,000	£23,000
		(R.S.A.)

2. The diagram on facing page shows in £m the value of imports and exports for a period of three-and-a-half years, each year being divided into its four quarters. Answer the following questions:

(*i*) What kind of graph is this?

(*ii*) What are the names given to the lines along which the £m and the years are shown?

(*iii*) At what period did imports exceed exports by the greatest amount?

(*iv*) In what periods did exports exceed imports?

(*v*) How large was the greatest gap between imports and exports?

(*vi*) What was the difference between the gap at the beginning of 1961 and the gap at the end of the second quarter of 1964?

(*R.S.A.*)

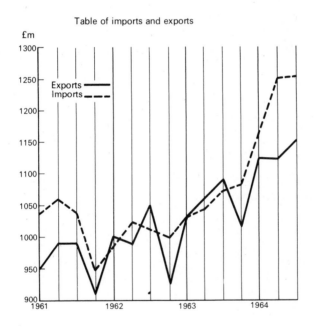

Table of imports and exports

3. Draw a pie chart showing the information given below:

The turnover of a garage consists of:

Sales of cars—50%
Sales of accessories—25%
Sales of petrol and oil—25%   (*R.S.A.*)

4. Explain, with illustrations, the purpose of

(*a*) a bar graph,   (*b*) a line graph,   (*c*) a pie chart.

                                          (*R.S.A.*)

5. The sales returns for your firm in the financial year 1968–69 were divided between branches in the following way:

       Plymouth   —25%
       Exeter   —12½%
       Bath   —12½%
       Southampton—50%

For 1969–70 the percentages were:

       Plymouth   —37½%
       Exeter   —10%
       Bath   —15%
       Southampton—37½%

Draw pie charts to illustrate this information.   (*R.S.A.*)

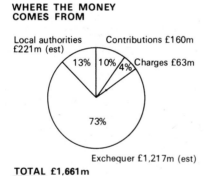

WHERE THE MONEY COMES FROM

Local authorities £221m (est)   Contributions £160m

13%   10%   4%   Charges £63m

73%

Exchequer £1,217m (est)

TOTAL £1,661m

WHERE THE MONEY GOES

Hospital services £821m

Miscellaneous, including administration £38m (est)

Local Health and Welfare services £268m (est)

2%

17%

6%

10%

8%

2%

6%

49%

Hospital capital expenditure £104m

Local authority capital expenditure £30m (est)

GPs £129m

Prescriptions £169m

Dentists and Opticians £102m

TOTAL £1,661m

6. The two charts shown on opposite page indicate National Health Service income and expenditure.

(*a*) What type of chart are they?

(*b*) What is the advantage of displaying information in this way?

(*c*) Set out in detail, but in list form, what you learn from them.

(R.S.A.)

7. Your employer runs a poultry farm. He has been experimenting by feeding one group of birds with food into which special chemicals are mixed, and the other on their normal rations. He wishes you to construct two graphs on the same axis in 4-week periods to compare the average number of eggs per bird laid by each group.

The figures are:

4-weekly periods	Group A (*fed with special chemicals*)	Group B (*fed on normal rations*)
1	14	12
2	18	15
3	22	19
4	20	18
5	17	15
6	15	13
7	15	13
8	12	12
9	15	15
10	4	5
11	6	7
12	11	12
13	11	9

(R.S.A.)

8. From the chart printed on p. 252, state:

(*a*) in which years home sales exceeded £10,000;

(*b*) in which years home sales exceeded 50 per cent of total sales;

(*c*) in which years total sales exceeded £35,000. (R.S.A.)

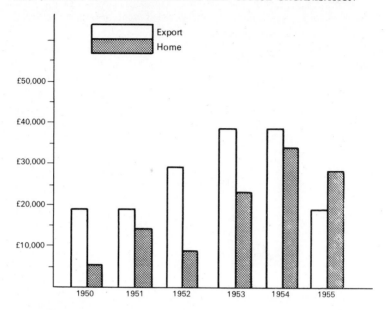

9. Describe and illustrate three different types of charts and give two examples in each case to show how such charts might be used in the office. (*L.C.C.*)

10. (*i*) What are the advantages of recording statistical data in graphic form?

(*ii*) Expalin the difference between a line chart and a bar chart and give an example to show when each might be used.

(*L.C.C.*)

CHAPTER 21

OFFICE MACHINES: I

REPROGRAPHY

THIS is a comparatively new word in the English language. It contains the prefix "re," meaning once more, the same again, repetition, and the suffix "graphy" which we get from the Greek word meaning writing. The meaning of the word reprography is therefore clear: writing or copying again; reproducing; duplicating: it is obviously used in connection with copying or duplicating requirements.

Reprography can be broadly divided into two main categories: duplicating, which conveys an idea of reproducing large numbers of copies, *i.e.* many copies made from one prepared master copy, and copying, which is normally associated with fewer copies or single copies made from one original. It will be seen from the description of the machines and their capabilities which follows that the dividing line between the two categories is not always very well defined, especially since the manufacturers of office equipment are constantly improving their equipment in an attempt to meet the ever-increasing office requirements. However, broadly speaking, the distinction between duplicating and copying remains as indicated above.

Whether a machine comes under the category of a duplicator or a copier depends on the length of run for which it is suitable. This is not the same as saying that it depends on the length of run with which it can cope. A brief example will show the difference: while a duplicator can duplicate from one master either a single copy or one hundred copies, it is obviously uneconomical and therefore unsuitable to prepare a master, to set up the machine and then to operate it for only a single copy or for a very short run of say four or five copies. The reverse is true of copiers: while a copier can make a copy of an original and the process repeated many times over for, say, one hundred copies, this becomes a very slow and very costly process and it is therefore unsuitable.

It can be said therefore that duplicators are suitable for long runs (over one hundred copies) and for medium runs (ten–100 copies) while copiers are suitable for very short runs (say up to ten copies).

DUPLICATORS

Although there are very many duplicators on the market, the different processes involved are (luckily for the student secretary!) comparatively few.

1. THE INK PROCESS

This method is also known as stencil duplicating. Basically, the master consists of a thin, wax-like sheet. The image is made directly on to the master either by writing (with a stylus—an instrument with a smooth point, not unlike a ball point pen) or by typing—an ordinary typewriter will do, providing the ribbon has been disengaged. As the master is quite flimsy, the impact of writing or typing on it makes holes through it: if the stencil is held up to the light it is possible to see the light coming through the outline of the image. Sometimes, if the typist's touch is too heavy, or if her typewriter cuts too sharply, the letter "o" may fall quite away from the stencil! If this remains uncorrected, the result will be a duplicated copy with all the "o"s shown as a blob of ink. The minute piece of stencil which has fallen out (or another piece cut from the unused end of the stencil)

Courtesy of Gestetner Limited

(a) Gestetner ink stencil machine, showing stencil master attached to the machine.

POSITION OF INK
SELECTOR KNOB   CYLINDER INKING   COPY DELIVERED

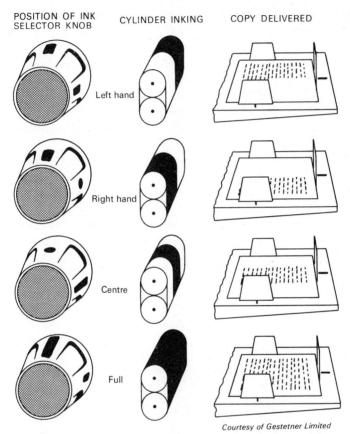

Left hand

Right hand

Centre

Full

Courtesy of Gestetner Limited

(*b*) Gestetner inking system, showing position control.

Fig. 57.—A Gestetner duplicator.

must be inserted in place. It can be stuck in position with correcting
fluid and the typist must then type over it (but not too heavily or the
whole operation will have been in vain). However, prevention is
better than cure and where this fault is troublesome it is well worth
buying those transparent protective sheets which are placed over
the stencil and which come between it and the keys of the typewriter, thus encouraging an even impression and avoiding too sharp
a touch.

When the stencil has been typed it is placed on the machine—face downwards—and ink applied to it. It is obvious that under pressure, the ink seeps through the perforations made in the stencil by the typing and when blank copy paper is applied to the stencil a copy is obtained.

In all reproduction work it is necessary to obtain a mirror image from which a positive picture is then produced; this is achieved in the stencil process by applying the stencil to the machine face downwards so that a reverse image is presented to the copy paper and from which a positive image is obtained by physical contact with the copy paper.

The best results are obtained on semi-absorbent paper: the ink is quickly absorbed and the paper dried before the next sheet is ejected from the machine (the idea being to prevent set-off on the reverse of each sheet which falls on top of one which has not completely dried). However, semi-absorbent paper may not always be suitable, *e.g.* it is unsuitable for subsequent writing by hand with a fountain pen, and it gives an appearance of cheap quality. It is therefore possible to use better quality, non-absorbent paper and to avoid set-off and smudg-

Courtesy of Roneo Vickers Limited

Fig. 58.—Roneo duplicator with spray attachment.

ing by the use of an attachment to the machine, which sprays each sheet with a chalk-like drying powder as it is ejected from the machine, thus drying each sheet before the next one settles over it (Fig. 58). Another method of avoiding set-off and smudging is by interleaving, but it will be appreciated that this method is slower since the blank sheets must later be withdrawn.

There are two main types of machine for ink stencils: one in which the ink is transferred to rollers which ink a screen against which the master is placed (Fig. 60(*a*))—an example is the well-known Gestetner duplicator pictured in Fig. 57—and the other has a hollow

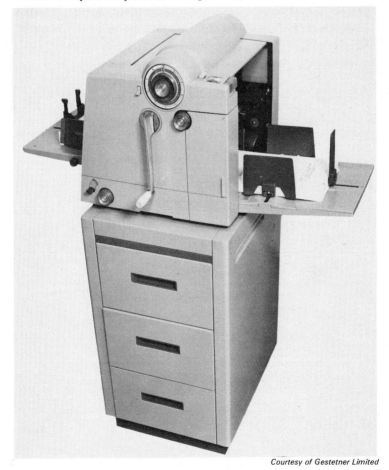

Courtesy of Gestetner Limited

Fig. 59.—A Gestetner duplicator.

drum into which the ink is poured (Fig. 60(*b*)). This drum or cylinder is part solid metal and part porous material. When the stencil is affixed to the porous part of the drum, the ink seeps through (by sheer gravity) and covers the stencil. Blank copy paper is then applied to the inked master and a duplicated copy is obtained in much the same way as with the machine previously described.

It will be seen that the process of obtaining copies is identical with both machines; only the type of machine by which the process is carried out is different. Where the machine used is of the type with a hollow drum into which the ink is poured, it is of course necessary to ensure that while the duplicator is at rest the porous part of the drum is uppermost otherwise the ink would seep through and the operator would have an inky mess to clear up!

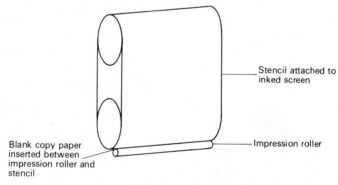

Stencil attached to inked screen

Blank copy paper inserted between impression roller and stencil

Impression roller

(*a*) Gestetner system.

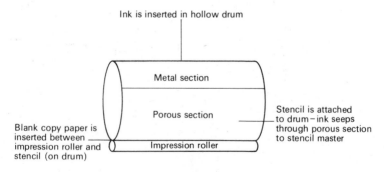

Ink is inserted in hollow drum

Metal section

Porous section

Stencil is attached to drum – ink seeps through porous section to stencil master

Blank copy paper is inserted between impression roller and stencil (on drum)

Impression roller

(*b*) Roneo system.

Fig. 60.—Diagrams of ink duplicating (stencil) systems.

(a) *Correcting an ink stencil.* Correcting fluid is available to fill the perforations made by typing or writing on the master. The method which gives best results is as follows: first rub lightly with the finger nail over the error to bring together the fibres of the material; now separate the master from its backing sheet either by keeping the two apart with the hand or by inserting a ruler or pencil between them; paint over the error and allow to dry (a matter of seconds) before removing the ruler and typing over the error with a sharp, even touch.

For correction of larger errors, grafting may be necessary. That part of the stencil containing the error is cut out—even if it is as much as a complete paragraph; the correct paragraph is then typed on another stencil and that piece is cut out and inserted in position on the first master. It is held in position—or stuck there—by painting around the edges with correcting fluid and "sticking" them together.

(b) *Storing an ink stencil.* If the stencil is to be used again, it must be cleaned after being removed from the duplicator. It is usually sufficient to lay it over a flat surface, *e.g.* a table, which has been protected with blotting paper or scrap duplicating paper. The master is then blotted several times to remove as much excess ink from it as possible. If a more thorough job of cleaning is required, the stencil may be cleaned further with a soft cloth dipped in special cleaning fluid, but this is not normally essential and is time-consuming. When all excess ink has been removed, the stencil must be stored in such a way that no pressure is applied to it, otherwise it will be damaged. For example, to store it flat and then place a heavy file on top of it would squash it and possibly damage the flimsy material. It is therefore possible to buy special frames which accommodate the stencils and which can be suspended from rods, in much the same way as coathangers are suspended from a rail.

(c) *Length of run for ink stencils.* Depending on the quality of the master stencil used, it is possible to obtain as many as 6,000 copies from one master. However, this is generally regarded as a maximum figure and the machine is normally used when runs ranging between say, 100 and 1,000 copies are required. These figures are of necessity a generalisation only. It will be appreciated that where the stencil is heavily ruled, especially where the lines cross one another, the life of the master will be considerably shortened, since these lines are the weakest parts of the stencil and will soon result in a tear. Similarly, if the operator is unskilled and allows the stencil to crease when affixing it to the duplicator, she will have to ease away these creases and this may also shorten the life of the master.

(d) *Multi-colour work with ink duplicating.* It is necessary to type two or more stencils, depending on the number of colours required. The duplicator must be cleaned each time a different colour of ink is used and when the required number of copies of one colour have been "run off," these same sheets are fed through once again, using a different master and a different colour of ink. The result will be two-colour work. Great care must be taken to ensure that registration is accurate, otherwise the effect will be spoiled.

It is probably easier to effect a change of colour with the machine of the type where the ink is accommodated inside a hollow cylinder, since the complete cylinder is easily removed and a spare one containing a different colour of ink can be inserted in its place. Obviously less cleaning is involved.

2. THE SPIRIT PROCESS

This method is also known as hectograph duplicating. In this process, the master is made by typing or by writing on a sheet of paper (preferably the special glossy art paper available, although this is not essential) which is backed by a separate, specially coated transfer sheet (Fig. 61). The transfer sheet looks like carbon paper but is in fact coated with a special dye which is easily removed by spirit. It is essential to remember to place the coated side of the transfer sheet against the glossy side of the master and to type on the matt side of the master (Fig. 62). The result will be a reverse image on the glossy side of the master. The transfer sheet is then discarded and the master placed—reverse image upwards—over the cylinder of the duplicator. As the blank copy paper is fed through the machine it is damped by a pad saturated with spirit and before the paper has time to dry it is pressed against the coated image on the reverse of the master. Since the dye on the image is easily removed by spirit, it will be understood that the spirit-damped copy paper will receive an impression from the master and a positive copy is thus obtained.

The best results are obtained by using non-absorbent paper, since

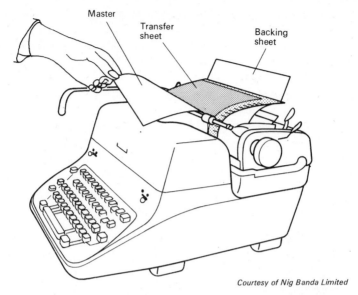

Courtesy of Nig Banda Limited

Fig. 61.—A typewriter showing spirit master, transfer and backing sheet.

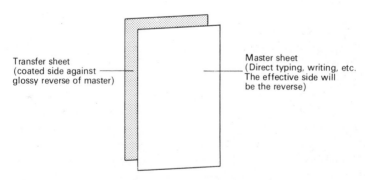

Transfer sheet
(coated side against
glossy reverse of master)

Master sheet
(Direct typing, writing, etc.
The effective side will
be the reverse)

Fig. 62.—Master for spirit duplicating.

the spirit would otherwise easily soak through and would dry before the paper was applied to the master.

No ink is used other than the dye on the transfer sheet and the only liquid is the spirit which is contained in a small tank in the machine. This process is therefore quite clean although the dye tends to "fly" and the operator may find some of it on her hands. It is, however, easily removed.

(*a*) *Correcting a spirit master.* Unlike ordinary carbon paper, the transfer sheet or special "carbon" paper can be used only once. When an impression has been taken from it, the dye from that part is removed from the sheet and affixed instead to the master: it is therefore necessary to remove the dye from the master and to overtype the correct word after a fresh piece of "carbon" has been placed over the original "carbon." The dye can be removed from the master by obliterating it (a special fluid is available to paint over the error), by erasing it (a soft rubber is available but this method tends to leave a smudge on the master which is not, however, reproduced on the copies), or by scraping it off with a sharp instrument (a safety razor blade is very effective). When all the dye has been removed from the error, a fresh piece of "carbon" must be found—possibly from the margin of the original transfer sheet—and this must be backed against the error. The typist can then type the correction and remove the small piece of added "carbon" before continuing with the typing. There is of course no need to erase the face of the master since the effective side is really the reverse on to which the dye from the transfer sheet has been transferred.

(*b*) *Storing a spirit master.* If the master is to be used again, it must be carefully removed from the duplicator and backed with a flimsy sheet of paper of equal size (to prevent the dye from setting-off on any other work) and stored in such a way that no pressure is applied to it, otherwise the pressure might remove some of the dye and thus considerably shorten the life of the master. Old masters can be "re-activated" by putting them through a heat copier, but the effect is only good for a small number of additional copies.

(*c*) *Length of run for spirit masters.* Much depends on the skill used in preparing the master and in obtaining copies. Thus a sharp, fairly heavy touch on the typewriter will ensure that the maximum amount of dye is transferred from the transfer sheet to the master which will obviously increase the number of copies obtainable. Similarly, skilful use of the duplicator by the correct application of fluid and pressure will also increase the length of life of the master. Too much fluid will soon wash off the dye and too much pressure will soon remove it: both must be used judiciously. The master is normally able to produce any number of copies up to about sixty or even 100 and with reasonable care, it can probably produce even more than this number. However the

higher figures must be regarded as a maximum and rather extra-
ordinary: it will be appreciated that each duplicated copy is
produced by being pressed against the master and thereby removing a small amount of the dye from it. It follows that with each
copy taken, the deposit of dye on the master is reduced until
eventually there is so little left that the copies become illegible.
Although in theory it might be argued that each copy is slightly
fainter than the preceding one, in practice it is impossible to notice
the difference between say the first copy and the second one but a

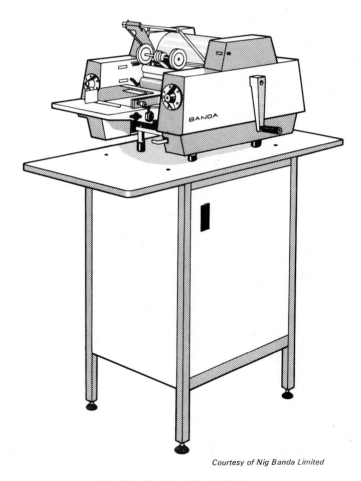

Fig. 63.—Banda spirit duplicator.

comparison of the first with the twenty-first would show a difference. However, as explained above, with careful operating of the machine, *e.g.* the careful application of spirit or of pressure, this drawback—if indeed it is a drawback—is minimised.

(*d*) *Multi-colour work with spirit duplicating.* Multi-colour work is possible—indeed it is particularly easy—with spirit masters. The transfer sheets come in a variety of colours (seven altogether: red, blue, green, black, purple, brown and yellow), and all that is necessary is to remove one transfer sheet and replace it with another of a different colour. The result will be that several colours are transferred to the copy paper in the process of duplicating. It will be seen therefore that there is no "messy" business of changing ink or cleaning down the machine and when multi-colour work is required, the spirit process of duplicating scores over other methods because of the ease and simplicity with which such work may be effected.

Figure 63 shows a spirit duplicator.

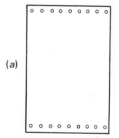

(*a*)

Courtesy of A. B. Dick Company
of Great Britain Limited

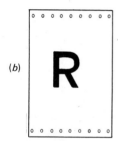

(*b*)

Courtesy of A. B. Dick Company
of Great Britain Limited

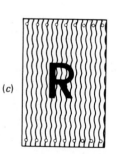

(*c*)

Courtesy of A. B. Dick Company
of Great Britain Limited

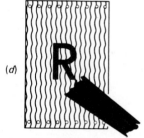

(*d*)

Courtesy of A. B. Dick Company
of Great Britain Limited

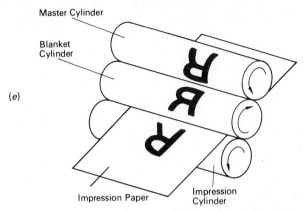

Courtesy of A. B. Dick Company of Great Britain Limited

(a) The basic principle of offset is that grease and water do not mix. The direct image-type master illustrates this principle, which applies to all masters and plates, paper or metal.

(b) The grease image is placed on the master, using offset ribbons, etc.

(c) A water solution is applied to the master surface. This will adhere to all parts of the master except where the grease image has been placed.

(d) A grease ink is then applied to the master. As the water solution repels the ink from the non-image area, the ink adheres to the image.

(e) The inked image is then transferred to the rubber blanket, paper is pressed against the blanket by the impression cylinder and the image previously printed on the blanket is off set on to the paper.

Fig. 64.—The offset process.

3. OFFSET LITHOGRAPHY
The name of this method is sometimes abbreviated to offset litho-duplicating. Originally, this was a printing process which had little application to the office. However, with the development of smaller duplicators which can be suitably accommodated in the office, e.g. table models, this machine has made tremendous strides in popularity, chiefly because of the high quality reproduction of which it is capable.

Briefly, the principle on which this process works (Fig. 64) is that grease and water do not mix (the one repels the other). The master is

Courtesy of A. B. Dick Company of Great Britain Limited

Fig. 65.—High-speed offset duplicator.

produced by writing or typing with a grease-retaining medium
(special typewriter ribbon or special pen/pencil) on to a paper master.
When the master is placed (face upwards) on the duplicator and
the machine (Fig. 65) set in motion, the master is washed over with
water and then with greasy ink. When the water is applied to the
master, those areas of it which have been impressed with an image
made by a greasy agent will repel the water and will therefore remain

quite dry, while the background on which no image has been made will accept the water and remain damp. When the ink is applied to the master, the reverse will happen, *i.e.* the ink will be accepted and retained by those parts of the master on which an image appears, while the white background of the master which has previously been damped with water will now repel the greasy ink and will therefore remain clear. At this stage, therefore, the master has wet ink over any writing that appears on it—rather like wri;ing with pen and ink while the ink is still wet. As the duplicating process continues, the wet master is applied to an intermediary cylinder—known as a blanket—and the image from the master is transferred to this blanket, in reverse. It is with this intermediary cylinder—the blanket—that the copy paper comes into contact and from which a correct (positive) copy is obtained (Fig. 66).

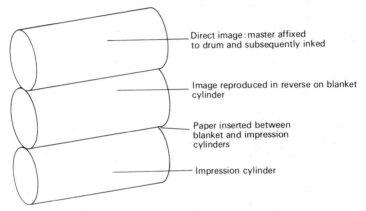

Direct image: master affixed to drum and subsequently inked

Image reproduced in reverse on blanket cylinder

Paper inserted between blanket and impression cylinders

Impression cylinder

Fig. 66.—The principles of offset lithography.

Any kind of paper may be used with offset lithography and the quality of reproduction is excellent. "Quality" in this context means that the duplicated copies closely resemble—indeed they are identical with—the image on the master. Thus, where high quality results are required, it is well worth taking trouble over the master, even to the extent of having it prepared by experts outside the office—since every copy subsequently made from that master will have an identical image to it. If the master has been prepared to look like print, the copies will look as if they too have been printed. This is an important advantage.

(*a*) *Correcting an offset master.* A very soft eraser must be used—special erasers are available—and only light pressure applied to remove the error. If too much pressure is applied, the error will be completely erased but the surface of the paper will have been damaged and when the master is processed in the duplicator, the spot where the surface of the paper was damaged will "pick up" the ink instead of repelling it, with the result that the copies will show an inky smudge.

Metal masters (which may be prepared by photographic means) cannot be corrected in the above manner. Only deletions are possible. These are effected with a Scotch Hone, a Glass Brush or a liquid Image Remover. No image can be superimposed for reproduction.

(*b*) *Storing an offset master.* If the master is to be used again it must first be cleaned and then coated with a sealing fluid which, when dry, forms a protective layer between the master and anything with which it might come into contact. The purpose of sealing the master is to protect it from contact with anything greasy; even fingermarks would show up on the copies if the masters were not protected. Before using the master again, the protective coating must of course be removed—this is easily done by rubbing lightly with cotton wool or a soft cloth impregnated with special cleaning fluid. It should be mentioned that the seal is entirely clear—like clear varnish—so that legibility of the master is not impaired.

Like other masters, the offset master must be stored in such a way that no pressure is applied to it, otherwise it may be damaged.

(*c*) *Length of run for offset masters.* Paper masters are available in a variety of qualities, *e.g.* suitable for runs of say, fifty, 500, 1,000 and 1,500. It is however possible to produce metal masters by photographic means. These are made of very thin pliable metal and are obviously much more durable than paper masters. It will easily be appreciated that the paper master has a very limited life since constant contact with ink and water and subsequent friction will soon wear through the paper. This just cannot happen when a metal master is used. Metal masters may be of two kinds: one type (the chemical transfer metal master) is easily prepared by photocopying the image on to the metal—an ordinary reflex photocopier may be used. Such a master is suitable for runs of up to 10,000 copies, after which the image deteriorates although the metal remains intact. The other type of metal master (pre-sensitised metal plate) is also prepared by photographing the image on to it—a negative is used—but in this case the chemicals used eat into the metal and the image is thus etched on the master. On such a master a maximum of some 100,000 copies may be made.

(*d*) *Multi-colour work.* This is possible on offset duplicators in much the same way as with ink duplicators, *i.e.* two or more masters must be prepared (one for each colour), the machine must be cleaned thoroughly before the different colour of ink is introduced and two or more "runs" are necessary, which create problems of registration. There are more sophisticated offset duplicators on the market (known as dual-headed or double-headed machines), which can cope with two colours but even with such machines the difficulties are not entirely non-existent.

4. OPERATING A DUPLICATOR

(*a*) *Wastage.* It is very easy to waste a great deal of duplicating paper unless proper care is taken by the operator.

If the copy paper is not "fanned" in order to let the air get between the sheets before it is placed in the feed tray, there is a risk that the feed mechanism will feed several sheets of paper through together, resulting in damage either to the machine or to the master, or at best resulting in a number of blank sheets having to be extracted from among the duplicated copies.

Another way in which much waste of paper can be avoided is by producing only one copy before setting the machine to the total number required. This copy should be carefully scrutinised for faults. Thus it might be desirable to adjust top or bottom margins, left or right hand margins, or density of image. If all adjustments are made and then a further single copy is produced to ensure that the material is now displayed satisfactorily, the duplicator can be switched on to produce copies at high speed without any wastage: only the first or second copies will have to be thrown away.

Above all, the masters should be thoroughly checked before they are put on the duplicator. Nothing is more calculated to enrage an employer than to receive say 1,000 copies of a duplicating job and then to discover that the finished product does not meet his requirements! Get him to approve the master before commencing "rolling off" operations.

(b) *Rotary and flatbed duplicators.* Most machines are now of the rotary type. That is, they incorporate a cylinder or drum to which the master is attached, and this drum revolves when the machine is in operation. Earlier models were of the flatbed type. Such machines have a flat table-top surface on to which the master is laid and the copy paper is brought into contact with the flat master which has previously been inked, to produce a copy.

(c) *Electric and manual operation.* Nearly every manufacturer produces duplicators which can be operated manually or by power. In some instances the machine is fitted with a handle and can be used manually if it is not plugged into a power point. In other cases a choice has to be made whether to purchase an electrically-operated duplicator or a manual one. The electric models are usually dearer (and heavier since they incorporate a motor) but where long runs are often required they have the great advantages that the operator is not fatigued by turning the handle hundreds of times; they are much speedier; and the operator, having pre-set the machine to the required number of copies, is free to turn her attention to other work, it merely being necessary to "keep an eye" on the duplicator. This last is a very real advantage

Type of duplicator	Quality of reproduction	Length of run	Storage of master	Correction of errors	Multi-colour work
Ink	Very good	Maximum 6000	Must be cleaned, stored flat, no pressure	Correcting fluid	Requires separate runs
Spirit	Good	Maximum 100	Must be backed with flimsy paper, stored flat, no pressure	Correcting fluid, soft eraser or razor	Merely use different colour transfer sheets. Seven colours available
Offset	Excellent	Maximum 100,000	Must be "sealed," stored flat, no pressure	Soft eraser	Requires separate runs. Dual-headed machines available

Fig. 67.—Types of duplicator compared.

in terms of economy of labour time. Figure 67 shows the main points of comparison between the different types of duplicators available.

COPIERS

These are often referred to as photocopiers although it is not true to say that in every case there is exposure to light, the developing of a negative and the printing of a positive copy. Be that as it may, the term is applied to all machines which are able to reproduce a copy from an original—not from a prepared master as in the case of duplicating.

There are three basic methods: (*a*) exposure to light; (*b*) exposure to heat; (*c*) electrostatic.

1. EXPOSURE TO LIGHT

(*a*) *Reflex*. These machines work on much the same principle as does the camera. The original to be copied, together with negative paper facing it, is placed on a flatbed-type copier (Fig. 68): the papers are exposed to light and the negative is then developed.

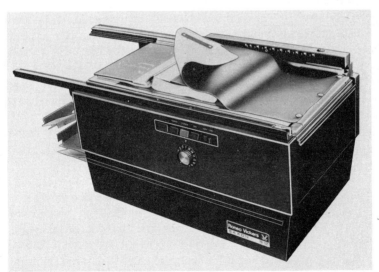

Courtesy of Roneo Vickers Limited

Fig. 68.—A flatbed copier.

This negative (which is of course a reverse image) is now placed on the flatbed together with a sheet of positive paper and the light switch is operated. When the exposure is effected (a matter of seconds) the positive paper is processed to develop and fix the printed copy. The negative is permanent and may be used again to produce further photocopies. This method is known as "reflex."

(b) *Diffusion transfer.* A variation of the above method also uses both negative and positive paper, but in this case instead of processing the negative alone and then processing the positive copy, both the negative and positive sheets of paper are fed through the machine together. A few seconds later the negative may be "peeled" away or separated from the positive, to reveal a copy of the original. The negative must now be discarded since its "transfer" properties (hence the name diffusion transfer) fade quickly. It is claimed that a quick and efficient operator might be able to make as many as six additional copies from the negative before it becomes useless but it is doubtful whether these will be satisfactory copies: they will appear fainter and, because the negative is still damp while the positive paper is dry, "squaring" is difficult and the image will appear to have "slipped," *i.e.* it will be crooked.

However, it is obvious that the diffusion method has the advantage of speed over the reflex method previously described. Since it is necessary to process the papers once only (the positive and negative sheets are developed together) the time taken is halved. Against this advantage must be weighed the fact that if more than one copy is required the whole procedure must be repeated (using up another sheet of negative paper) whereas with the simple reflex method a permanent negative is obtained and only positive sheets are required for second and subsequent copies. The result is a saving in paper, which is quite costly.

The above methods of photocopying are sometimes referred to as "wet" methods as the chemicals required for developing and fixing the image are liquid. Machines using the "wet" process are normally of the flatbed type which has the advantage of being able to copy from a bound book. The quality of reproduction is particularly good and any colour may be copied (although the copy will of course be in black and white). Disadvantages are that the paper is expensive (compared with other methods), the copies may discolour slightly in time, and liquid chemicals are used (with consequent danger of spilling and the necessity of refilling).

(c) *Dyeline* (*or diazo*). This method works on the principle that light bleaches and therefore discolours material which is exposed to it. The original, which must be on translucent paper (to allow the ultra violet light rays to penetrate), is placed against specially treated paper (sensitive to light) and the two are exposed to light. The light passes through the translucent original, reaches the sensitive copy paper and bleaches it white. However, where an image appears in black on the original, the light is prevented from penetrating through to the copy paper and that part is therefore not bleached. The result is a copy of the image. The copy is then processed with chemicals.

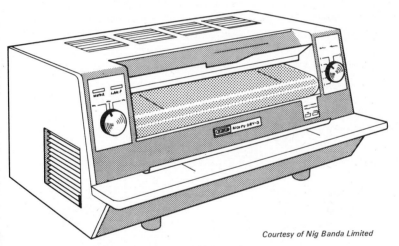

Courtesy of Nig Banda Limited

Fig. 69.—A dyeline copier.

While essentially a copying machine (Fig. 69), the process has been adapted by some manufacturers to produce multiple copies and in this instance the dividing line between copying and duplicating becomes rather thin.

I can personally recall the application of the above principle under rather primitive conditions. While working abroad in a hot country, it was necessary to make copies of architects' drawings and plans. The originals were placed in contact with the sensitive paper, and the two were then exposed on a balcony to the hot sunshine. Soon, the sensitive paper discoloured, leaving an unbleached image of the original on the copy paper!

2. EXPOSURE TO HEAT

This method is sometimes known as the "dry" method or the "thermal" method. The principle here is to use paper which is sensitive to heat. This paper is then placed in contact with the original and both are passed through the copier while being exposed to heat. The image on the original retains the heat and reacts on the sensitised paper, resulting in a copy of the original which has been "burned" on to the copy paper.

A great advantage of this method is that it employs no chemicals, hence there is no danger of spilling and no trouble in cleaning out the trays of fluid. It also has the advantage of speed since no negative has first to be produced. However, it is not without disadvantages: the machines are normally of the "roller" type, which means that a copy cannot be made from a bound book; the quality of reproduction may be poorer, especially with the cheaper paper; the paper must be fairly flimsy; and most coloured inks contain a dye which prevents the heat from penetrating to the sensitised paper, which means in effect that this method cannot copy from colour.

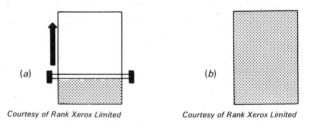

(a)   (b)

Courtesy of Rank Xerox Limited   *Courtesy of Rank Xerox Limited*

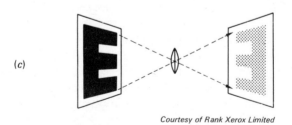

(c)

Courtesy of Rank Xerox Limited

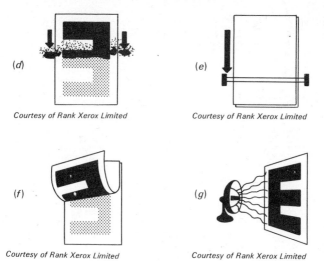

(d)

Courtesy of Rank Xerox Limited

(e)

Courtesy of Rank Xerox Limited

(f)

Courtesy of Rank Xerox Limited

(g)

Courtesy of Rank Xerox Limited

(a) The surface of a coated plate (or drum) is sensitised by an electrically charged grid which moves across it.

(b) The coating of the plate is now fully charged with positive electricity.

(c) The original document (E) is projected on to the coated plate. Positive charges disappear in the areas exposed to light.

(d) A negatively charged powder is dusted over the plate and adheres to the positively charged image.

(e) A sheet of paper is placed over the plate, and receives a positive charge.

(f) The positively charged paper attracts powder from the plate, forming a direct positive image.

(g) The print is fixed by heat for a few seconds to form the permanent image.

Fig. 70.—The Xerographic process.

3. ELECTROSTATIC METHOD

This process is sometimes referred to as Xerography. Xerography stems from the Greek words meaning "dry writing." No liquid ink is used in this process (Fig. 70).

Briefly, this method exploits static electricity. Thus the surface of a plate within the machine is charged with positive electricity. An image of the original to be copied is then projected on to the plate. With exposure to light the positive charges disappear from the plate on those areas which were blank (*i.e.*, the background) on the original. Now, a negatively-charged powder (the so-called ink) is dusted over the plate. This powder is attracted to the positively charged image on the plate. Copy paper (any kind is suitable) is now placed over the plate and receives a positive charge. The paper now attracts the powdered "ink" from the plate and an image is ob-

Method	Advantages	Disadvantages
Reflex: (light)	1. Copies from colour 2. Flatbed type copies from bound books 3. Very good quality reproduction 4. Permanent negative may be re-used 5. Versatile - can make transparencies for overhead projector; masters for offset duplicator	1. Liquids are used - spilling, cleaning, replenishing 2. Slower than other methods 3. May require dimmed light
Dyeline: (diazo)	1. Good quality reproduction	1. Originals <u>must</u> be translucent
Heat: (dry; thermal)	1. Quick 2. Dry, clean, no refills required 3. Adequate quality of reproduction - good on dearer quality paper 4. Versatile - makes masters for spirit duplicator	1. Cannot copy from colour 2. As the original is processed with the sensitised paper, there is a risk (albeit a small one) of damage to the original 3. Copy paper must be fairly flimsy
Electrostatic:	1. Quick 2. Dry, clean 3. Adequate quality of reproduction 4. Uses any paper for copies, which makes it cheaper to run 5. Copies from colour 6. Can copy 3-dimensional originals, e.g. book, key	1. Possibly servicing is more costly

Fig. 71.— Types of photocopier compared.

tained. This image is permanently fused to the paper by means of heat. Some of the advantages of the electrostatic process are that it is quick, it requires no training for the operator, it is dry and clean and above all, it makes use of any ordinary paper for copying purposes. This last point is a very real advantage as all other methods of photocopying require treated paper which is expensive to buy.

Machines have been developed to cope with multiple copies and it can be said that xerography is now entering the field of duplicating. At the present time there are no machines commercially available (at reasonable cost) which can copy in colour, but it will not be long before manufacturers overcome their problems in this field. Indeed, Rank Xerox hope to market a limited number of colour photocopiers very shortly.

Figure 71 shows the main points of comparison between the different types of copiers available.

OPERATING THE PHOTOCOPIER

It must be remembered that in most cases the paper used in photocopying is specially treated, making it expensive to buy. It is essential therefore to take care that wastage is eliminated. With a little training and experience and by reference to the manufacturers' instructions, it should be possible to discover the correct exposure times, thus reducing the "guesswork" and ensuring that satisfactory copies are produced at the first attempt. Similarly, where chemicals are employed, the containers must be kept clean in order to keep the copying process trouble-free.

CHOOSING A MACHINE

It may happen that the secretary is called upon to give an opinion on the choice of machine to be purchased, and this is no easy matter. There is such a bewildering variety of duplicators and photocopiers available that the inexperienced secretary—and some experienced secretaries as well—may not know where to start.

The first point to consider is what *type* of machine will be most suitable. Let us take office duplicators as an example.

1. WHAT QUALITY OF WORK IS MOST OFTEN REQUIRED?

If an extremely high quality of reproduction is consistently necessary, then it may be worth buying an offset duplicator, having an operator specially trained, and going to the somewhat greater trouble of setting up the machine.

2. WHAT LENGTH OF RUN IS MOST COMMONLY REQUIRED?

The ink duplicator can cope with medium and long runs but the offset duplicator would be more suitable for *extremely* long runs if they are required on *numerous* occasions. Little operator training is required for ink duplicating.

3. IS MULTI-COLOUR WORK REQUIRED?

The spirit duplicator can, without doubt, cope with multi-colour work with the least possible trouble, both in preparation of master and in duplicating. But if such work is only occasionally required and the office already possesses say, an ink duplicator, then the latter can, of course, cope with occasional changes of ink without too much difficulty.

4. WHAT OTHER MACHINES ARE ALREADY AVAILABLE IN THE OFFICE?

This question really means: is a new machine really necessary, or can existing equipment cope?

5. CAN FUTURE REQUIREMENTS BE ESTIMATED?

Existing needs may point to one kind of duplicator but if, in the near future, it seems likely that requirements will be altered, then it would be unwise to invest in equipment that will soon become inadequate.

6. SYSTEMS ADAPTATION

This really means: can the new duplicator be integrated with existing *other* equipment, *e.g.* a photocopier? For example, a heat photocopier can make masters for the spirit duplicator. A "wet" photocopier can produce offset masters, and so on. Therefore the new piece of equipment must be seen as part of a *whole* system.

7. COST

This is really a secondary consideration, because once it has been established that enough money is available to buy new equipment, then the type of machine required is more important than the difference in cost between two different types. However, once the kind of machine has been decided upon, the cost factor does enter into consideration because rival manufacturers, or different models produced by the same manufacturer, will show some variation in price. The question of cost also covers cost of masters (although here also this point is secondary to the quality of reproduction) and cost of duplicating, *e.g.* the duplicating paper used.

Much the same arguments will apply to any other piece of equipment.

ELECTRONIC STENCIL CUTTER

A machine (Fig. 72) has been developed in recent years which is able to cut a stencil from an original document. This is particularly

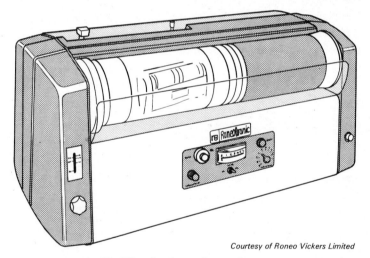

Courtesy of Roneo Vickers Limited

Fig. 72.—An electronic stencil cutter.

advantageous as it reduces the time which would otherwise have to be taken in typing a copy; it enables stencils to be cut of documents containing diagrams, etc. which could not easily be reproduced by hand and, of course, it eliminates the possibility of error and therefore does away with the necessity for tedious and time-consuming checking.

A stencil is affixed to the machine, as is also the original to be copied. A scanning process then takes place and the image to be copied is reproduced on to the stencil. The master can then be used for ink duplicating in the normal way.

Short-answer Questions

1. Which method of duplicating gives the best quality of reproduction?

2. How may two-(or more) colour work be obtained with the spirit duplicating process? Is two-colour work possible with other duplicating methods?

3. Why is duplicating paper for ink (stencil) duplicators usually semi-absorbent? Is it possible to use paper which has a smoother surface?

4. Of what material are offset masters made?

5. Name three different types of (*a*) duplicating and (*b*) photocopying processes.

6. What is a "flatbed" type of machine? Has it any special advantages?

7. Give other words which describe (*a*) ink duplicating; (*b*) spirit duplicating; (*c*) dyeline copying; (*d*) electrostatic copying.

8. Are there any disadvantages to the heat photocopying process?

9. State which method of photocopying or duplicating you would use to obtain:

(*a*) twenty-five copies of a typewritten sheet in multi-colour type;

(*b*) 200 copies of a pricelist;

(*c*) three copies of a map which includes small print.

10. State the principle on which offset duplicating works.

Past Examination Questions

1. List four steps (excluding typewriting) in the preparation of a stencil for duplicating.   (*R.S.A.*)

2. State, with reasons, whether you would or would not suggest using a photocopier in the following circumstances. If you would not recommend using a photocopier, what other machine would you use, assuming its availability?

(*a*) ten copies of a two-page report which is required for internal use. It is in draft form and needs re-typing;

(*b*) 200 copies of a three-page report which is to be sent to customers. It is already in its final form;

(*c*) six copies of a page of a book which is required for internal use. The page must not be torn out;

(*d*) a customer's letter which has to be dealt with by three departments.   (*R.S.A.*)

3. (*a*) Give two materials of which offset-litho plates can be made.

(*b*) Give two ways in which offset-litho plates may be prepared for offset-litho printing.

(*c*) Give two advantages of using an offset-litho machine instead of a stencil duplicator.   (*R.S.A.*)

4. Your firm has agreed to make available to your department a sum of money which will enable you to purchase either an electrically operated ink duplicator or a good photocopying machine. What considerations would you take into account when deciding which machine would be most suitable for your work?

5. How would you correct errors: (*a*) on a wax stencil; (*b*) on a spirit master?   (*R.S.A.*)

6. Draw up instructions for "cutting" a stencil to include grafting, clearly indicating what this is.   (*L.C.C.*)

7. The copying work in your office has increased materially and your employer is considering the purchase of a photocopying machine. He knows very little about photocopiers and has asked you to advise him on a suitable model. Write a memorandum to him setting out your recommendations and how you have obtained the information.   (*L.C.C.*)

8. (*a*) Explain how corrections may be made, if at all, on the following master sheets and state the degree of effectiveness in each case:

(*i*) Spirit; (*ii*) Ink; (*iii*) Offset.

(*b*) List some of the possible causes for ink patches occurring on copies duplicated by the offset lithography process.

(*L.C.C.*)

9. Explain the difference between the heat transfer and the diffusion transfer methods of reproduction. Technical details are not required, but you should give the advantages and disadvantages of

each method and any other uses to which the machines can be put.   (*L.C.C.*)

10. Complaints have been made that the ink duplicating department has produced poor quality copies from an ink duplicator. The main faults are:

(*i*) Smudging on both sides of the paper.

(*ii*) Vertical streaks of very light inking in contrast to the general heavy inking on the rest of the page. Suggest possible causes and remedies.   (*L.C.C.*)

CHAPTER 22

OFFICE MACHINES: II

MICROFILMING

ALTHOUGH microfilming is a means of copying or of reproducing, it would not normally be used for the same requirements as the photocopying or duplicating methods described previously.

Microfilming consists of taking a photo of documents and reducing their size on film, so that large quantities of information may be represented on a small roll of film or separate frames of film. The original documents may then be destroyed or retained as required.

There are two main advantages of microfilming in the office.

1. A tremendous saving in storage space can be achieved. Space is at a premium, especially in London, and files take up an enormous amount of space. Thus, where it is not essential that the documents be retained in their original form, they may be microfilmed and whole filing cabinets emptied!
2. A great saving in time and labour may be effected. Where it is necessary to extract certain information from documents a tedious and time-consuming task of copying is avoided if the *whole* document is filmed, from which any information may be taken as required.

There are several models of microfilmers (Fig. 73) available to suit the particular requirements of an organisation. Thus one model on the market at the present time can microfilm at the rate of 615 cheque-size documents per minute. Another model available is designed to microfilm continuous forms (as in computer print-outs) at the rate of 2,000 inches per minute. Again, there is a choice of reduction ratios, so that a variety of requirements are catered for.

The most efficient use is made of microfilming when large quantities of documents of similar size have to be filmed, *e.g.* a batch of used cheques. If the size of the original varies from one document to

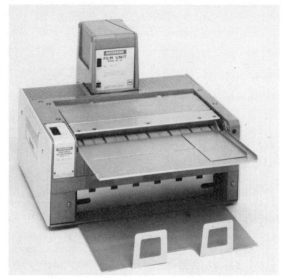

Courtesy of Kodak Limited

Fig. 73.—Recordak 16mm portable microfilmer.

Courtesy of Kodak Limited

Fig. 74.—Recordak Starfile microfilmer.

the next, it will be appreciated that the process is slowed down since adjustments will have to be made to deal with each size.

Some libraries are now making use of microfilming. The model pictured in Fig. 74 can photograph library cards (and other documents, *e.g.* cheques, file cards, coupons, etc.) at a speed of up to sixty documents per minute. The reduction ratio is 21 : 1.

When it is necessary to read a document, the film may be projected on to a "reader" in magnified and therefore readable form (Fig. 75) and this reader also has a paper print facility. A reader

Courtesy of Kodak Limited

Fig. 75.—Recordak Magnaprint reader.

(Fig. 76) recently put on the market by Kodak Ltd. now makes micropublishing (the widespread distribution of information on microfilm in the home, shop, office and even in a car) a practical proposition. This reader, which can work off a car battery, is no bigger than a telephone, weighs less than 5 lb and can be used indoors or out, even in bright sunlight. Thus not only businessmen may use it, but also students, engineers working on sites, etc.

Other equipment available includes processing machines, developers and printers.

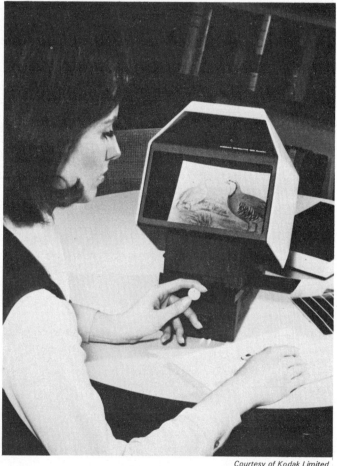

Courtesy of Kodak Limited

Fig. 76.—Ektalite portable reader.

Processing may of course be undertaken within the organisation if the operators and equipment are available. However, the manufacturers operate a very rapid and efficient processing service at reasonable cost.

It will be appreciated that careful indexing must be maintained, since it might otherwise be an impossible task to retrieve a document which was pictured minutely *somewhere* on a roll of film! Coding and indexing systems are also marketed by the manufacturers.

TYPEWRITERS

A little background history might be interesting. It may be a surprise to find that the present keyboard arrangement differs very little from that shown on the original typewriter (Fig. 77). No one seems able to say with any certainty whether the letters were intended to be arranged in any particular order, although there is a theory that the first row of the keyboard was fitted with the letters which appear in the word "typewriter" and these letters were subsequently re-arranged, although they still appear in the first row. Be that as it may, the fact remains that the present keyboard is not scientifically arranged to produce the most economic results in terms of mastering the skill and speed required in typing. A professor of education at Washington University whose name was Dvorak (pronounced Vorjak) claimed to have developed a keyboard which is now known by his name and which is designed to assist the learner in mastering the keyboard. Apart from quicker keyboard mastery, it is also claimed that the typist can get on with the actual typing at a higher rate of strokes per minute, since the letters on the keyboard have been so displayed as to take account of hand and finger movements (as in time and motion study).

While machines "for simulating handwriting" might have been thought of as long as 200 years ago, it is only in the last sixty or seventy years that typewriters have become such a commercial proposition as to make no office complete without one. From early models incorporating awkward methods of shift key change, we have progressed at high speed through standard and portable models (each successive year seeing more gadgets and time-saving devices incorporated), to the current electric typewriters, automatic typewriters and indeed other machines linked to the typewriter idea, *e.g.* the teleprinter, the adding machine, and so on.

Courtesy of Imperial Typewriter Company Ltd.

Courtesy of Imperial Typewriter Company Ltd.

Fig. 77.—Some early typewriters, an illustration

Courtesy of Imperial Typewriter Company Ltd.

Courtesy of Imperial Typewriter Company Ltd.

from *A Catalogue of Historical Typewriters* (*contd. overleaf*).

Courtesy of Imperial Typewriter Company Ltd.

Courtesy of Imperial Typewriter Company Ltd.

The great advantages as compared with manual writing are that personal style of handwriting is eliminated, thus ensuring legibility, several copies may be made simultaneously and, of course, after the initial period of training, typing is infinitely quicker than writing by hand.

1. THE STANDARD MANUAL TYPEWRITER

There is little to choose between the models made by reliable manufacturers. Each manufacturer tries to overtake the others by incorporating additional devices supposed to alleviate the typist's job (but not invariably achieving this aim), and to please the typist or the employer by a more attractive and streamlined design than that of a competitor.

If the selection of typewriter is left to the secretary, personal preference will invariably dictate the choice.

2. THE NOISELESS TYPEWRITER

This model aims to soften the noise made by the typist at her work, thus making it easier for the chief to carry on his own work, or to speak over the telephone, without asking the typist to stop typing. Such machines, while admittedly making a muted sound, are not very popular because they "feel" different to the touch. For example, it is not necessary—indeed it would be wrong—to depress the keys with as much force as on a manual machine and the typist has to "flick" her fingers over the keys, almost (but not quite) in the same way as when using an electric typewriter. Another disadvantage lies in the fact that because there is no force behind the striking of the keys, more than one or two carbon copies cannot be successfully taken.

These machines are not in very general use, but some manufacturers will supply them on request.

3. THE ELECTRIC TYPEWRITER

This development of the typewriter has been in common use in offices in this country for about twenty-five years. It has gained steadily in popularity both with employers who consider electric typewriters something of a status symbol and also a means of pleasing a good secretary, as well as with the typists who enjoy the light touch and the even appearance of the typescript. The following are some of the advantages claimed for electric typewriters:

1. Less fatiguing for the typist since less energy is expended in striking the keys and in effecting a carriage return. Some keys are fitted with a repeat mechanism, thus making it possible to underscore, type continuous full stops, etc. with even less effort.
2. Following on from the above, it is obvious that the typist's output may be increased if she needs less resting time.
3. As the force with which the keys are struck is electrically controlled, it follows that a more even appearance of the type is achieved—it makes no difference whether or not a key is struck with as much force as the next one. Also, "ghosting" (or double impression) is eliminated from the inexperienced typist's touch.
4. It is possible to regulate the force of impact, therefore more carbon copies may be taken. It has been claimed that a maximum of some twenty copies is possible, but much depends on the quality of carbons, the thickness of paper and on the machine itself.
5. Greater speed has been claimed for the electric typewriter, but this must be qualified. For example, while it is undeniable that the keys may be struck faster than with a manual model, even manual machines are capable of being operated faster than any typist could make them work, so that the greater potential of electric machines cannot be fully realised. Similarly, although the carriage return can be operated from the keyboard, *i.e.* without any hand movement to speak of, this operation is in fact slower than manual operation due to "waiting time" while the carriage returns automatically.
6. Improved stencil cutting due to sharper impression and even touch.

Some of the disadvantages of electric typewriters when compared with manual machines are:

1. They are heavier. This is important where a typewriter has to be lifted. It is the electric motor incorporated into the machine which makes it so much heavier.
2. Dependent on power. Power cuts are not a daily occurrence, but they have been known to happen! Another point to be considered is that the location of the electric typewriter must

iiii iiii	Most typewriters, having regular
oooo oooo	spacing, give every character—even
wwww wwww	capitals—the same space, irrespective
mmmm mmmm	of the differences between their shapes.
MMMM MMMM	Proportional spacing gives each character
WWWW WWWW	its natural width, as in printing, and
OOOO OOOO	matches the additional height of
IIII IIII	capitals with additional width.

Courtesy of IBM United Kingdom Limited

(*a*) Example of proportional spacing.

Courtesy of IBM United Kingdom Limited

(*b*) Selectric typewriter.

*Courtesy of IBM United
Kingdom Limited*

(*c*) Selected golf-balls.

Fig. 78.—Typewriter with interchangeable golf-ball heads.

be within reach of a power point. The flex could also be an unnecessary hazard.

3. If a typist has been trained on, or is used to, a manual typewriter, a (short) conversion period is necessary before she feels completely "at home" with an electric machine.

4. Electric typewriters are usually dearer to buy than manual ones.

5. Servicing is more specialised.

Some electric machines are built to give *proportional spacing* (Fig. 78(*a*)) (apparently first introduced by IBM in 1940). This lends an attractive print-like effect to the type. Basically each letter uses up an amount of space in proportion to the size of the letter; thus the letter "l" uses two units of space while the letter "w" uses five. Capital letters take up more space than lower case letters. It is also possible to achieve a flush right-hand margin (but this necessitates the typing of a draft first). Such a typewriter, when fitted with a special "once only" ribbon designed to give a denser and sharper outline obviously enhances the appearance of any typewritten text.

A comparatively recent development in electric typewriters is the IBM 72 (sometimes known as the "golf-ball" machine because of the appearance of the metal "ball" on which the letters are embossed). This machine was introduced by IBM in 1961. While the operation of the keyboard is no different from that of any other typewriter, the mechanics are entirely different, there being no type bars. The characters are embossed on a metal ball (Figs. 78(*b*) and (*c*)) which revolves so as to present to the paper that character which has been depressed on the keyboard. The carriage does not move (thus minimising vibration)—it is the "ball" which travels across the page. The main advantage here is the ease with which this hollow metal sphere may be removed and be replaced, if desired, by another fitted with a different style of type, *e.g.* italics. Other advantages are that there are no type-bars to clash and pile as might happen with fast typing. Also there is a built-in device to "store" the characters for a fraction of a second, making it impossible for the typist to type at a speed faster than that with which the machine is able to cope.

4. THE AUTOMATIC TYPEWRITER

This is sometimes referred to as the "robot typist" because the machine can function without the need of a typist to depress the keys.

Indeed, it can be curiously fascinating to see such a machine in operation, for the keys may be seen to move and yet there is no typist there to operate the keyboard! In fact, these machines are electric typewriters connected to units known as "readers" into which punched tape or punched card is inserted. The tape or card is coded according to the wording of the text required and when the type-writer is set in motion, it automatically transcribes and types from the code. This type of machine makes it possible to despatch individually typed letters to a large number of people, *e.g.* customers or potential customers: the communication assumes a personal touch and does not get labelled "circular," thus minimising the risk of its getting put into the waste paper basket without being read.

As it is possible to code not only complete letters, but a number of individual paragraphs (something in the order of 50 different para-graphs), a selection can be made from a variety of paragraphs to give a large number of possible texts.

As mentioned previously, the typewriter itself is an ordinary electric one connected to the special unit for automatic typing: these typewriters are capable of achieving high speeds, especially when fitted with a "sphere type head" (similar to that found on the golf-ball type IBM 72 typewriter previously described). The manufacturers claim that a speed of something in the region of 175 words per minute is possible.

If required, it is possible to buy the unit for preparing the punched tape or card, and thus to prepare one's own material in the office; the operation itself is quite simple, the input tape or card being inserted into the unit and the text being punched from keyboard operation. Alternatively (since these extras are quite costly) the input material may be produced by the manufacturers to the customers' orders.

An example of the use of such machines may be seen in some Accounts Departments where standard letters are sent out to cus-tomers with overdue accounts. Each debtor gains the impression that the reminder to pay has been typed especially for him, whereas in reality only his name, address and the amount payable (*i.e.*, the variable information) is inserted by the typist, the rest of the "stan-dard" text being used to remind other defaulters!

Another example is to be found in direct mail advertising where it is important that the letters avoid the appearance of a circular.

It is worth remembering that apart from the time saved in actual typing time, a further saving in time is made by the elimination of proof-reading. If one copy is accurate, so will all the other copies be.

"VARITYPER" DESK-TOP TYPE COMPOSING MACHINE

This machine (Fig. 79) is designed to give a print-like effect to the written text—it is sometimes called a composing machine—and a variety of type fonts is available. These fonts are in the shape of segments which are easily fitted to the machine and can be changed with no trouble at all, to produce a variety of types and sizes of print. The machine can accommodate two different fonts for use at any one time, so that one piece of display work may incorporate matching or contrasting print without the need to change the font.

(On some composing machines, *e.g.* that produced by IBM, the type element is not in the form of a segment but in the shape of a sphere, similar to the "golf-ball" found on the IBM 72 typewriter, but the basic idea is the same: a variety of fonts is available, and the changeover from one to the other is achieved with no trouble at all.)

The "Varityper" has a carriage which is open ended on both sides to accommodate particularly wide sheets of paper, *i.e.* they may "hang

Courtesy of Addressograph-Multigraph Limited

Fig. 79.—Varityper model 1010.

out" of the sides of the carriage. The carriage itself is available in a variety of lengths, the maximum being 24 in. Some other special features of the "Varityper" are:

1. It is possible fully to justify the copy to varying widths.
2. Proportional spacing is possible, *i.e.* each letter takes up the amount of space it requires, rather like print.
3. A variety of thicknesses for ruling is available, making the machine particularly useful for forms design.

The above features are not all necessarily incorporated in every "Varityper" model, and the price range is a wide one varying between something like £1,200 and £2,500.

The "Varityper" is a machine designed to give a professional appearance to work produced in the office and is particularly suitable where masters are to be prepared for duplicating. If the duplicator selected is an offset litho (which it will be remembered gives particularly good quality reproduction) the result will be very professional indeed.

However, this machine is not suitable for normal use as a typewriter. The "mechanics" of the "Varityper" are quite different from those of a typewriter and although the type is in the front of the machine and the keys are depressed in much the same fashion as the keys of a typewriter, the hammer action comes from behind, thus pressing the paper against the type, through the paper carbon ribbon. This means that carbon copies may not be satisfactorily obtained and are not normally taken on the "Varityper." As the hammer action comes from the rear, through the copies to the top copy, it could well be that the top copy, being "cushioned" by the carbon copies, becomes poor. It can therefore be said that the taking of carbon copies is not really a good proposition on the "Varityper" which is, in any case, not designed for that purpose, but for the purpose of producing professional looking print-like composition in the office.

A good example of the use commonly made of the "Varityper" is in the production of masters or the preparation of artwork for litho reproduction. In view of the variety of rulings available good forms design can be obtained.

THE TELEPRINTER

This machine (Fig. 80) really serves the interests of communication: many modern companies subscribe to the Post Office telex system which means that the teleprinter finds a place in most modern large and medium-sized companies.

This machine has a keyboard very similar to a typewriter, thus making it easy for a trained typist to operate it. The machine is used to transmit written messages over long distances, even abroad.

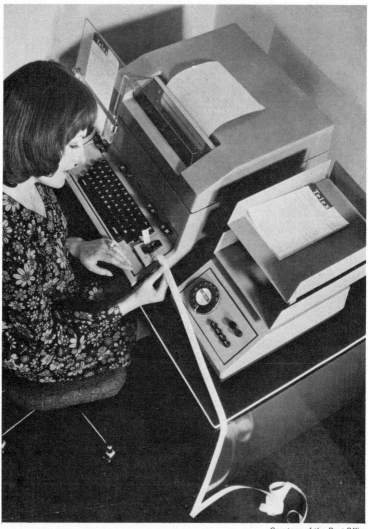

Courtesy of the Post Office

Fig. 80.—Telex with teleprinter and automatic transmission.

Subscribers to the telex system have a teleprinter installed on their premises (with a telex number, rather as subscribers to the telephone have a telephone installed with a telephone number) and by dialling the number of any other subscriber they wish to contact, it is possible to be connected with that other subscriber (providing that their teleprinter has been switched on to receive messages and that it is not itself engaged in receiving or sending a message). A message may then be typed (and as many as six copies may be taken if required) and this message automatically appears in typed form on the receiving teleprinter. Indeed, it is quite fascinating to watch the message appear—as if from nowhere—being typed out as though by an invisible typist!

It is said that the telex system is to written communication what the telephone is to verbal communication. Indeed, it may be called "the written telephone call!"

An additional refinement incorporated on many machines is a punched tape attachment (Fig. 81). The value of this attachment is easily assessed: if it is desired to send out a message which might be difficult to type accurately at the first attempt, *e.g.* tabular or statistical information, or if the operator is not yet well trained, an attachment for using punched tape is extremely useful as it cuts the cost of the time spent in sending the message. The device is particularly useful for messages to be sent over long distances, *e.g.* abroad, since the time bought is—as in the case of the telephone—quite costly. The machine is switched to "local" and the message is typed out in the normal way. Simultaneously the message is punched into paper tape. If errors are made, they are corrected, thus ensuring that the punched paper tape is absolutely accurate. Once the message is completed, the paper tape is fitted to the machine, the teleprinter is connected to the subscriber who is to receive the message and the message is then sent automatically (from the tape, not by the typist). The great advantage is that no time is now lost in displaying the "tricky" message—the tape takes over, and the message is typed at a speed of something like sixty-six words a minute—a great time saver when the cost of time is high, as it would be if the message is to be sent abroad.

Some advantages of the telex system are:

1. Messages are received almost simultaneously, as they are sent out.

Courtesy of the Post Office

(*a*) Automatic telex installation with reperforation and tape transmitting attachments.

2. Messages are in written form, thus preserving a written record.
3. As many as six copies may be made (the paper is either carbon-backed or carbon-interleaved).
4. The punched tape attachment enables messages to be sent accurately at high speed, thus effecting a saving in time and therefore in money.
5. Messages may be received at any time: the advantage is that where messages are to be received by a country where there is a difference in the time between the two countries, the machine may be left switched on to receive messages, and the messages will be received outside office hours, and will be typed and ready for action to be taken the following morning.

Courtesy of the Post Office

(*b*) Telegraph teleprinter showing tape transmission more closely.

Fig. 81.—Attachments to teleprinter installations.

It is interesting to note that telex is less than fifty years old. A form of telex service was provided from 1932 onwards over the telephone network; this was not entirely satisfactory and the service did not grow significantly. It was later decided to institute an entirely separate network designed for the needs of telex. This network was set up in 1954 and since then the system has grown until it is now comparable with the telephone and is, indeed, a "written telephone call."

DICTATING MACHINES

Audio machines are now firmly established in the business world, in spite of the great initial gloom and opposition that came from those concerned with shorthand who saw the advent of this mechanisation as a challenge to the survival of the shorthand-writers of the world. However, audio-typing can be most efficiently combined with shorthand-writing and large numbers of busy executives now employ secretaries who are able to take "live" dictation as well as audio dictation. Audio-typing does of course lend itself admirably to pooling, but there are probably as many personal secretaries using dictating machines as a small part of their duties as there are audio-typists in a typing pool.

Some of the advantages of using dictating machines are listed below:

1. The secretary may be engaged on other work, *e.g.* filing, transcription from shorthand notes, reception duties, etc. while her chief dictates into the machine such work as letters, or reports which require considerable thought and which would otherwise necessitate the secretary sitting idle while waiting for the chief to express his ideas. Audio dictation is also particularly suitable for the poor dictator who requires constant "play back."

2. The system is particularly adaptable to centralisation of typing work. Banking systems facilitate pooling of work and the dictator may be quite remote from the typing pool. He is connected to the recording machine by telephone instrument, the machine itself being located in the typing pool; the dictator, however, has complete control of the machine while he is dictating. In the typing pool, a supervisor allocates the work load in the most efficient way.

3. The chief may dictate outside the office merely by taking the machine with him: in the home, while travelling, etc.

4. Some recording media, *e.g.* non-magnetic belts, may be filed (instead of a written carbon copy) but this seems to have little practical value.

5. Where it is not essential to keep a written record of the communication, the tape (or other recording medium) may be posted direct to the recipient who is known to have play-back facilities.

6. Other applications include use for recording proceedings of meetings or other discussions, including telephone conversations.

There are some disadvantages in complete reliance on dictating machines:

1. Like any other machine, a dictating machine is liable to break down; it requires servicing.

2. The location of the machine is dependent on availability of power points; the leads from the machine to the power point may be a hazard.

3. The machine cannot be operated if power cuts occur.

4. A high calibre of typist is required to cope with spelling, punctuation and correction of errors on the tape.

5. Poor dictation technique, *e.g.* where instructions are given at the end instead of the beginning of the letter, can delay the typist's work and cause frustration if retyping becomes necessary.

6. Unlike a shorthand writer who sits opposite the chief, taking down dictation, the machine cannot be helpful in supplying information, or in suggesting an appropriate phrase or an elusive word to the boss.

7. It is sometimes claimed that personal contact with the chief is lost through the use of dictating machines, but this accusation must be qualified. Certainly in an audio-typing pool where only typing is undertaken, personal contact may be limited to receiving the tape and returning the typed letters; (and even this contact can be eliminated by an internal messenger service). Again personal contact is reduced considerably where remote dictation systems operate. But where a *secretary* uses a dictating machine, audio-typing will only be a fraction of her duties and personal contact still remains.

1. DICTATION TECHNIQUE

The secretary does not often have to dictate letters but no doubt she often believes (usually with justification) that she could do the dictation better than her chief! A few hints on dictation technique may prove helpful and the clever secretary will find a means of bringing these points to the notice of a poor dictator.

1. Instructions, *e.g.* additional copies, special notepaper, etc. should be given at the commencement of the dictation, not when the typist has already completed the letter.

2. Unusual words, technical material, proper nouns, should be spelled clearly.

3. Special punctuation such as parentheses, dashes, should be indicated.

4. Speech should be clear—no mumbling, turning away from

the microphone, looking in desk drawers or out of the window (or holding a pipe between clenched teeth!).

5. When interruptions occur, the machine should be switched off otherwise it would be wasteful of typist's time and of recording medium.

2. RECORDING MEDIA

Either magnetic or non-magnetic material may be used. The magnetic material may take the form of tape, sheets, discs or wire, and makes the correction of errors particularly easy since this may be effected simply by superimposing the correct words over the error. It is also possible to erase the whole dictation with a special "brush" or by rubbing over a metal bar, so that the tape may be used many times over. Quality of playback is only affected when the tape really becomes ancient or when it has been crumpled. Magnetic wire is not often used nowadays, because the fine wire is prone to breaking and although this is easily remedied by knotting the ends together, threading the knotted wire becomes a nuisance. The advantage of wire is that it maintains the quality of playback while other media eventually deteriorate.

Non-magnetic plastic belts are very much cheaper to buy than magnetic media, but as they cannot be used over and over again this advantage is negatived. Also as corrections cannot be superimposed over the error they have to be indicated to the typist by some other means which makes the procedure rather cumbersome. The advantages of non-magnetic belts lie in the permanence of the record—it is not possible to erase the dictation inadvertently—and in the fact that the length of the dictated letter can be assessed at a glance from the grooves which appear on the belt, also they are relatively cheap.

3. AUDIO EQUIPMENT (Figs. 82–87)

(a) *The executive's equipment.* Apart from the recorder itself, which may be a small pocket unit or a sturdier desk model, the chief only needs a microphone and of course blank recording media.

(b) *The secretary's equipment.* Some manufacturers make a recorder for the executive and a transcriber for the secretary, while others merely manufacture one machine which travels between the chief and his typist. Whichever manufacturer is selected,

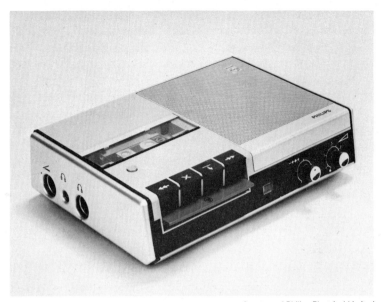

Courtesy of Philips Electrical Limited

Fig. 82.—Philips 86 transcriber.

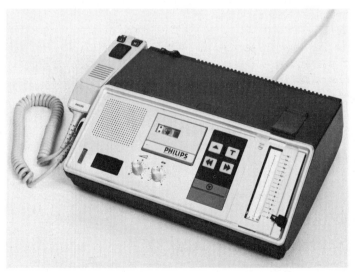

Courtesy of Philips Electrical Limited

Fig. 83.—Electronic (mains-operated) desk dictating machine.

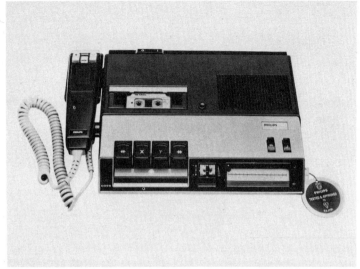

Courtesy of Philips Electrical Limited

Fig. 84.—Dictation/transcription machine.

Courtesy of Philips Electrical Limited

Fig. 85.—Pocket-sized battery-operated note-taker.

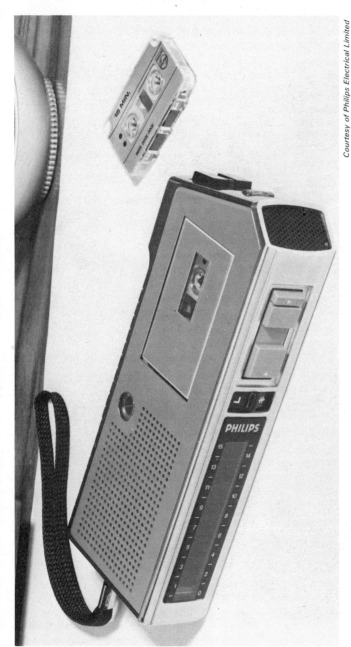

Courtesy of Philips Electrical Limited

Fig. 86.—Battery-operated portable dictating machine.

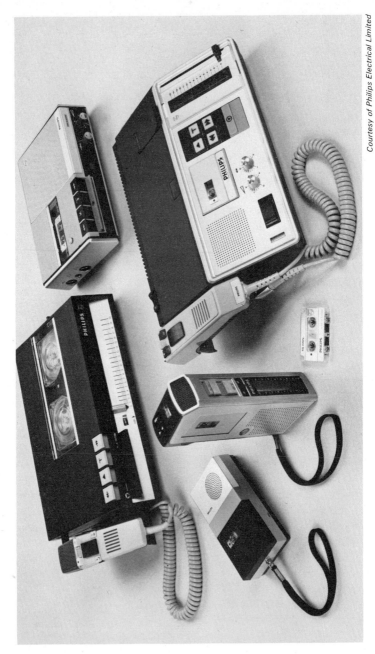

Courtesy of Philips Electrical Limited

Fig. 87.—Various types of audio equipment.

the secretary must have the machine from which to play back. In addition, she needs a foot control which enables her to stop, start, or reverse the dictation. Unless the dictation is to be aloud, she also requires a head-set, or earphones through which the dictation is fed. It is not essential that both ears should receive the sound and for those ladies who fear that earphones may disturb an elegant "coiffure" earphones are now made to hang down from the ears, rather like a doctor's stethoscope. An objection is also sometimes raised by the typists that it is uncomfortable to have the earphones in the ears, and the manufacturers have obligingly produced a small plastic ear-shaped device which can be "hooked" on to the ear, thus allowing the sound to reach the typist without actually inserting the plugs into the ear.

4. CENTRALISED DICTATION

This is sometimes called remote control dictation, or the banking system (Fig. 88).

The system involves a number of recording machines located in the typing pool, under the care of a supervisor. The dictators may be quite remote from the typing pool and are connected to the machines by telephone (which may be the existing P.A.X. or P.A.B.X. system or it could be directly wired). The dictator speaks into the telephone instrument and the material is recorded on the machine in the typing pool. Controls, *e.g.* stop, playback, record, are in the form of push buttons on the executive's telephone. When the dictation is over the supervisor in the typing pool has to place a fresh tape on the recorder.

A variation of the bank system is known as the tandem system (Fig. 88). Here, each typist has her own unit of two machines (hence the name "tandem"). An executive who wishes to dictate is routed to the first available unit and during dictation he has complete control of the machine. In this system, the executive is able to speak with the typist prior, during and after recording so special instructions may be given direct, and as dictation is automatically routed to the first available unit there is no need for a supervisor to be involved in allocating the work.

STENOTYPING MACHINES

This is an abbreviated writing system performed on a typing machine (Fig. 89). It is well known that shorthand (or other brief writing systems,

(*a*) The bank unit (ten receivers), incorporating the Grundig SL machine.

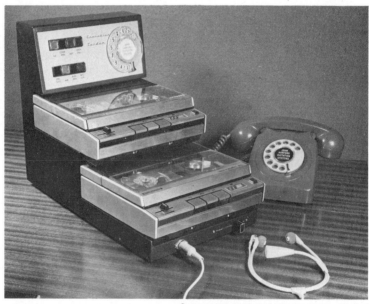

(*b*) The tandem unit, incorporating the Grundig SL machine.

Fig. 88.—Bank and tandem units.

(*a*) Stenotyping machine.

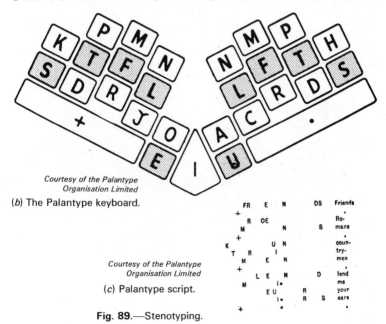

SKPTD+MFRNLJOEAUI·NLCMFRPTDSH

(*b*) The Palantype keyboard.

(*c*) Palantype script.

Fig. 89.—Stenotyping.

e.g. speedwriting) is faster than writing longhand; add that to the fact that typing is also faster than longhand writing and it will be seen how fast stenotyping (a combination of the two) can become. Stenotyping machines are small and easily carried; they are also quite silent, making them useful for, say, court reporting. The drawback lies in the fact that the user normally has to buy (or hire) her own machine and this is obviously costlier than buying a shorthand notebook and a pencil. It is also bulkier then a notebook to carry around.

ADDING AND CALCULATING MACHINES

Adding machines (Figs. 90–91) may be subdivided into add-listing and non-listing machines, the difference being that the listing machines provide a written record of the additions or subtractions. The advantage in having a "tally roll" will be appreciated if it is

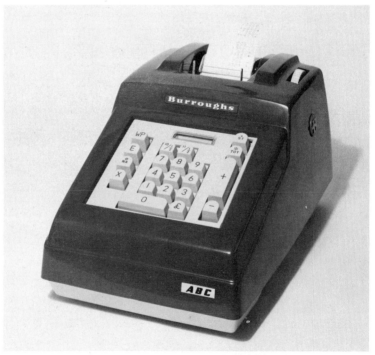

Courtesy of Burroughs Machines Limited

Fig. 90.—Hand-operated adding machine.

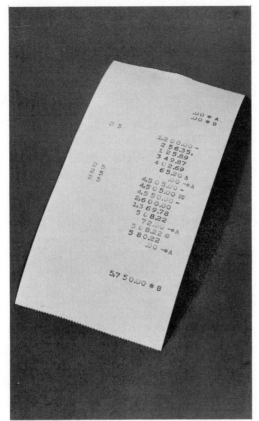

Courtesy of Burroughs Machines Limited

Fig. 91.—The list produced on an adding machine.

required to "check off" the items listed, if an error is later detected or if, for any purpose, a written record is to be kept. On the other hand, the non-listing machines display the figures in little "windows" which are subsequently cleared; no written figures are available, but since the printing operation is eliminated these machines are quicker to operate and there is no need to feed the roll of paper into the machines, nor is changing of the ribbon (similar to a typewriter ribbon) ever necessary since printing has no application here.

Adding machines may also be sub-divided into key-driven and lever-set categories, the former being operated by depressing keys (rather like the typewriter keys) and the latter being operated by setting small levers into the correct figure positions. The latter type is sometimes called "rotary" or "barrel" type, although rotary calculators may also be key-driven.

Like most other machines, adding machines may be manual or electric.

Although it is possible to multiply and divide on these machines, the process is rather cumbersome, the calculation being effected by a series of addition or subtraction. Thus, if it is required to multiply five by three, the figure five would be depressed three times, resulting in the total of fifteen. Some machines are of course provided with "repeat" keys to speed up the operation. There are also "correction" keys, to nullify a wrongly depressed key, "clear" keys to clear the machine of any figures it might be carrying, "total" and "sub-total" keys. On the listing machines, it is usually possible to indicate on the list whether the total shown is the final total or a sub-total, *e.g.* the letter "T" might appear to indicate "total," or the letter "S" to show that the figure was merely a sub-total, and the machine was not cleared of that figure.

Calculating machines come in varying shapes and sizes, ranging from a comparatively small desk model to a large "monster" occupying more floor space than a clerk and his desk. They also come in varying degrees of sophistication, ranging from fairly simple, mechanical machines to complex (and costly) pieces of equipment incorporating an electronic "brain." Like the simpler adding machines, calculators may incorporate a tally roll or simply show the results in little "windows," no printed record being available. Apart from adding and subtracting, calculators allow faster multiplication and division than is possible on an adding machine; according to the type of machine, they will also calculate percentages and square roots at high speed.

MAILROOM MACHINES

The postal department of a large organisation houses much machinery and equipment, the most commonly used types being listed below:

1. LETTER OPENER

This machine (Fig. 92) incorporates a sharp blade (similar to a guillotine), and as the envelopes are fed through, a minute strip is cut from the edge of the envelope. These machines are capable of operating at extremely high speeds and would only be used where the volume of incoming mail warranted the expenditure. Prior to being put through the opener, the envelopes should be sorted into sizes (the opener may be adjusted to cope with various envelope sizes) and the envelopes should then be tapped lightly against a flat surface, *e.g.* the table, to ensure that the contents fall away from the top. If

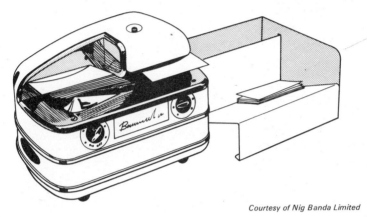

Courtesy of Nig Banda Limited

Fig. 92.—Letter-opening machine.

this is not done, there is a risk that the letter inside the envelope may be cut as the guillotine slices a thin strip from the top of the envelope.

2. FOLDING MACHINE

This ingenious piece of equipment (Fig. 93) will fold sheets of paper into pre-determined sizes. There may be provision for one or more folds, and the position of the folds is easily adjusted. A whole stack of statements, or circulars, will be dealt with in a matter of minutes, and be ready for insertion into envelopes.

3. INSERTING AND SEALING MACHINE

Linked to the folding machine may be a further piece of equipment which will guide the folded sheets into their envelopes and seal down the envelopes.

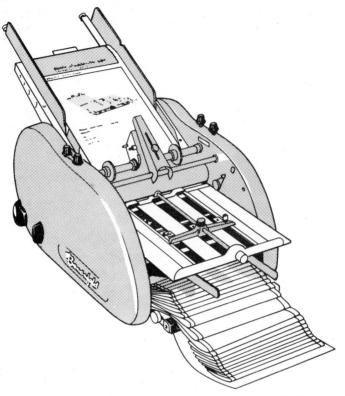

Fig. 93.—Folding machine.

4. COLLATOR

It often happens in business that a circular, price list, report, etc. which runs into many pages has been prepared. When all these pages have been duplicated, they must then be put together in numerical (or other required) order: in other words, they must be collated. It is obviously time-consuming to do this by hand, and it also requires much space: imagine spreading fifteen or twenty "piles" over a desk. They would spill over on to the floor! Collators may be electrically or manually operated, and consist of a number of slots into which the sheets are placed in the required sequence. When the machine is operated, each slot releases one sheet and these sheets either drop down in the correct order into a receiving tray or "pop up" ready for collection in the correct order, according to the type of machine. The great advantage is of course speed of operation: some machines can collate up to 15,000 sheets per hour.

5. FRANKING MACHINE

This machine (Figs. 94 and 95) "prints" the postage required on each

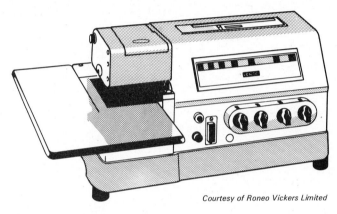

Courtesy of Roneo Vickers Limited

Fig. 94.—Hand-operated postage machine.

envelope, thus effecting a saving in the time taken to affix stamps. Apart from speed of operation, there are other advantages in the use of franking machines.

1. Pilfering of stamps is eliminated, since there is no need to keep postage stamps in the office.
2. Employees' private mail is less likely to be put through the office post when the envelopes are franked since it becomes obvious that the sender has not troubled to buy a stamp.
3. It is possible to incorporate a short slogan, thus affording a cheap means of additional advertising.
4. Envelopes which are spoiled or for any other reason not used after franking may be retained and the postage refunded.
5. The machine registers the amount of postage spent and this is then paid direct to the Post Office in a lump sum, so that the risk of "running out" of stamps is eliminated. It is, however,

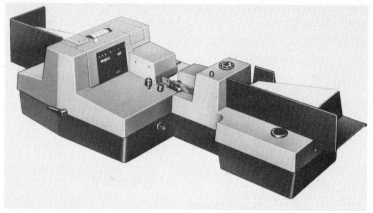

Courtesy of Roneo Vickers Limited

Fig. 95.—High speed franking machine that automatically feeds, seals, franks, stacks and counts in one operation.

necessary to take care that the amount of credit allowed is not exceeded.

On the other hand, there are certain disadvantages and conditions which must be complied with, for example:

1. A licence must be obtained from the local Head Post Office.
2. Payments *in advance* in respect of postage must be made from time to time at a specified Post Office where the machine must be presented for meter setting or registering.
3. The correspondence franked must be faced, securely tied in bundles and handed in at a specified Post Office. (It is possible to make special arrangements to post into a mail box or have the mail collected from the office premises by a postman.)
4. Each week a control card must be tendered to the Post Office showing the readings of the meter as at the end of each weekday.
5. The machine must be inspected and maintained at least twice in each six months to ensure clear and distinct marking and accuracy in recording.

The following are some manufacturers licensed by the Post Office to rent or sell franking machines:

Acral Ltd.,
Bush Fair,
Harlow, Essex.
CM18 6NG

Hasler (Gt. Britain) Ltd.,
Hasler Works, Commerce Way,
Croydon, CRO 4XA

Pitney-Bowes Ltd.,
The Pinnacles,
Harlow, Essex.
CM19 5BD

Roneo-Neopost Ltd.,
Roneo House,
74 Upper Richmond Road,
Putney, London, SW15 2TY

The Singer Company (U.K.) Ltd.,
Friden Division, Friden House,
101 Blackfriars Road,
London, SE1 8HP

6. ADDRESSING MACHINE

This useful piece of office machinery (Figs. 96–98) enables the same name and address or any repetitive data to be reproduced as many times as required from one master plate. The most common application is of course where a large number of addressees,

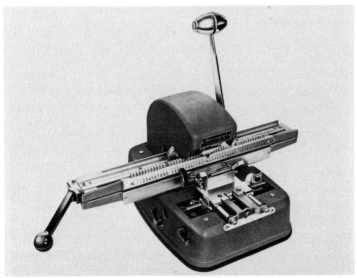

Courtesy of Addressograph-Multigraph Limited

Fig. 96.—Addressing machine for maintaining small or medium lists or as anciliary equipment in larger installations.

Courtesy of Addressograph-Multigraph Limited

Fig. 97.—Hand-operated portable addressing machine with application to many business routines, especially where repetitive information has to be written on to unit documents and lists.

e.g. customers, shareholders, employees, have to be written to periodically. The procedure is to prepare a master plate, check it for accuracy and file it until required. When the envelopes have to be addressed they are passed through the machine, and as they come into contact with the plates, so the address is reproduced on the envelope or other document. There is no need for further checking' for accuracy once the plate has been checked. Addressing machines may be hand- or electrically-operated—the latter of course being capable of high speeds. One manufacturer claims something in the region of 6,000 impressions per hour.

The masters may be either embossed plates of metal or plastic for which an embossing machine is necessary (but not difficult to operate) or stencil plates prepared on a typewriter, the principle being similar to that for stencil duplicating. Embossing may be done in the office if the machine is available; otherwise an efficient service is operated by the manufacturers.

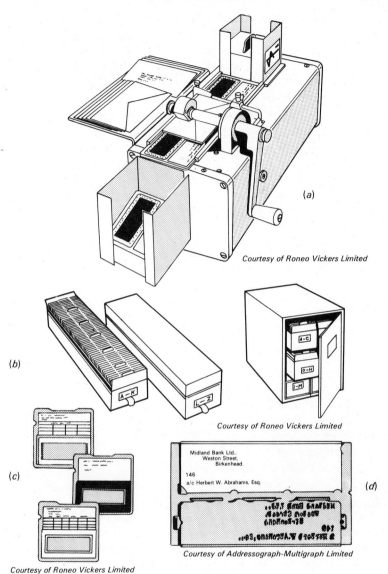

(a)

Courtesy of Roneo Vickers Limited

(b)

Courtesy of Roneo Vickers Limited

(c)

Midland Bank Ltd.,
Weston Street,
Birkenhead.

146
a/c Herbert W. Abrahams, Esq.

(d)

Courtesy of Addressograph-Multigraph Limited

Courtesy of Roneo Vickers Limited

(*a*) Hand addressing machine.

(*b*) Cabinets for standard-sized cards.

(*c*) Stencil cards that can be prepared on an ordinary typewriter.

(*d*) An embossed plate.

Fig. 98.—Addressing machine equipment.

While the primary use of addressing machines may be the addressing of envelopes, they can be used for several other purposes, *e.g.* addressing such communications as statements, invoices, and orders, which are then posted in window envelopes. They may be used to list names and addresses where credit transfers are being made; they may be used to list shareholders' names in dividend lists; to address dividend warrants; and of course they can be used for any information (not merely addresses) which has to be repeated over and over again.

7. SHREDDER

Where the work is of a highly confidential nature it becomes necessary to destroy all unwanted material (Fig. 99). Shredding is neater

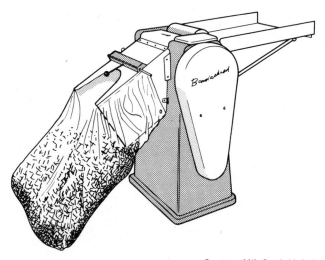

Courtesy of Nig Banda Limited

Fig. 99.—A shredding machine which delivers the shreds automatically into sacks.

and cleaner than burning, and, if required, it is possible to use the shredded paper for packing.

8. OTHER MAILROOM EQUIPMENT

Invariably, the post room will be equipped with a weighing machine, a guillotine, staplers, punches, string, simple envelope sealers like sponges or a roller in a water container, coloured pencils, airmail stickers, wrapping paper and other paraphernalia required to ensure the safe despatch of mail.

ACCOUNTING MACHINES

These machines (Fig. 100) are usually calculators linked to a modified typewriter provided with a small number of keys to print key words, *e.g.* "cash," "goods," "balance," "total," etc. Operation is

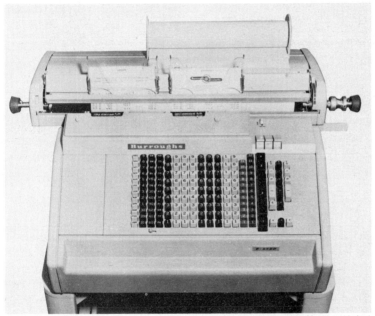

Courtesy of Burroughs Machines Limited

Fig. 100.—Dual printing accounting machine.

from the keyboard and a pre-determined control provides printing and calculating with a minimum of effort on the part of the operator. For example, when the operator depresses only one or two keys, the machine may continue to type out not only those figures which have been depressed from the keyboard, but also the calculations to be effected therefrom, as well as any words or sentences required, and all this is placed in the correct position on the paper, *e.g.* in columnar or other required form, without further effort on the part of the operator.

The same calculating machine may be used for a variety of procedures depending on the number of "registers" or "controls" (Fig. 101) which it is designed to accommodate. It is these registers which "tell" the machine its orders, *e.g.* at what point on the page to start printing, whether the figure printed is to be added or subtracted

Courtesy of Burroughs Machines Limited

Fig. 101.—Accounting machine programme selector. Each programme control centre contains two or four different programming schedules, each of which can be programmed for one or more accounting jobs: turn the knob to change from one job to another.

from another, whether the result is subsequently to be cleared from the machine or whether it is to be retained for further processing, and so on.

Wages, sales ledger and purchase ledger postings are typical examples of accounting procedures which can be conveniently mechanised.

PUNCHED CARD EQUIPMENT

A punched card installation is mainly used for sorting and processing data at high speed. The system makes use of small cards, not too different in size from a postcard. These cards are pre-printed with columns or "fields" displaying figures, and a small amount of key information is shown around the edges of the cards. When it is desired to insert certain information on the cards, the figure in the appropriate column is punched through (for this operation a punching machine, known as a *key-punch* is required), and the information thus recorded may be subsequently "read."

It must be appreciated that accuracy is essential and when the cards have been punched by the machine operator, they are then put through another process which verifies the original operation. Verification is by means of a machine which performs a similar job to the original, with the difference that if there should be a variation between the original punching and the verification, this is made evident by the machine "jamming" or "locking." The machine used for this operation is called a *verifier*.

When it is required to sift the information contained in the cards they must obviously be sorted, or analysed. This may be done by a machine which can be represented quite simply as a conveyor belt with a number of pockets or containers immediately underneath it. At one end of the machine is a hopper into which the unsorted cards are stacked; when the machine is set in motion, the cards are sent on their travels along the "conveyor belt" and those which contain the material for analysis, *i.e.* those with punched holes in certain positions, will be dropped *en route* into the containers below. The rest of the cards, *i.e.* those which are not required for analysis, because the punched holes they display are not in the positions which indicate relevant data, will travel to the end of the journey and drop into a hopper at the other end of the "conveyor belt." The above description is, perhaps an over-simplification, but it gives a good idea of the operation. It only remains to be said that with this machine cards are sorted at fantastically high speeds. The machine just described is known, not unnaturally, as a *sorter*.

There remains a *tabulator*, which is capable of printing the information contained on the punched cards in lay language. This machine can also perform calculations, *e.g.* where it prints a series of figures, it will, if required, calculate a total and show it in printed form.

While the above are some of the basic machines used in a punched card installation, it will be appreciated that many more auxiliary machines exist of which use is made in accordance with the purpose for which the system is being used.

The great advantages of punched card installations are not merely speed of operation, which in itself is considerable, but accuracy and, not least, the vast amount of information which can be produced from the analysis or "sorting" of the cards.

COMPUTERS

Electronic computers have made a tremendous impact on office work. Since they can perform at very high speed, a great number of clerical functions have been mechanised, thus reducing the number of clerks involved on work which the computer has "taken over." At first sight, this might be interpreted as a saving to the organisation which has installed the computer as the wages bill will of course be reduced. This, however, is not always so; in fact, even after allowing for the not inconsiderable initial cost of installing a computer, it might be found that wages are still as large an item as in the past. It might be asked how this paradox comes about since the computer now performs calculations which previously required the services of many clerks. It is true that *clerical* labour has been reduced but another type of labour has increased. To cope with the computer, the organisation will require programmers, systems analysts, accountants, to say nothing of a host of engineers, technicians and machine operators! The fact will probably emerge that more staff has been recruited (albeit not clerical staff)! It will be seen later that the saving in labour—although in some instances extremely important—is by no means the only advantage of installing a computer.

The great speed at which the computer operates is attributable in large measure to the electronic impulses of which it makes use, these impulses travelling at practically unimaginably high speeds, and also to the fact that calculations are performed by using the binary system of arithmetic instead of the system commonly used and known as the denary system of arithmetic. The difference between the two systems is that whereas the denary system consists of ten digits as its basis, binary makes use of only two, 1 and 0. Thus, in the binary system:

1 as we know it remains	1
2 becomes the figure 1 moved one digit to the left	10
3 becomes 10 plus 1	11
4 becomes the figure 1 moved three digits to the left	100
5 becomes 100 plus 1	101
6 is indicated by moving the last digit in 101 one place to the left	110

The important point to note is that only two digits: 1 and 0 are ever used, thus allowing for much greater speed than in the conventional denary method.

The basic components of a computer are not difficult to learn: they consist of the *input* unit at one end and the *output* unit at the other end. Between the two come three other units: the *arithmetic* unit, the *store* and the *control* unit.

(*a*) *Input* is fed into the computer usually by magnetic or punched means, *e.g.* where a punched card installation already exists, input may be in the form of punched cards.

(*b*) *Output* is also often in punched or magnetic form, but if the unit is linked to a printer, then of course the information is interpreted and translated into readable print.

(*c*) *Arithmetic unit.* Here are performed the actual calculations which are required.

(*d*) *Store.* This is really the "memory" of the computer. There are two types of store, the immediate access store and the random access store, and most computers make use of both. Information is actually stored here until required.

(*e*) *Control unit.* The control unit tells the computer what to do, *i.e.* what operations to perform, in what sequence they shall be done, what shall be done with the information when it becomes available, whether it is to go into the store for later use, and so on.

The units may be visualised as in Fig. 102.

It will be appreciated that apart from the basic parts of a computer there must be much ancillary equipment. This could take the form of a complete punched card installation, of a high-speed printer (capable of printing perhaps a complete page at a time, *i.e.* not line by line) and any number of other machines.

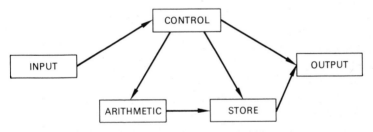

Fig. 102.—Flow chart of control units.

As explained earlier, it appears that the fears that mechanisation or computerisation would bring about reduction in staff have been unfounded and in many cases more staff have actually been recruited. However, it must be admitted that it is a different category of staff that needs to be recruited and while redundancies might genuinely occur in clerical staff as a result of mechanising certain operations, many firms have been able to give (and maintain) assurances that staff would not be made redundant as a result of mechanisation. After all, natural wastage of staff over a period of time will effect the required reduction (without hardship) if no replacements are made;

people who work in offices leave for a variety of reasons: to get a better job, to get married, to have babies, to retire and so on.

Speed of operation is invariably counted as one of the main advantages of using a computer. In fact, while this advantage cannot be denied it is not always the main one. *Accuracy* is an important factor; so is the *saving in clerical labour.* But perhaps most important of all is the amount of *information which can be made available to management.*

Short-answer Questions

1. How is it possible to read documents after they have been microfilmed?

2. Give three advantages of an electric typewriter over a manual one.

3. What are the main features of a "Varityper"?

4. Why is the telex system sometimes described as the written telephone call?

5. What equipment is used in audio-dictation and audio-typing, other than the transcriber itself?

6. Why might you prefer an add-listing machine to a non-listing one?

7. Name five machines commonly found in the postal department of a large organisation.

8. Distinguish between an adding machine and an accounting machine.

9. What are the main machines used in a punched card installation?

10. Give three advantages to be gained from installing a computer.

Past Examination Questions

1. If an employer spells technical words when dictating into a tape recorder, suggest how he may make sure that the transcriber will not confuse letters which sound similar.

Give one point in favour of each of the following recording media:

(*a*) magnetic; (*b*) non-magnetic. (*R.S.A.*)

2. Describe briefly two types of machines which might be used to speed the despatch of correspondence. (*R.S.A.*)

3. Give four reasons to support the theory that electric typewriters are more efficient than manual typewriters. (*R.S.A.*)

4. For what purposes are the following used:

(*a*) a VariTyper; (*b*) a teleprinter? (*R.S.A.*)

5. The Post Office offers the Telex service. What is this?
(*R.S.A.*)

6. Write a full note on each of the following:

(*a*) authomatic typewriter; (*b*) typewriter with variable type; (*c*) electric typewriter.

Your answer should include two examples of the purposes for which each of these machines may be used. (*L.C.C.*)

7. Your chief is proposing to purchase an audio machine which you will have to use. Before making the purchase he has asked for your views on:

(*a*) Whether the idea is a good one and (*b*) any particular machine you prefer.

Try to justify your answer with good reasons and examples.
(*L.C.C.*)

8. What calculations other than addition may be performed on an adding/listing machine? Explain briefly how these are made. Give an example to illustrate when this machine might be used in preference to a lever set rotary calculator. (*L.C.C.*)

9. You have been asked to furnish information on microfilming to your employer who is considering its introduction into your office. Write a memo to him setting out quite clearly the advantages and disadvantages of the system. (*L.C.C.*)

10. The Managing Director of your Company has asked you to visit the Business Efficiency Exhibition to report on any one piece of equipment which you feel is long overdue in your office. Prepare the necessary report. (*L.C.C.*)

CHAPTER 23

THE DAILY ROUTINE . . .

INTRODUCTION

EVERY job of work can be broken down into a routine. The whole *year's* work is probably divided broadly into work leading up to (*a*) the annual statutory audit and the Annual General Meeting, (*b*) the launching of a new product, (*c*) the annual visit to agents abroad, and so on. (Note these events occur once in the yearly cycle.) A more detailed study of the work might reveal that in a *month* there is also a routine which may be established: thus price lists are issued or revised, work schedules and progress reports are made out, monthly profit and loss figures are extracted, statements are sent out to debtors, the bank reconciliation statement is made out, the petty cash book is balanced. (These—and of course many other jobs—are probably done only once in the monthly cycle.) Even the *day's* work is punctuated by tasks which occur regularly each day. This does not mean that work goes on humdrum every day with monotonous regularity: certainly some tasks are monotonous; certainly some tasks recur at the same time in the same way each day; but this need not be a bad thing: it could for instance mean that such tasks are carried out with less effort; that familiarity with the routine makes for anticipation of such tasks and allows the secretary to carry them out with that efficient, "unflustered" look which is so often used to describe the perfect secretary. It follows from the very fact that some tasks are familiar in every detail and can be anticipated that this must allow the secretary more time to organise and deal with those exceptional tasks which also occur as part of her day's work.

It is not only the secretary who has a routine to follow; of prime importance is the establishment of the boss's routine: once this is known she can arrange her day to fit in with his requirements. After all, it must be remembered that a secretary's prime function is to be of assistance to her chief. She must not try to bend him to suit her routine (unless in exceptional circumstances she is in a position to judge that such action would be to his ultimate benefit). Rather should she try to mould her day's work into his.

THE BOSS'S DAY

This must do some extent vary with the individual boss and the particular department in which he finds himself, but it is fairly safe to assume that one of the first things he will do when he arrives in the morning is to look at his diary to note any particular appointments or meetings for the day. (His secretary will have seen that his desk is tidy and his diary laid in a prominent position on it, not necessarily opened for all to see.) Depending on the time for meetings and appointments, the next item on the boss's agenda for the day is probably dealing with correspondence. This will have been arranged for him by his secretary, who will not of course have forgotten to take in any reminders for action on previous correspondence. When he has had time to sort through the correspondence to be dealt with, he may ask her in to take instructions. Some letters may be dictated in full; others may be given to her in outline only: "Say we can only offer £500 and don't make it sound as if we are too keen"; "Find out what we ordered last year and place a similar order again"; "say, yes, I am interested in his proposals for advertising our Mark II and could he come and discuss these with me—make an appointment for some time next week." Other instructions again may come to the secretary in the form of a terse "No"; "Yes"; "Accept"; written on the incoming letter itself.

Probably before the correspondence has been fully dealt with, it is time for tea or coffee; perhaps there is time to relax before attacking the rest of the work; if not, tea must be sipped in between letters. Correspondence out of the way, the chief is left to carry out the rest of his work on his own: he may have accounts to balance, reports to draft, meetings to attend, visitors to receive. If possible, the secretary should know in outline how his day will go and where she may contact him if need be. Before the end of the day he will deal with any new urgent work, will sign the letters his secretary has typed for him and will give any necessary instructions for the next day's work.

THE SECRETARY'S DAY

It has been said before that she must mould her day to fit in with her boss's routine. Eventually a pattern will emerge for all but the most erratic of bosses and the secretary will be able to plan her own day. Her diary must be consulted as well as her boss's. The mail must be opened, sorted, collated with files or other documents and made ready for dictation. Reminder folders must be searched for letters requiring action and all must be placed, preferably in order of urgency, on the boss's desk for attention. It might be a good time to clear the filing tray of last night's copy letters while he is glancing through the correspondence; then she is probably called in for dictation. An hour or so later, it is time for morning break. Dictation completed, she must now see what other work has to be dealt with. There may be travel arrangements to make, hotel reservations to make, itineraries to prepare for her chief. If he has to attend a meeting, there will be papers to be got ready in his brief case. Meanwhile, there will be the day's letters to type, telephone calls to answer, visitors to be ushered in and others to be discreetly put off. The chief is probably not sitting quietly in his office all this time. He punctuates the secretary's day with additional instructions, last minute requirements, urgent work to be done before anything else!

The secretary's day has been condensed into a single paragraph! But each of her duties could be developed—they sometimes take days to complete! Let us take just one or two examples:

1. TRAVEL ARRANGEMENTS

Is his passport valid? If not, apply to the Passport Office, Clive House, Petty France, London, SW1H 9HD and try to give them adequate notice, not just a day or two. Are entry visas required? Find out from the foreign Embassy and/or the travel agent whether any special requirements apply for the particular country. Make reservations (road, rail, sea, air) noting any special requirements of the chief, *e.g.* reserved seat, window seat, sleeper, etc. Make hotel reservations either through travel agent or personally.

Make a note of any office papers he must take with him, so that you can pack them in his brief case at the last moment. Order foreign currency from the bank and note the chief's requirements as to travellers' cheques, currency, etc. Here also, try to give adequate notice if possible, not just a day or two. When arrangements have reached the final stages, prepare the chief's itinerary. This should show clearly times and places of arrival and departure, hotels booked in each town, and where meetings have been definitely arranged, these should also be shown. If the travel is extensive, it may be preferable to have an itinerary for the actual travel and a separate diary to show the activities arranged for each day. Whatever method is adopted, there are two overriding factors: *it should be absolutely clear to understand* and *the secretary should retain a copy in the office.*

2. RECEPTION DUTIES

It is often one of the secretary's duties to receive visitors for her chief and conduct them to his office. Where appointments have been made in advance, these callers will of course be expected, and it is pleasant (and politic), to show the caller that he is indeed expected and welcomed. A few words like "Mr. Brown is expecting you, Mr. Jones" or "Go right in Mr. Jones" (note that the visitor is addressed by name) is generally sufficient. If it is necessary to keep the caller waiting, the inconvenience should be minimised as much as possible by supplying him with interesting reading material, a cup of tea or coffee and, of course, a plausible excuse for the chief!

Some visitors are not so welcome, and the secretary may be instructed to divert them from her chief. On no account should she take it upon herself to assume that a person should not be seen by the chief: he should always be consulted. Where it is clear that a caller is not to be taken to the boss, the secretary may suggest some other appropriate person in the office whom the visitor could contact; see him herself, make note of his requirements and promise to pass these on to her chief; invent a plausible excuse why the chief may not be seen. Circumstances (and the secretary's ingenuity) will dictate which line of action should be taken, but she should be polite and tactful at all times. Even if the visitor is a nuisance there is no need to be discourteous.

It will be seen that the daily routine can itself be quite exacting and often varied, but occasionally things happen that are totally unforeseen and could not by any stretch of the imagination be classed as part of a secretary's regular duties.

Short-answer Questions

1. Sometimes the chief will give his secretary an "outline" of his reply to a letter. What does this mean?

2. Name two tasks which should be performed in the morning before the chief arrives.

3. Where would you go to obtain a new passport?

4. Where could you obtain information about a foreign country to which your chief intended to travel?

5. How could you tactfully keep some would-be visitors away from your chief?

6. Give three points to which you should pay attention before your chief goes on a trip abroad.

7. What is an itinerary?

8. If a visitor for whom an appointment has been made arrives, but your chief is not yet ready to receive him, how can you minimise the inconvenience?

9. Suggest briefly a daily routine for the secretary.

10. What is one of the last tasks a secretary does before going home from work?

Past Examination Questions

1. "A secretarial post calls for much initiative because it is possible for a good private secretary to save her employer a great deal of time by the quick anticipation of his requirements and possible future action." Justify this statement. (*L.C.C.*)

2. Reception duties form part of many secretarial posts and some callers do not have appointments. Describe the secretary's role in:

(*a*) receiving callers with appointments;

(*b*) dealing with callers without appointments. (*L.C.C.*)

3. (*i*) Your employer will shortly be travelling abroad. Where will you obtain:

(*a*) Passport; (*b*) Visa; (*c*) Foreign currency?

What other arrangements might you be expected to make in order to ensure a trouble-fr*e journey for your employer?

(*ii*) How will you deal with incoming mail while your employer is away? Your answer should cover routine correspondence as well as matters which need to be referred to your employer before you can deal with them satisfactorily. Your employer expects to be away from the office for one month. (*L.C.C.*)

4. The private secretary's work is mainly concerned with assisting her immediate employer. Describe some aspects of her job which demonstrate how this aim can be achieved. (*L.C.C.*)

5. As secretary to the junior partner in your firm, you are asked to assist him with arrangements for the visit to this country of three potential customers from abroad. They will be accompanied by their wives, and are expected to stay for three days. List the points to which you will need to give attention and add any suitable comments.

(*L.C.C.*)

6. What work is normally undertaken by the secretary before her chief begins his day at the office? Why is it necessary for her to perform these tasks? May any such work be done at any other time?

(*L.C.C.*)

7. Apart from shorthand and typewriting, which parts of your training in secretarial duties do you feel will be of most value to you in modern office life? Give your reasons.　　(*R.S.A.*)

8. (*a*) Explain what different items you might expect to find in your own and your employer's office diaries.

(*b*) List the actions you would take after you had made an appointment by telephone for your employer to attend a business meeting the following week.　　(*R.S.A.*)

9. Your employer has left you the following note: "Tuesday, Miss Smith—After you went home today, I got a message to say I was to go to Head Office tomorrow. I had a luncheon date with a Mr. Jones for tomorrow, and, I think, some other appointments, but although I looked in your drawer I couldn't find the office diary. Please see to all necessary things, and order a car to meet the train from N. . . . I think it leaves at 5.40 p.m., but check. I have to go to the Executives' dinner at the Savoy. I have left a cheque for you to cash at my bank, and my dinner jacket is at the cleaners round the corner, being pressed." State in what order you would deal with the necessary matters.　　(*R.S.A.*)

10. Your employer will be away from the office all day tomorrow as he has a number of outside appointments and is also attending a meeting with business colleagues. He asks you to get his papers ready for him and to give him a note of his appointments. How would you prepare his papers? What information would you give him, and in what form?　　(*R.S.A.*)

CHAPTER 24

...AND EMERGENCIES
(including safety in the office)

ALL the characters and events described in this chapter have existed in the author's experience. They bear relation to and have been inspired by individuals and occurrences known to the author, and none of the incidents is pure invention!

SAFETY IN THE OFFICE

Safety is more than a matter of implementing the provisions of the *Offices, Shops & Railway Premises Act* 1963. It is a matter of using one's common sense; of anticipating and thereby avoiding the possibility of accidents. (Did you know there is a theory that there are no "accident-prone" people, only stupid ones who are unable to foresee the dangers?) Trailing telephone flexes could trip you up, but so could the lead of any electrical machine: is your electric typewriter close to a power point? Do you remember to pull out the plug before leaving in the evening? (It is not enough to merely switch off.) Open drawers, especially the bottom drawer of a filing cabinet, can be a real menace. Have you ever lifted a typewriter? Well, don't, especially if it is an electric one. They are even heavier. Just as you would do in your own home, avoid putting things too close to the edge of the desk. Finally, if you are working with machinery, duplicators, calculators, etc. remember to switch off the current before investigating any faults, avoid poking with your fingers and always, BE CAREFUL.

IS FIRST AID A NECESSARY PART OF YOUR SECRETARIAL TRAINING?

After reading the following incidents, you may feel that a certificate in First Aid is as useful as (if not even more useful) than a certificate in shorthand or typing!

(*a*) Some bosses, perfect in every other way, have irritating habits that will not be cured. Mr. A is a portly gentleman: he likes to tilt back and forth in his chair while he concentrates on his dictation. The floor is highly polished and there is no carpet under his chair. At first this makes Miss Smith highly nervous: she tends to concentrate more on the degree of the angle between his chair and the floor than on her dictation but weeks go past and nothing happens. She begins to think that he has great expertise in judging just how far he can go. She is lulled into a false sense of security. Suddenly one morning, in the middle of dictation (a lengthy and complicated report which required much concentration) IT HAP-PENS! There is a loud crash and when a startled Miss Smith looks up from her notebook she sees, where her chief sat facing her across the desk but a moment ago, nothing but a blank wall! There is a moment of stark, stunned silence, then little noises, splutterings and growls give an indication of where he is. Miss Smith looks under the table: amid a confusion of papers and files, chair legs and table legs, human legs and wastepaper baskets, Mr. A struggles up. He is holding a handkerchief to his face, (both are very red—both the handkerchief and his face, that is). When he removes the handkerchief, Miss Smith sees that he is bleeding profusely from the nose.

WHAT WOULD YOU DO?

(*b*) Mr. B is a dapper little man, foreign, with all the charm and endearing mannerisms which English girls find irresistible in men from his country. There is only one thing wrong: when he concentrates on his dictation, he likes to play with a thin rubber band. He pulls it this way and that way, winds it round his fingers, pulls it taut until Miss Smith is sure that it will snap and fly into her face. It has snapped many times but always misses her. Miss Smith has tried everything, from "tut-tut" and frowning looks, to hiding all the rubber bands in the office, but he must have an inexhaustible supply at home. One day, of course, the inevitable happens. Miss Smith feels a sharp sting right in the middle of her forehead.

WHAT WOULD YOU DO?

(*c*) It isn't only the chief who does foolish things. Sometimes Miss Smith herself is guilty. Her office is in one of those nice modern blocks, with picture windows and her desk is near the wall by one of those windows. The only trouble is that they are just a little too high for her to reach by hand and . . . well . . . sometimes it's too much trouble to go and find the window pole to use. So, ingeniously, Miss Smith has discovered that if she pulls open the bottom drawer of her desk and stands on it, she can just reach the window to close it. She has done it often, nothing can happen . . . or can it? One day there are two heavy ledgers on the right side of her desk in addition to the usual telephone, typewriter, In and Out trays, etc. She balances on that drawer just once too often and this time it is the chief in his adjoining room who is startled by a loud crash. Miss Smith finds herself on the floor in a welter of over-turned desk and chair, a tangle of telephone wires and share ledgers. The telephone receiver is draped over her shoulder, the In tray is balanced on her head and Mr. C is peering anxiously over the corner of the desk.

WHAT WOULD YOU DO?

OTHER POSSIBLE SITUATIONS

AN APOLOGY TO MR. D

Once again Miss Smith is to blame. She is working abroad in a sun-drenched Mediterranean town. She is taking dictation, sitting in a large, comfortable armchair. She was up very late last night, at a party and today, sitting in a comfortable armchair, with the sun streaming in, shining its gentle warmth over her . . . well, Mr. D, you really were an impossibly slow dictator. The next thing she knew, something had awakened Miss Smith, but what? A surreptitious glance at Mr. D reveals nothing: he is busy leafing through a file. How long has she been asleep? Has Mr. D noticed?

WHAT WOULD YOU DO?

WOULD YOU LIE FOR HIM?

Mr. E is young, gay, friendly. He has innumerable girl friends who telephone him often at the office. Young Miss Smith shares an office with Mr. E and has an extension of his telephone on her desk. This is most convenient, for when the telephone rings, they both pick up the receivers simultaneously. As expected, it is one of the girl friends. "Is Mr. E there, please?" An enquiring glance at Mr. E finds him gesticulating wildly. Miss Smith says:

"No, I'm afraid he isn't in at the moment; may I take a message?"

"When do you expect him back?" Mr. E shakes his head violently.

"I'm afraid he didn't say."

"Are you sure he isn't there?"

"Why, yes, of course I am."

"Well, you don't sound too sure."

Miss Smith blushes to the roots of her hair. She glances at Mr. E whose angry frown does nothing to restore her confidence. She takes a deep breath: "I assure you, Mr. E is out at a conference. Would you like him to ring you back?"

"No, don't bother; I'll 'phone again later." There is a sharp click, Miss Smith replaces the receiver and breathes again.

"Well done, Miss Smith!" cries Mr. E.

Poor Miss Smith. If her typical English aversion to lying has been slightly tarnished, it is all in a good cause.

IS POSING PART OF YOUR JOB?

Mr. F is the editor of a newspaper. He is often out of the office on business and one afternoon, while he is out at a conference, the newspaper artist asks Miss Smith if he may sketch a portrait of her. Miss Smith's vanity succumbs. While the sketching is in progress . . . you've guessed it: Mr. F unexpectedly returns!

WHAT WOULD YOU DO?

COULD YOU COPE WITH A BURGLARY?

One morning, Miss Smith arrives at nine o'clock in the morning to find two or three juniors talking in whispers outside her door. Curiously she asks what is wrong but as soon as she looks inside her office she can see what has happened. Her desk is turned upside down, the four legs in the air. Part of the underside of the desk has been hacked through to get at the middle drawer which was locked. The safe door is wide open but no money was kept there, only ledgers and papers. These are now outside the safe, strewn all over the floor; some crumpled, some torn. Her chief has not yet arrived.

WHAT WOULD YOU DO?

DON'T SHOOT YOURSELF!

Miss Smith likes to arrive a few minutes before her chief in the morning, and to dust his desk and tidy it. One morning she accidentally knocks over and breaks a small statuette which stood on the corner of his desk. Her chief had once told her it had great intrinsic as well as sentimental value for him.

WHAT WOULD YOU DO?

EVERYTHING IN ITS PLACE

Miss Smith is busy collating the pages of a lengthy report which her chief has to take to a meeting the next day. Because her desk is full of papers, she carefully places an important photostat out of the way on the floor. The next day her chief telephones from his conference to say that she has forgotten to put the photostat in his brief case with the rest of the papers. Miss Smith remembers she had left it on the floor near her desk, but the cleaners have already done their work. There is no sign of the photostat.

WHAT WOULD YOU DO?

IS THERE A THIEF ABOUT?

Miss Smith works in a small office which she shares with one other girl. On her way home from work Miss Smith opens her purse to find her bus fare and discovers that her money is missing.

WHAT WOULD YOU DO?

EXTRA-CURRICULA DUTIES

Miss Smith's chief is away on holiday with his family. He has asked her, as a special favour, to look in at his home once a week to water his plants. One day, as Miss Smith goes to his house to perform this duty, she finds that a serious leak has developed in a water pipe in the kitchen and the flooding has damaged carpeting and furniture. There is water everywhere.

WHAT WOULD YOU DO?

SOMETIMES IT'S SAD

This is the saddest thing that happened to Miss Smith in all her working life: After many years of working for her chief, she arrives one morning to be met by the caretaker. He tells her that her chief had been working late the previous evening when he suddenly had what appeared to be a heart attack and died.

WHAT WOULD YOU DO?

DETERMINATION

The following story has nothing to do with emergencies or with safety, but it is a charming story, and a true one, and it illustrates clearly how common sense and determination can triumph over obstacles.

Mr. G is in his late fifties: he is a very large, very tall, very imposing gentleman. He appears almost perpetually crotchety and discontented; expects perfection from his staff. He travels a great deal, during which time his secretary's days are somewhat slack, but makes up for this on his return when he dictates very lengthy, technical reports. These must be quickly and impeccably transcribed. He is impatient and makes this obvious to all who attend him.

His secretary has been recruited in his absence: she is young, rather timid, but eager to learn and very determined to make a success of her job. From the other secretaries in her office, she hears how her chief is quick to find fault, grumbles perpetually, dictates too quickly, uses difficult, technical words . . . the list is endless. In short, no one likes him; everyone pities her.

Is it impossible to like this gentleman? In her chief's absence the young secretary daydreams about working so well that she achieves the perfection he is seeking. When he returns, she sets about translating the dream into reality. Through her tireless devotion to work a team spirit is forged between them. When technical words are incomprehensible to her, she firmly asks him to "spell them out, please." Next day, she quietly asks if she may purchase a technical dictionary "out of petty cash, please." In time, she discovers that a little "mothering" is acceptable. She is firm about such things as "have your tea before it gets cold, Mr. G"; or "I made the appointment for 2.30 p.m., as I thought you wouldn't want to rush through your lunch."

At first, Mr. G is amused; he doesn't think this timid little thing will last a week. But he begins to feel like an ogre; he must try not to frighten her: look at the way her eyes open wide when he growls. Miss Smith is winning. She lasts more than a week. By the time a month has gone by her chief would be sorry to see her go. A certain dry humour creeps into his attitude; mutual respect develops between them. Wonder of wonders! They get on like a house on fire!

CONCLUSION

I am occasionally asked for advice by secretaries who have a good, well-paid job, but do not really get on well with their chief. Is it really necessary to like your chief? In my opinion, there can be no doubt over the answer: emphatically yes. In fact, I would go so far as to say that if you cannot get on well with your chief, you should look for another job. As his secretary you must be prepared to work for him and with him; if necessary to start early and leave late; to learn enough of his "line of work" to become more useful to him; to anticipate his requirements. If necessary you must be reassuring, give confidence; at times perhaps be critical. You must be ready to shield him, to cover up for him, to make excuses for him, and, sometimes, to excuse him. Ask yourself, can this be achieved without mutual genuine liking and respect? Feelings cannot be disguised—not for long anyway; so for your sake be sincere; for his sake be loyal.

You will discover likeable traits in even the most formidable of bosses, but you must give yourself a chance to really get to know him; first impressions are not always right and, in any case, it helps to remember that you're not perfect either.

No attempt has been made to find answers to most of the situations described in this chapter as there may be more than one correct answer. The situations and emergencies which occur must be dealt with in the light of the particular circumstances prevailing at the time they happen. The seriousness of the situation, the degree of urgency, the extent of the damage, all have some bearing on the course of action upon which the secretary will decide. The important thing is to try to *think clearly*, to *appreciate the consequences of action taken* and to *act in the best interests of the chief.*

Short-answer Questions

1. Is it necessary to like your chief before you can be a good secretary to him?

2. What should you do if your chief dictates too fast for you?

3. What is the best remedy for a nosebleed?

4. You arrive in the office to find it has been burgled. What is the first thing you should do?

5. Should you refuse if your chief asks you to do some private work for him during office hours?

6. What should you do if your chief takes out some of the other

girls in the office even though, to your knowledge, he is a married man?

7. Should you accept if your chief's superior asks you if you would like to work for him instead of your chief; it would mean promotion for you?

8. Should you try to cure your chief of mannerisms which irritate you?

9. What would you do if you discovered you were a pound short in the petty cash box?

10. How could you assess if your work was giving satisfaction?

Past Examination Questions

1. Your employer is attending an important conference (not on the office premises); he expects to leave the conference at 5.30 p.m. At 4 p.m. his wife telephones you. She is most distressed, informs you that there has been a serious fire at your employer's home and although she is unharmed, she has been treated for shock and is now resting at her sister's home. She will not of course attend the dinner party at 7 p.m. to which she and her husband had been invited that evening. Describe in numbered paragraphs the action you would take. *(L.C.C.)*

2. Your chief normally arrives at the office at 9.30 a.m. You arrive at 9 a.m. You have made various appointments for him throughout the day; these include attendance at a directors' meeting (your chief is Company Secretary) and a trip to the airport to meet a foreign customer. At 10.30 a.m. you receive a visit from a police officer who informs you that your chief has been involved in an automobile accident and has been taken to hospital. How will you cope:

(*a*) with the appointments;
(*b*) with any urgent work requiring his attention;
(*c*) with any other matters that you think necessary?

(L.C.C.)

3. Your employer and his wife are touring by car and you can contact them only every few days. You go each day to their house to collect mail and to see that everything is all right. One day you find a cable from their adult son to say that he is arriving from Kenya the next day and will be staying with them for a few days. He gives his flight number and time of arrival. What would you do? *(R.S.A.)*

4. You work for a personnel officer. While she is on holiday you are left to deal with emergencies, although you are, of course, able to ask the advice of the executive members of the staff. A telephone operator does not turn up for work two days and neither telephones nor writes. Decide what you would do in these circumstances and write a memorandum describing your actions so that the personnel officer will be fully informed on her return. (*R.S.A.*)

5. You work for an architect who is an official of his professional association. He has been asked to represent his association at an international conference in Paris. He decided to combine the conference with a holiday in France and, therefore, is travelling in his own car. The day before the conference, he telephones from a small French village to say that he has crashed his car and, although not seriously hurt, he is feeling very shaken and quite unable to continue his journey to Paris. He asks you to take whatever action you consider appropriate with regard to the conference.

What action would you take in the circumstances? (*R.S.A.*)

6. The firm for which you work owns a small house which it has converted into offices. One evening, having agreed to work till 6.30 to finish some letters, you are the last to leave. You decide to go across the road to the letter box to post the letters and to come back for your things. When you get back you find that the latch on the front door has dropped (there is no back door) and your handbag, keys, meat for dinner and the work which you had promised to deliver on the way home are inside. What would you do?

(*R.S.A.*)

7. You work for an executive who often travels abroad for the firm. Before going on a three weeks' tour of America, he stays late in the office and dictates a number of letters, using a magnetic tape machine. He leaves the tape and the correspondence he has been dealing with on your desk with a note asking you to transcribe the letters and sign them on his behalf. You do not have time that day, so leave the tape in a tray on a table in your office. The next day, the tape is missing. You are very worried and spend most of the morning trying to find out what has happened to it. You eventually find that one of the younger girls in the department saw the tape lying about, as she thought, and put it in the box with other tapes awaiting re-use. The office manager had come in early in the morning, taken the top tape from the box, and had dictated for about a quarter of an hour.

You know that some of the letters dictated by your executive were related to the introduction of a new product and were not connected with the correspondence which he left on your desk. What would you do? (*R.S.A.*)

8. Your firm proposes to send a member of the staff on a fortnight's offset-litho course for which the firm will pay 20 guineas. This member of staff will then be available to assist the offset operator on a part-time basis. You are keenly interested in the offset machine and ask to attend the course. While you are there, you are invited by a friend's father to join his firm as a full-time offset operator at a salary which is much higher than the one you earn at present. He suggests that you should give a week's notice to your firm on returning from the course. How would you deal with this situation? Give the reason for your decision. (*R.S.A.*)

9. You are secretary/receptionist to a veterinary surgeon. He is on holiday and there is a locum (replacement) who does not know the district. The locum is visiting several scattered farms, and you are in the yard feeding a dog, when the telephone rings. You come in to find that the daily cleaner has answered it, and the only information she can give you is that a veterinary surgeon is wanted urgently at Blackhurst Farm. You can find no record of previous visits to this farm, and you cannot find it on a map. Describe what actions you would take and in what order to get the locum there as quickly as possible. (*R.S.A.*)

10. Your employer and his wife are on holiday abroad. Their twelve-year old son walks into your office and says he has run away from boarding school. What would you do? (*R.S.A.*)

CHAPTER 25

LEGISLATION

IN recent years much legislation affecting offices, employers and workers has been passed by Parliament. The following is a resumé of the contents of those Acts with which every senior secretary should be familiar.

THE OFFICES, SHOPS AND RAILWAY PREMISES ACT 1963

Based on earlier Factories Acts, the *Offices, Shops and Railway Premises Act* 1963, deals with the health, safety and welfare of persons employed to work in offices, shops and certain railway premises. It is worth noting that the provisions of the Act do not apply to premises in which only the employer's close relatives are employed, *e.g.* spouse, parent, grandparent, son, daughter, grandchild, brother or sister; nor does the Act apply to premises where "outworkers" work, *e.g.* where a person does work in his own home which is not also the employer's home. Finally the Act does not apply to premises used for no more than twenty-one hours work per week.

1. CLEANLINESS
All premises, furniture, furnishings and fittings within premises to which the Act applies must be kept clean. Dirt or refuse must not be allowed to accumulate and floors and steps must be cleaned at least once a week by washing, sweeping or other effective method.

2. OVERCROWDING
No room is to be so overcrowded as to cause risk of injury to the health of persons working in it. Account must be taken not only of the number of persons working in the room but also of the space occupied by furniture, fittings, machinery, etc. Each worker must have at least 40 sq. ft of floor space or 400 cu. ft capacity.

3. TEMPERATURE

Every room in which employees work (other than for short periods) must be maintained at a reasonable temperature and if the employees are not engaged in work involving severe physical effort, the minimum temperature after the first hour should be 16° C (60·8° F). The method of heating must not produce fumes or otherwise be likely to cause injury to the health of the workers. Finally a thermometer must be provided on each floor, in a conspicuous place and in such a position that employees may easily see it and the temperature determined.

4. VENTILATION

Every room must be well ventilated and this may be effected by the circulation of adequate supplies of either fresh or artificially purified air.

5. LIGHTING

Sufficient and suitable lighting must be provided throughout the premises. Artificial lighting is of course permitted providing it is properly maintained. Glazed windows and skylights used for lighting must be kept clean (inside and out as far as practicable) and free from obstruction.

6. SANITARY CONVENIENCES

Suitable and sufficient sanitary conveniences must be provided for employees at places conveniently accessible to them. These must be kept clean, properly maintained and effectively lighted and ventilated. If necessary, there should be proper separate accommodation for persons of each sex.

7. WASHING FACILITIES

Suitable and sufficient washing facilities must be provided for the employees, including a supply of clean, running hot and cold or warm water and in addition soap and clean towels or other means of cleaning and drying must also be provided. Washing facilities must be conveniently situated, effectively lighted and properly maintained. If necessary separate accommodation for persons of each sex should be provided.

8. DRINKING WATER

An adequate supply of wholesome drinking water must be available at conveniently accessible places for the employees. If the water is not piped then it must be kept in clean containers and must be renewed at least once a day. If the water is not available from a jet from which it is convenient to drink, then either disposable cups must be available or if glasses, etc. are provided then there must be an adequate number of them together with facilities for rinsing them in clean water.

9. ACCOMMODATION FOR CLOTHING

Suitable and sufficient accommodation must be made available where the employees may leave such clothes as hats, coats, rainwear, etc. There must also, so far as practicable, be some arrangement to enable such clothing to be dried if necessary. If the employees wear special clothing at work which they do not take home with them (*e.g.,* overalls for duplicating work, etc.) similar provisions must be made for such special clothing.

10. SITTING FACILITIES

Where employees have reasonable opportunities to be seated without detriment to their work, the employer must provide suitable seats for them in the ratio of not less than one seat to three employees.

11. SEDENTARY WORKERS

Where most of the work is (or can be) done sitting, employees must be provided with suitable seats and, if necessary, foot-rests.

12. EATING FACILITIES

Persons who are employed to work in shop premises and who eat their meals there must be provided with suitable and sufficient facilities for eating them.

13. FLOORS, STAIRS, PASSAGES, ETC.

All such spaces must be of sound construction, kept properly maintained and free from obstruction which might cause persons to slip. Staircases must have handrails on the open side(s) and all openings in floors must wherever practicable be securely fenced to prevent accidents.

14. MACHINERY

Dangerous moving parts, etc. must be securely guarded, fenced or otherwise made safe for the operator of such machinery. This requirement does not necessarily apply when the machine is being serviced but such servicing may only be carried out by persons who have attained the age of eighteen years.

Similarly, no person under the age of eighteen years may be allowed to clean any machinery if this would expose him to risk of injury.

Finally, no person, regardless of age, may be required to work at any machine of a dangerous character unless he has been fully instructed as to the dangers and has received sufficient training or is under proper supervision.

15. HEAVY WORK

No employee may be required to lift, carry or move a load so heavy that there is risk of injury to him.

16. FIRST AID

A properly equipped first aid box or cupboard must be readily accessible for each unit of 150 employees; each first aid box must be in the charge of a responsible person. At least one person in charge of first aid boxes must be properly trained in first aid treatment; he must always be available during working hours and these facts together with his name must be prominently displayed for the notice of employees.

17. FIRE PRECAUTIONS

Proper means of escape in case of fire must be provided and maintained free from obstruction. Exits must be distinctively marked, fire alarms must be installed and properly maintained, fire-fighting equipment must be provided and maintained, and finally the employees must be made familiar with means of escape and the routine to be followed in the event of a fire occurring. A Fire Certificate must be obtained if:

(*a*) more than twenty persons are employed on the premises at any one time;

(*b*) more than than ten persons are employed other than on the ground floor of the premises;

(c) any person is employed where highly inflammable materials are stored or used.

18. ACCIDENTS

If an accident occurs which causes the death of an employee or disables him from doing his work for more than three days it must be notified to the local authority.

> NOTE: It will be seen that the standards imposed by the *Offices, Shops and Railway Premises Act* 1963 are minimum standards and many responsible employers have been providing standards in excess of the minimum for many years. However, those employers who in the past have provided less than these standards for the welfare of their employees now have a legal obligation to improve the conditions under which their employees perform their work. It is interesting to note that the Act forbids the levying of charges on employees for any expenses which might be incurred for bringing the premises and conditions of work up to the standards required by this Act.

THE CONTRACTS OF EMPLOYMENT ACT 1972

This Act embodies the requirements of the *Contracts of Employment Act* 1963, as amended by subsequent legislation, *e.g.* the *Redundancy Payments Act* 1965 and 1969 and the *Industrial Relations Act* 1971. The main provisions are set out briefly below.

1. MINIMUM PERIOD OF NOTICE

The employer now has to give his employees the following *minimum* periods of notice:

> At least one week after thirteen weeks' continuous employment.
> At least two weeks after two years' employment.
> At least four weeks after five years' employment.
> At least six weeks after ten years' employment.
> At least eight weeks after fifteen years' employment.

The employee must also give his employer at least one week's notice after thirteen weeks' continuous employment, but this does not increase with longer service. These are minimum requirements and the two parties are of course at liberty to agree to longer notice. Similarly, the employer or the employee may waive the right to notice or may accept a payment in lieu of notice. Finally, either party may terminate the contract of employment without notice if the behaviour of the other justifies it.

2. WRITTEN STATEMENT OF TERMS OF EMPLOYMENT

Not later than thirteen weeks after the employment commences, the employer must give to the employee a written statement recording the more important particulars of the contract of employment. The following information must by law be included in the statement:

(*i*) The names of employer and employee.

(*ii*) The date when employment began (if five years ago or more, it is enough to state that the employee has been employed for not less than five years).

(*iii*) Rate of pay.

(*iv*) Intervals at which remuneration is payable, *e.g.* weekly, monthly, or other.

(*v*) Hours of work.

(*vi*) Holidays and holiday pay.

(*vii*) Provision for sickness and sick pay.

(*viii*) Pensions and pension schemes.

(*ix*) Length of notice to be given by employer and employee to terminate employment.

In the event that no specific terms have been agreed under certain of the above headings, then the written statement must specifically state this.

(*x*) The employee's rights in relation to trade union membership.

(*xi*) To whom the employee may apply in the event of a grievance about his employment, how such application is to be made and the procedure for dealing with the matter.

It is not essential for the written statement itself to set out in detail the full particulars under the above headings. It may, for example, refer the employee to other documents (*e.g.*, regulation handbooks, pension scheme booklets, etc.) which he has an opportunity of reading in the course of his employment.

The written information must be kept up to date. Thus changes in the terms of employment must be notified to the employee in writing within one month. Personal notification of changes is not essential; thus a circular notice which remains available for reference would be sufficient.

If a written contract of employment which covers all the required particulars exists between the employer and employee, and a copy is made available to the employee, then the written statement required by the Act need not also be given to the employee.

3. EMPLOYEES EXCLUDED

The Act does not apply to close relatives of the employer (*e.g.*, father, mother, husband, wife, son or daughter of the employer); nor does it apply to certain specified categories of employees.

THE REDUNDANCY PAYMENTS ACTS 1965 AND 1969

1. PAYMENT OF COMPENSATION

These Acts require employers to make compensation or redundancy payments to employees who are dismissed on grounds of redundancy. The amount of the payment is related to the pay, length of service and age of the employee, as follows:

(*a*) For each complete year of service after the forty-first birthday ... $1\frac{1}{2}$ weeks' pay.

(*b*) For each complete year of service after the twenty-second birthday ... 1 week's pay.

(*c*) For each complete year of service after the week which began before the eighteenth birthday ... $\frac{1}{2}$ week's pay.

There are reductions where the employee is over sixty-four years of age (fifty-nine for a woman) and in certain circumstances where a pension is due.

2. REDUNDANCY FUND

A Redundancy Fund is established from contributions collected with the employer's flat-rate National Insurance contribution for employees over the age of eighteen years. Employers who have to make redundancy payments as required by the Act are entitled to claim a rebate of 50 per cent of the cost from the Fund.

3. TIME LIMIT FOR CLAIMING

A redundancy payment cannot be claimed by the employee more than six months after the termination of his employment, so that if there is any dispute about entitlement to payment or the amount due, or if payment is agreed upon but not effected by the employer, the employee must serve a written claim on the employer within six months of the termination of employment, otherwise he loses his entitlement to the payment.

Similarly, an employer who makes a redundancy payment must submit a claim for the rebate to which he is entitled within six months of the date of making the payment. Disputes are settled by Industrial Tribunals.

4. EMPLOYEES COVERED BY THE ACT

Most employees in any kind of employment are covered by the provisions of the Act, but there are certain exceptions, *e.g.* close relatives of the employer, employees with less than two years' continuous service, part-time employees who work less than twenty-one hours a week, and certain other specified categories of employees.

THE EMPLOYER'S LIABILITY (COMPULSORY INSURANCE) ACT 1969

This Act came into force on 1st January, 1972. It applies to most employers with certain specified exceptions, *e.g.* local authorities, police authority, nationalised industries and certain others.

1. REQUIREMENT TO INSURE

Employers covered by the Act are required to insure against liability for injury or disease sustained by their employees in the course of employment. The insurance cover must be for at least £2 million in respect of claims arising out of any one occurrence. Most employees have to be insured, but there are certain exceptions, *e.g.* close relatives of the employer, employees not ordinarily resident in Great Britain and who are working here for fewer than fourteen consecutive days, and certain other specified categories of employees.

2. CERTIFICATE OF INSURANCE

This must be issued by the insurer to the employer within thirty days of the insurance contract being entered into, and similarly at each renewal. As from 1st January, 1973, employers must keep copies of their certificate prominently displayed at each place of business where the employee may see and read it.

THE EQUAL PAY ACT 1970

The object of this Act is to eliminate discrimination between men and women in regard to pay and other terms and conditions of employment. It comes into force on 29th December, 1975, thus giving employers an opportunity to effect the transition gradually, but it is noteworthy that the Act provides that if orderly progress towards equal pay is not being made, an Order may be made requiring the partial implementation of equal pay by 31st December 1973. In particular, women's rates of pay would have to be raised to at least 90 per cent of men's rates.

The Act applies to both men and women. It covers most employed persons, but there are minor specified exceptions, *e.g.* persons employed wholly or mainly outside Great Britain.

Short-answer Questions

1. Mention five aspects to which the *Offices, Shops and Railway Premises Act* 1963 relates.

2. What is the minimum temperature which must be reached after the first hour of work in premises to which the *Offices, Shops and Railway Premises Act* applies?

3. Name three Acts of Parliament which have been passed in the last ten years and which affect employers and employees.

4. What are the main requirements of the *Contracts of Employment Act* 1972?

5. What is the minimum period of notice of termination of employment which an employer may give an employee after thirteen weeks' continuous employment?

6. Must the employee give his employer any notice of termination of employment? If so, how long?

7. Mention three aspects of the employee's terms of employment which must be shown in the written statement which an employer must give to the employee.

8. At what stage of the employment must this written statement be given to the employee?

9. What is the object of the *Employers' Liability (Compulsory Insurance) Act* 1969?

10. What is the time limit within which an employee must serve notice of his claim to a redundancy payment?

CHAPTER 26

TIPS FOR THE EXAMINATION ROOM

UNLESS you are exceptionally talented, there is little point in attempting an examination without proper preparation. Some people think they are getting the benefit of a "trial run" if they enter for an examination even though there is little hope of gaining a pass but I would not advise this for a number of reasons: In the first place, you cannot hope to give of your best if you know in advance that you are not going to pass; then there is the psychological aspect. It is a well known fact that success breeds success—what then does failure breed? Finally consider the waste: the money for your entry fee, the time spent getting to and from the examination centre, the time and energy spent writing out the answers and the examiner's time reading these answers—all spent to no purpose.

PREPARATION

Proper preparation starts several months (sometimes years) before the ultimate examination. You must learn your subject and you must keep the ultimate aim before you like a carrot dangling in front of your nose, urging you forward whenever your efforts tend to flag. Knowledge may be gained in a number of ways: by experience, by reading, by listening, by looking, by questioning. If you can gain practical experience in the subject you are studying you will be "learning by doing"—one of the most effective ways of learning. Experience in an office is invaluable but if this is impossible to achieve the next best thing is to do project work and to make the most profitable use of simulated office conditions (often available in schools and colleges). It is a fallacy to think you can get by without reading: you might just scrape through the examination, but if you want to be *assured* of a pass then you must read what the experts have to say about the subject. And one expert is not enough. Only by reading a number of books (at the very least three) can you gain a proper appreciation of the depth of your subject; in this way also (sheer repetition) you will remember some of the masses of information which the examiners expect you to have at your fingertips. Listen to what other people have to say about the subject: listen to lecturers who are experts, listen to older friends who have already gained experience, listen to anyone who has something worth saying about the subject you are learning. Ask questions. If you do not understand, do not be too timid to question a lecturer; ask for opinions; question your friends. If you do not ask you will not be told. Always keep your eyes open. In most places where people work, there is an office of some sort not far away. If you cannot gain first hand experience of working in a commercial office yourself, try to watch other people at work in an office—any kind of office. There are offices in colleges and schools, in stores, in hospitals and wherever documentation is dealt with.

By assimilating the information gained from a *number* of experts, and by profiting from the experience of others, you will be developing something which is exactly what the examiners are looking for in your answers: *an informed opinion of your own.* This is more than a mere regurgitation of something you have read, it is more valuable than the sum of reading and experience, it adds a third quantity: your *own* interpretation.

PAST QUESTION PAPERS

Another valuable aid to the preparation for examinations is to invest in past question papers. These are cheap and easy to obtain from the examining bodies and can give a very real guide to the kind of questions that you may expect at your own forthcoming examination. They will also give you an idea of how well prepared you are for the examination, and finally they provide excellent material for you to work on when you give yourself practice in actually writing out answers under examination conditions. Another booklet well worth getting from the examining body is the Examiner's Report. This rarely costs more than a few pence and is really a mine of information and guidance. It is from the Examiner's Report that you get constructive criticism; that you gain a glimpse of the pitfalls which other candidates have stumbled into; that you find out what the examiner is really looking for. Reading the Examiner's Report in conjunction with the question paper to which it relates is one of the cheapest and yet most effective ways of learning to please the examiner.

STYLE

One other sure way to please the examiner is to cultivate a good style of writing. It is weak style, for example, to use the second person. Compare "You should try to anticipate your chief's requirements" with "The Secretary should try to anticipate her chief's requirements," (the examiner does not want you to tell him what he should do, nor does he really want you to address him in this chatty style).

Unless very sure of yourself, try not to be too assertive or dogmatic in your answers. Compare "The following is a list of the contents of the *Offices, Shops and Railway Premises Act* 1963" with "The following are some of the main provisions of the *Offices, Shops and Railway Premises Act* 1963." (Be big enough to admit that you may not be able to list them all and indicate at the same time to the examiner that you know that there are probably some other provisions not listed by you.)

Adopt the language, the jargon even, to suit the subject in which you are being examined. Compare "In duplicating work it is essential to make sure the text appears exactly where it is required" with "In duplicating work it is essential to secure accurate registration." This lends sophistication and a hint of expertise to your writing.

Set out your answers so that the evidence of knowledge contained in them is displayed to the best advantage. Make liberal use of paragraphs to indicate fresh ideas, underline headings, even words, for emphasis. Where the answer lends itself to such a style, listing is not only permissible but is concise and saves valuable time. And remember, if the question asks for a list you will not get get full marks by writing an essay; but an introductory paragraph and a conclusion are of course permissible. Conversely, if a discussion is required you will not completely satisfy the examiner by offering a *list* of ideas.

CONCISENESS

Try to show how wide your knowledge is *without digressing.* For example in dealing with a question on, say, carbon copies, it would not be out of place to devote a line or two to electric and noiseless typewriters and their effect on the number of carbon copies obtainable; but it would be a useless digression to write about the advantages and disadvantages of these machines.

LEGIBILITY

Above all, write legibly. Always remember that your script is a drop in the ocean of scripts which the examiner has to mark. If you want to be assured of a pass, your handwriting must do justice to the knowledge you have acquired. It is your only means of communication with the examiner; if he can't read what you have written he will have no means of discovering whether you know the answer to the question or not—and if there is one thing you can be sure of it is that the examiner does not like to waste time deciphering poor handwriting when hundreds of other scripts are waiting to be marked. From a potential secretary, perhaps more than from any other candidate, the examiner has a right to expect neat, legible handwriting; thoughtful, logical answers and well displayed, carefully presented essays. Always remember that there are probably hundreds if not thousands of other scripts to be marked. To be *assured* of a pass, you must try to "sell" your script to the examiner, you must try to make it a little neater, a little more pleasing, a little more knowledgeable than the other scripts.

Do not be too brief: two or three lines will rarely earn a good mark. However, if time is running out and you realise that you will be unable to complete all the answers then at least jot down in list form the ideas you would have developed: this will earn you a few marks.

If, just prior to the examination date, you can honestly say to yourself that you have prepared yourself to the very best of your ability, then you will secure a pass.

THE EXAMINATION ROOM

Having worked for so many months in preparation for the examination, do not risk spoiling it all by arriving late on the day itself. Make sure you know the location of the centre, and check that the transport you will use to get there is reliable. See to it that you allow enough time to get to the centre well in advance of starting time (half an hour is not too early), and take a sweet to suck or a book to read if you like for the interval before the examination starts.

From the word "go," your aim must be to communicate your knowledge to the examiner. The time at your disposal is limited, and you must make the best use of it.

RULES TO REMEMBER

RULE 1
Read the instructions and make up your mind to follow them. Next note the time allowed, subtract ten or fifteen minutes, divide the answer by the number of questions *to be attempted* (not the total number of questions) and you arrive at the approximate length of time you should devote to each question. Don't worry if you exceed this time on one or two questions, you will be able to make it up on one of the other questions, and in any case you have ten or fifteen minutes (which you allowed in your calculation) to fall back on if need be.

RULE 2
Now read the instructions again and note whether there is a compulsory question, whether some questions carry more marks than others, whether you must answer a specified number of questions from a particular section of the paper and any other requirements of that nature. Next, read through the questions and choose those you intend to answer.

RULE 3
Unless you are specifically told to answer the questions in numerical order *and* your answerbook is not in loose leaf form, you would be well advised to answer first those questions which you feel you know best. There are several reasons in favour of this procedure:

(*a*) As you get warmed up to your answers, so your thoughts and ideas flow more spontaneously and you gain confidence.

(*b*) While you still have plenty of time at the beginning of the session you are able to use your full quota (and more if necessary) of time for each question, thus ensuring maximum marks.

(*c*) If, towards the end of the examination you are faced with some questions to which you can only give a meagre answer, it will matter little that you have not much time to spend on thinking up "waffle," and if, luckily, you find yourself with enough time left over then you can afford to rack your brains for ideas.

RULE 4
Before you begin to answer each question, read it over more than once, and make sure that you understand what the examiner is trying

to find out. You will get no marks whatsoever if you write a wonderful essay which does not answer the question asked. It helps if, half way through your answer, you stop writing and read the question again. Thus, if you have begun to digress from the subject, you may be able to spot this and save the answer without having to rewrite it.

RULE 5

When you have finished all your answers, arrange them neatly in numerical order (if the pages are in loose leaf form), and read over your work. Look out for small errors like a misplaced apostrophe, a word left out or written in twice. Check that each answer clearly shows the number of the question to which it relates.

RULE 6

At every examination, a small number of candidates are guilty of the following (make a resolution that you will not be one of them):

(*a*) They write their name contrary to instructions instead of (or as well as) their number on the script.

(*b*) They laboriously write out the question before beginning the answer.

(*c*) They answer more questions than are required.

These are the things that exasperate an examiner. Do you honestly think they should award a secretarial certificate to a girl who appears incapable of following simple instructions?

CONCLUSION

If, at the end of the examination, you are not too confident that you have answered the questions well enough to pass, try not to worry too much. It may mean that you have in fact appreciated only too well the extent and depth of the questions and that, having answered reasonably well, you will get a pleasant surprise when the results come out. The examiners do not expect perfection. They know that candidates may be nervous, that the time allowed is not over-generous, that there may be more than one solution to a question. Remember, also, that you don't need 100 per cent to gain a pass—half that figure will usually see you through!

CHAPTER 27

THE PERFECT SECRETARY

INTRODUCTION

YOU may wonder whether the perfect secretary exists, and if so, how she achieved perfection.

Of course she exists. She is perfect because she suits her particular employer: change the employer, the environment, or the employer's business and she may become less than perfect. A secretary is a person who has acquired the basic secretarial skills of shorthand and typewriting plus enough knowledge and practical experience in office work to be able to cope with filing, simple office machinery and reception duties. A *good* secretary needs also to have accumulated enough knowledge about commercial work in general and office organisation in particular to be able to run her own office and to organise as much of her chief's work as he will let her. She must be able to exercise initiative and diplomacy; she must be able to keep her eyes open and her mouth shut. She becomes the *perfect* secretary when in addition to the foregoing list of attributes she is able to add an interest in and knowledge of her chief's particular line of business, enough experience in her chief's employ to be able to anticipate his requirements, and absolute loyalty to her chief.

It will be seen that perfection in secretarial work can be achieved. But it requires assiduous application, a genuine liking for the work and for the chief, and practical experience. All this takes time and I would venture to suggest that it is impossible to achieve anything near perfection with less than, say, three years' practical secretarial experience. In the majority of cases it will take much longer—but it is the same with any career: only when the basic qualifications are gained does the climb to perfection begin. And the greater her practical experience the more quickly and easily will a secretary be able to make the transition from good to perfect secretary for a new employer.

QUALIFICATIONS

Some employers require proof of a candidate's ability before they are willing to engage them, and it is very satisfying to be able to produce certificates of passes in the relevant subjects, together with good references from past employers. To get the latter, it is only necessary to ask the chief for a reference before leaving his employ. To obtain the former it is necessary to sit for formal examinations by recognised examining bodies.

Passes in one or more of the following secretarial examinations would be a great asset to any potential secretary:

1. THE JUNIOR SECRETARY'S CERTIFICATE

This is offered by the London Chamber of Commerce Commercial Education Scheme. As its name implies, this examination is particularly suitable for the younger or the less experienced candidate.

2. THE PRIVATE SECRETARY'S CERTIFICATE

Offered by the same examining body, this examination is more demanding and is suitable for students of a higher calibre. It is the next logical step up from the Junior Certificate, and is suitable for secretaries to middle management.

3. THE PRIVATE SECRETARY'S DIPLOMA

This examination is also offered by the same examining body. The standard required by the examiners is high and a student who gains this qualification can justifiably be proud of her achievements. This examination is suitable for secretaries to higher management and for those who have already taken the Private Secretary's Certificate. Successful candidates are eligible to apply for full membership of the Institute of Qualified Private Secretaries Ltd.

4. THE DIPLOMA FOR PERSONAL ASSISTANTS

This examination is offered by the Royal Society of Arts. It is designed for persons who aspire to positions as personal assistants or secretaries to higher management. Here also, the standard required by the examiners is high and a student who gains this qualification can justifiably be proud of her achievement.

5. SINGLE-SUBJECT EXAMINATIONS

Many examining bodies offer single-subject examinations (*e.g.*, shorthand, typewriting, secretarial duties, office practice) which a candidate may attempt *one at a time*. In some cases a number of individual certificates may be converted into a Group Certificate. Single-subject examinations are usually offered in a variety of speeds (for shorthand and typewriting) and at elementary, intermediate and advanced levels (for other subjects).

SPECIALISATION

We are living in an age of specialisation and for those secretaries who wish to identify more specifically with the employer's work or who require a qualification in a specialised field, the opportunities are many.

1. THE BI- (OR TRI-) LINGUAL SECRETARY

Most popular shorthand systems are phonetic, and providing the secretary's knowledge of the foreign language(s) is adequate, she may practise her skill in any number of languages. The more commonly used languages (other than English) in this country are French, German and Spanish but opportunities exist for linguists in most of the modern languages. Adaptations to the English shorthand system are easy to master and with Britain's entry into the Common Market it is a safe assumption that the bi- or tri-lingual secretary will be in greater demand. The Bi-lingual Secretary's Certificate and the Bi-lingual Secretary's Diploma are examinations offered by the Royal Society of Arts in the more popular European languages. Apart from the general secretarial skills these examinations test the candidate's ability to speak, write and type in the foreign language, to translate and (optionally) to take shorthand dictation in the foreign language.

2. THE MEDICAL SECRETARY

Secretaries who have a *penchant* for work in the medical field will find opportunities for well-paid posts with general practitioners, consultants, in hospitals and in the public health service. The Medical Secretary's Diploma and Medical Secretary's Certificate are offered by the Association of Medical Secretaries and candidates who take this examination are tested not only in general secretarial work, but also in first aid, in medical stenography and in other relevant background subjects. The work is extremely interesting and offers a measure of specialisation within the field itself as secretaries may work for doctors who are themselves specialists.

3. THE FARM SECRETARY

For those who are tired of working in the big city or who have a genuine liking for work in the country, a secretarial course with an agricultural content seems to be the answer. Opportunities exist for work on farms, estates, with agencies and with government departments and commercial or industrial concerns connected with agriculture. Apart from the basic secretarial skills, training is given in farm accounts and records, animal husbandry, farm machinery and other relevant background subjects. Examinations which may be taken are the National Certificate in Agriculture or the Ordinary National Diploma in Business Studies (Agricultural Secretary). Courses may be residential.

4. THE LEGAL SECRETARY

The law has a fascination for many secretaries and the legal profession offers interesting and remunerative posts to girls who have mastered legal terminology and who are accurate typists. Apart from fast and accurate shorthand and typewriting, it is useful for legal secretaries to have some knowledge of the general principles of law and legal procedure. Single subject examinations may be taken.

5. THE COURT REPORTER

Experienced secretaries and shorthand typists who are able to combine high speeds in shorthand with a liking for and some knowledge of legal work and court procedure may find an interesting and rewarding career in court reporting. The basic requirements are a sound knowledge of the English language and the ability to write shorthand at high speed and to transcribe accurately. In-service training is given by firms who employ successful applicants and examinations may be taken both of a practical nature and in law and in court procedure, leading ultimately to membership of the Institute of Shorthand Writers. Work may be involved with criminal cases, appeals, civil actions, divorce cases, public inquiries, conferences and affords opportunities of hearing and observing the judges and lawyers at work. Salaries offered to trainees compare very favourably with those offered to secretaries in the commercial field.

USEFUL ADDRESSES

The Royal Society of Arts,
18 Adam Street,
London, WC2N 6AJ.

The London Chamber of Commerce and Industry,
Commercial Education Scheme,
Marlowe House, 109 Station Road,
Sidcup, Kent DA15 7BJ.

The Association of Medical Secretaries,
Tavistock House South,
Tavistock Square,
London, WC1H 9LN.

The Association of Farm Secretaries,
9 Willes Terrace,
Leamington Spa.,
Warwickshire CV31 1DL.

The Institute of Shorthand Writers,
2 New Square, Lincoln's Inn,
London, WC2A 3RU.

When the secretary has learned her trade, gained experience, passed examinations, is there anything left for her to do? If she wants to stimulate her interest in secretarial work, to exchange views and ideas with other secretaries (this, incidentally, is also an ideal way to gain knowledge, and keep up-to-date) and to encourage recognition of her qualification, she may apply to join:

The Institute of Qualified Private Secretaries, Ltd.,
126 Farnham Rd.,
Slough,
SL1 4XA.

The aims and objectives of this body are concerned with establishing and promoting the status of the qualified secretary. Membership would also provide opportunities to obtain advice, attend meetings, and generally stimulate interest.

THE PERFECT SECRETARY—THEN WHAT?

If you are happy in your work and enjoy performing the individual tasks which all together combine to form your complete job; if you find your work not so easy that it becomes boring and not so difficult that it becomes frustrating, but just sufficiently challenging; if you can see periodical salary increases in the future; if your employer and colleagues are pleasant to work with; in short if your job satisfaction is adequate, then do no more than concentrate on maintaining the peak perfection you have achieved. You have done extremely well in your career. From a junior secretary you have ascended through the ranks of private secretary, personal assistant, top executive secretary. You are at the top; concentrate on staying there.

It would be outside the scope of this book to go into any detail on career opportunities (other than in the secretarial field), but as secretarial work, more perhaps than any other clerical work, affords an insight into a variety of careers and professions, it may be that for some persons, achievement of secretarial success is the beginning of a new stage. After all, no one gets a better opportunity than a secretary to see what is involved in being a solicitor, an accountant, a sales representative, a gemmologist, an architect, a company secretary ... the list is endless. The secretary may find she becomes so involved in her chief's work that she aspires to a similar qualification to his for herself. In such a case she will usually get encouragement from her chief, because in gaining more specialised knowledge herself, she becomes a more valuable member of his team. Instead of remaining his secretary, she may become his assistant or even his partner (but she must be prepared to see another secretary take her former place!).

Apart from dropping secretarial work and embarking on a course of full-time study (which most working girls are unable to do), a practical course of action is for a secretary to seek to make the transition in gradual stages, combining her employable secretarial skill with her inexperience of the new career. As she learns more about the new job, so she should offer her employer less secretarial expertise, if necessary changing employers several times to bring about the desired reversal in the work content.

Her rewards should be ample: the salary potential of her new career may well extend beyond that of a secretary or personal assistant; her ambition and desire for status may be better satisfied in her new role (she may become a qualified member of a recognised professional body and have a secretary of her own!); her interest in the new work may be more stimulating and satisfying.

For the secretary who wants to take such a step, however, the road is not an easy one. From being a top secretary, she becomes a learner in the new career; from being an expert in one field, she becomes a beginner in another. Because she has spent years learning to become a secretary, she may find herself older than most of her fellow-learners in the new profession: she must learn to accept, in the early stages of her transition, routine work normally delegated to junior staff. She must be prepared to undertake years of further study, usually in the evenings and at weekends; to sit for new examinations; to look for jobs in a new field. Above all, she must be prepared to give up what she has worked so long and so hard to achieve: being a first-class secretary.

CHAPTER 28

THE SECRETARY IN EUROPE

ALONG with other workers, the secretary may now practise her skill in any member country of the European Community. These countries are:

Belgium France Italy Luxembourg Netherlands The Federal Republic of Germany	Known as the founder Six who signed the Treaty of the European Community in Rome (known as the Treaty of Rome) on 25th March, 1957. This treaty came into effect on 1st January, 1958.
Denmark Great Britain The Irish Republic	Joined the European Community on 1st January, 1973.

GENERAL INFORMATION ABOUT THE E.E.C.

More than twenty-five years ago, Sir Winston Churchill spoke of "a kind of United States of Europe" (19th September, 1946) and this is indeed the sort of pattern which is emerging. Each member country retains its cultures, traditions, customs, but "harmonisation" and "unity" are the aims. Thus common trade policies are adopted, a single currency is envisaged, free movement of labour and services is allowed.

A sort of Civil Service for the European Community has been established, employing nearly 100,000 persons in the research establishments, the Commission, Secretariats of the Council, the Parliament, the Court and the Investment Bank. The official languages are Danish, Dutch, English, French, German, Irish and Italian. The most commonly used languages are French and German.

1. FREE MOVEMENT OF LABOUR AND SERVICES

Since 31st December, 1969, free movement of labour anywhere in the Community became operative for workers of member countries and from 1st January, 1973 United Kingdom nationals have enjoyed this privilege. This does not mean of course that nationals from non-member countries may never work within the European Community, but workers from member countries are given priority in filling vacancies. Furthermore, member countries are not allowed to give priority to their own nationals over applicants from other Community countries but it is possible (subject to approval of the Commission) for the rate of immigration of community workers to be reduced if there is a danger that workers already employed might suffer through an influx of immigrant workers.

2. WORK PERMIT
This is no longer required for workers within the European Community. It is not necessary for person to show that he has an offer of employment before he moves to a member country, nor even that he has applied for a vacancy. Indeed, workers may remain in a member country for three months to look for work. During that period and throughout their stay in member countries, workers, their families and dependants have the same rights as the nationals of the member country in which they are working so far as housing and ownership of property, terms and conditions of work, pay, vocational training, social security and trade union representation are concerned. However, this freedom does not, for obvious reasons, extend to work in the public service of the member country.

3. RESIDENCE PERMIT
Although no working permit is required, foreign nationals must obtain a residence permit; but this may be done *after* not before arrival. The residence permit is normally issued on application to the police authorities in the foreign country; evidence of employment and a medical certificate may be required. The permit is valid for five years and is automatically renewable except of course where there are strong and genuine objections (*e.g.*, a threat to public health, or public security).

4. GUIDANCE IN FINDING JOBS
Member countries supply one another with details of vacancies in their own country; thus intending immigrant workers may obtain guidance not only from the country concerned, but also from their own national Department of Employment.

WHAT DOES THIS MEAN TO THE SECRETARY WHO WISHES TO WORK IN THE E.E.C.?

1. First of all, having decided which country you want to work in, you should apply to that country or to its Embassy in this country to find out any special regulations which may apply. (Some addresses are given at the end of this chapter.) For example, in France the age of majority is twenty-one, not eighteen years, and you may be asked for evidence of your parents' permission; a medical certificate of health may be required, and so on.

2. You should have a valid passport (a British visitor's passport is not sufficient if you intend to look for work) and your passport should be endorsed by the Passport Office "Holder has the right of abode in the United Kingdom."

3. Prepare a checklist of some important questions which you want answered and make sure you know the answers. (Some ideas for a checklist are given later in this chapter.)

4. Go to your local Department of Employment and gather as much information as they are able to give you. A leaflet entitled *Working in Europe* is particularly helpful.

5. To find employment, you may apply to local national Labour Exchanges, to local private employment agencies, where they exist (*e.g.*, in France there are no private employment agencies), to commercial firms direct or in reply to advertisements in local newspapers and, of course, to your own Department of Employment in this country.

6. Written applications for employment are best made by sending a formal covering letter setting out a brief explanation of your reasons for emigrating, your contemplated length of stay in the foreign country and your reasons for feeling that you can satisfy your prospective employer's requirements. The tone and style of your letter should be respectful and should always put the employer's requirements in the foreground, not your own. (It is not his concern that you want to learn the language, want to see the world, want a change. . . .) Your covering letter should be accompanied by a separate sheet which gives concise but full particulars of your name, address, age, nationality, education, qualifications, experience, etc.

CHECKLIST

1. What salary will you be paid?
2. What will be your terms and conditions of work. (Although these will be the same as those offered to that country's own nationals, they may be quite different from what you are used to. Thus some firms may offer a two-hour break for lunch, but start work at 8 a.m. and not end before 6 p.m. Others (few) insist on Saturday morning work.)
3. Have you found accommodation? If not, is it easy to find, and where can you apply for help? The Labour Attaché in the foreign Embassy in this country may be able to supply addresses of hostels, etc.
4. What are the health and social security facilities like in the foreign country? (Again, you will have the same rights as local citizens, but these will not be the same as those you enjoy in the United Kingdom.) For example, although in France the State bears a high proportion of the cost of medical services, these must be met by the private individual in the first instance and only later are they reimbursed by the State.
5. What annual and public holidays will you have? (Must you take your holidays within a certain period, *e.g.* between May and October?)
6. What period of notice will you be required to give your employer (and vice-versa); and is there a probationary period to serve during which time your employment may be terminated without notice?
7. Will you be paid weekly, monthly?
8. Pension rights must be ascertained (if you are contemplating long-term employment).
9. Are your qualifications and certificates gained in this country acceptable to your prospective foreign employer?
10. Do you realise (but honestly realise) that in spite of all your enquiries and research, unless you have been to the foreign country before (a holiday is not always long enough), you are bound to find many differences in customs, etc. that you cannot possibly anticipate at this moment? (Did you know that Christian names were "out" in French offices and a formal approach was the "done thing"?)

11. Is your knowledge *of the actual work* adequate? You may, for example be able speak Dutch, French, German, etc. fairly fluently, but can you set out a letter in the style commonly adopted in European countries?

(*a*) The date is often preceded by the town from which the letter is being sent, *e.g.* Paris, le 2 janvier 1974.

(*b*) In most European correspondence it is customary to write the name and address of the addressee in the top *righthand* side of the letter.

(*c*) A distinction may be made in the complimentary close of a letter according to whether the addressee is a customer (a very gracious close); a supplier (a rather less flowery close); a debtor (a very terse close)!

Your prospective employer is not bound to engage you if you cannot offer him services which local workers are unable to offer. You will be in an ideal position if you can find an employer who needs to make use of your knowledge of English; otherwise, unless you speak and write the foreign language really well, you will be at a disadvantage since local citizens will of course be better able to cope with his work.

It is an excellent idea to try to find a job with a branch of a British company in the European Community. In this way, you will be concerned with writing letters in English (*e.g.*, to Head Office in the U.K.) but will be working in the foreign environment (*e.g.*, local customs, regulations, telephone enquiries). This is by far the better alternative to plunging in at the deep end with a job where you will be competing with local citizens on their own home ground. It is also an excellent way of gradually improving your fluency in the foreign language and your ability to cope with general office routine (and queries) in an unfamiliar environment. You can imagine how embarrassing (not to say inefficient) it would be to answer each telephone call with "*Un moment, s'il vous plait; je ne vous comprends pas—je suis étrangère!*" And, believe me, when your caller is unable to make his meaning clearer by frowning or smiling or by using his hands for emphasis, you may well have to call for help unless you speak the language fluently.

Many British Embassies employ a limited number of locally-engaged staff and here again if you are lucky enough to obtain a locally-based job in a British Embassy, you will be in an ideal position—working in a British environment in a foreign country. Furthermore, you will probably enjoy additional benefits, *e.g.*, British national holidays.

ARE YOU AFFECTED IF YOU DO NOT INTEND TO GO ABROAD?

Workers from other member countries may now come to the United Kingdom with as little restriction as will be applied to you if you go abroad within the European Community. And it is well known that many foreigners have learned English better than the English have learned foreign languages. If therefore you intend to work in this country and to make use of foreign European languages you have learned at school or in training, you will have to be a better "employment prospect" to an employer than a European applicant whose mother-tongue is French, German, etc. and who has acquired a good knowledge of English. You may not be able to compete on the foreign language side, but secretaries, even bi- or tri-lingual secretaries have a lot more to offer than knowledge of foreign languages. Your basic skills, your personality, your willingness to work, the extent of your involvement with your employer's business, the degree of your sincerity and loyalty to your employer—all these ingredients to go make a complete secretary—YOU.

THE UNITED NATIONS

Secretaries whose mother tongue is English may be recruited for work at the European Headquarters of the United Nations in Geneva. Recruitment is normally by examinations which are taken in London and which are advertised in the national press, *e.g. The Times*, the *Daily Telegraph*. Candidates should preferably be bi-lingual (English plus French or Spanish) and should have minimum speeds of 100 w.p.m. and 50 w.p.m. in shorthand and typing respectively. It is not essential to have these speeds in the subsidiary language.

SOME USEFUL ADDRESSES FOR INFORMATION AND WORK OVERSEAS

European Communities Press and Information,
200 rue de la Loi,
1040, Brussels, Belgium.

Commission of the European Countries,
20 Kensington Palace Gardens,
London, W8 4QQ.

27 Merrion Square,
Dublin, 2.

244 rue de la Loi, Brussels

61 rue des Belles Feuilles
Paris 16ᵉ.

1 Berlin 31,
Kurfürstendamm 102,
Berlin.

Via Poli 29, Rome.

Centre Europeen,
Kirchberg, Luxembourg.

Alexander Gogelweg 22,
The Hague.

The Personnel Division,
United Nations Office at Geneva,
Palais des Nations,
1211 Geneva 10,
Switzerland.

United Nations Information Centre,
14–15 Stratford Place,
London, W1N 9AF.

INDEX